Hegel's Philosophy of Action

The Hegel Society of Great Britain
and
the Hegel Society of America

These are the Papers Delivered at the 1981
Oxford Conference

Hegel's Philosophy of Action

edited by
LAWRENCE S. STEPELEVICH,
Villanova University
and
DAVID LAMB,
University of Manchester

HUMANITIES PRESS
Atlantic Highlands, N.J.

First published in 1983 in the United States of America by Humanities Press Inc., Atlantic Highlands, NJ 07716

©Copyright 1983 by Humanities Press Inc.

Library of Congress Cataloging in Publication Data
Main entry under title:

Hegel's philosophy of action.

  Papers delivered at the joint meeting of the Hegel Society of America and the Hegel Society of Great Britain held at Merton College, Oxford, Sept. 1-4, 1981, to mark the 150th anniversary of Hegel's death.
  1. Hegel, Georg Wilhelm Friedrich, 1770-1831–Congresses. I. Stepelevich, Lawrence S., 1930-   . II. Lamb, David, 1942-   . III. Hegel Society of America. IV. Hegel Society of Great Britain.
B2948.H3545   1983   193   82-23335
ISBN 0-391-02823-5

MANUFACTURED IN THE UNITED STATES OF AMERICA

Editor's Preface

During the course of the sixth biennial meeting of the Hegel Society of America, held at Trent University in October, 1980, Professor Zbigniew A. Pelczynski, president of the newly formed Hegel Society of Great Britain, proposed that both societies should hold, in 1981, a joint meeting to mark the one hundred fiftieth anniversary of Hegel's death. Under this rather short notice, Professor Quentin J. Lauer, the new president of the Hegel Society, and the conference chairman, Professor W.A. Walsh, prepared for a meeting of both societies to be held at Merton College, Oxford, September 1—4, 1981. The papers in this volume were those delivered during this meeting.

This Oxford Conference found most of its audience and participants among American and British students of Hegel, but there were—as the program indicated — a number of scholars from West Germany, France, and the Netherlands. The lectures were heard, appropriately enough, in the G.R.G. Mure Room at Merton College, and the portrait of this renowned Hegelian looked over the whole of the conference. Indeed, were Mure yet alive, this vigorous display of Hegelianism would certainly have come as a pleasant surprise, for Hegelianism, during his lifetime, had found little honor either at Oxford or elsewhere. But at this Oxford Conference, the extent and depth of the resurgent interest in Hegel was no longer a matter to question but rather to enjoy, and so the following essays not only add to the already abundant treasury of Hegelian scholarship but, in their theme, betray a confidence that looks even beyond that scholarship into a future of action.

In this confidence, the general topic of the Conference — "Hegel's Philosophy of Action" — addressed itself directly to a problem that is always to be found in the immediate background of any successful school of philosophy: what does this philosophy demand in practice?

As this question of practice was asked by Hegelians of Hegelianism — and not by Marxists whose practice has long since been decided for them — the answers were expectedly diverse and wide-ranging. Under the general topic, the papers focused upon three areas: Hegel's system as a framework for practical action; Hegel's political and economic views; and Hegel's philosophy of history in the light of future action. In sum, Hegel's theoretical philosophy, his practical philosophy, and his philosophy of history — the concrete embodiment of thought and action.

Four papers can be categorized as directing themselves to the topic of relating Hegel's system to a philosophy of action: those of Professors Charles Taylor, Guy Planty-Bonjour, Quentin Lauer, and Murray Greene. Six papers concerned themselves with articulating some of the various aspects of Hegel's practical philosophy: those of Professor H.S. Harris, A.S. Walton, M.J. Petry, Ludwig Siep, Errol Harris, and Richard D. Winfied. Hegel's philosophy of history was the topic of papers by Walter Jaeschke, Raymond Plant, and Lawrence S. Stepelevich.

The ordering of the thirteen papers in this volume simply follows the order in which they were presented to the Conference. Any editorial reordering along the lines of a "logic" would require a justification, a justification which could not avoid being lengthy, questionable, and superfluous.

LAWRENCE S. STEPELEVICH
DAVID LAMB

TABLE OF CONTENTS

Editor's Preface

Hegel and the Philosophy of Action
  Charles Taylor, Oxford University   1

Hegel's Concept of Action as Unity of Poiesis and Praxis
  Guy Planty–Bonjour, The Sorbonne   19

Hegel's Last Year in Berlin
  Walter Jaeschke, Hegel-Archiv Bochum   31

The Social Ideal of Hegel's Economic Theory
  H.S. Harris, University of Toronto   49

Hegel: Individual Agency and Social Context
  A.S. Walton, Open University   75

Is There a Future in the Philosophy of History?
  Raymond Plant, University of Southampton   93

Religion and Culture in Hegel
  Quentin Lauer S.J., Fordham University   103
  Comment: Robert Bernasconi, University of Essex   115

Hegel's Criticism of the Ethics of Kant and Fichte
  M.J. Petry, Erasmus University of Rotterdam   125

The "Aufhebung" of Morality in Ethical Life
  Ludwig Siep, Duisburg Universität   137

Hegel's Theory of Political Action
  Errol E. Harris, Northwestern University   157

Freedom as Interaction: Hegel's Resolution to the Dilemma of
  Liberal Theory
  Richard D. Winfield, New York   173

Cognition as an Act of Freedom
  Murray Greene, Baruch College   191

Between the Twilight of Theory and the Millenial Dawn:
  August von Cieszkowski and Moses Hess
  Lawrence S. Stepelevich, Villanova University   213

Index of Names   227

HEGEL AND THE PHILOSOPHY OF ACTION

by
CHARLES TAYLOR

I want to attempt in this paper to relate Hegel's thought to a set of perennial issues that have been central to the philosophy of action in modern times. The objective is twofold. Understanding Hegel's contribution to the developing modern debate on the nature of action helps us to understand the historical development of this debate; and this, I want to argue, is important for understanding the debate itself. At the same time, articulating the theory of action that is central to Hegel's philosophy helps us to see this philosophy itself in a new light.

Of course, for any highly systematic body of thought like Hegel's we can reconstruct the whole from many perspectives. Each one gives us something, though some are more illuminating than others. I believe that looking at Hegel's thought from the angle of the underlying conception of action provides one of the more interesting perspectives on the whole.

I

We can, perhaps, identify one fundamental issue that has been open in the philosophy of action in modern times. To do so, of course, requires some interpretation of the history of modern philosophy, and this, as always, can be subject to controversy. The precise question that defines this issue was not asked in the seventeenth and eighteenth centuries, and is rather one that is central to our twentieth century debate. But I want to claim, nevertheless, that different

Before the decision was made to publish the papers presented at this conference, Professor Charles Taylor granted permission to another publisher to publish this paper. The editors would like to thank that publisher for permission to publish Professor Taylor's paper. It will appear, slightly amended, in *Contemporary Philosophy,* ed. by G. Flistad, vol. IV, *Philosophy of Mind* (The Hague and Boston: Martinus Nijhoff, 1983).

1

answers to this question were espoused earlier, as one can see from a number or related philosophical doctrines that were expressly propounded, and that depends on these answers. I hope the plausibility of this reading will emerge in the course of the whole argument.

This being said, I will baldly identify my central issue in an unashamedly contemporary terms: what is the nature of action? Or, otherwise put, what distinguishes (human) action from other kinds of events? What are the peculiar features of action?

One family of views distinguishes actions by the kind of cause that brings them about. Actions are events that are peculiar in that they are brought about by desires, or intentions, or combinations of desires and beliefs. As events, actions may be described, among other ways, as physical movements (although one would have to be generous with the term "physical movements," so as to include cases of nonmovement, as, for example, with the action we would describe as "He stood still."). In this, they resemble a host of other events that are not actions. What distinguishes them is a peculiar type of psychological cause, that they are brought on by desires or intentions. Of course, to hold this is not necessarily to hold that psychological explanations are ultimate. One can also look forward to their reduction to some neurophysiological or physical theory. But in that case the burden of distinguishing action from nonaction would be taken over by antecedents differently described: perhaps some peculiar kind of firing in the cortex, that was found to be the basis for what we identify psychologically as desire.

A view of this kind seems to have been implicit in much of Donald Davidson's work.[1] But the basic conception goes back, I believe, at least to the seventeenth century. A conception of this kind was, in a sense, even more clearly at home in the basically dualist outlook common both to Cartesian and empiricist philosophies.

Qua bodily movements actions resembled all other events. What distinguished them was their inner, "mental" background. Within the bounds of this outlook, there was a clear ontological separation between outer event and inner background.

Against this, there is another family of views that sees action as qualitatively different from nonaction, in that actions are what we might call intrinsically directed. Actions are in a sense inhabited by the purposes that direct them, so that action and purpose are ontologically inseparable.

The basic intuition here is not hard to grasp, but it is difficult to articulate it very clearly. What is in any case clear is that this view involves a clear negation of the first: we cannot understand action in terms of the notions of undiscriminated event and a particular kind of cause; this is to explain it in terms of other primitive concepts. But for the second view, action is itself a primitive:

there is a basic qualitative distinction between action and nonaction. To the extent that action can be further explicated in terms of a concept like "purpose," this turns out not to be independently understandable. For the purpose is not ontologically separable from the action and this means something like: it can only exist in animating this action; or its only articulation as a purpose is in animating the action; or perhaps, a fundamental articulation of this purpose, on which all others depend, lies in the action.

This second view thus resists the basic approach of the first. We can't understand action by first identifying it as an undifferentiated event (because it is qualitatively distinct), and then distinguishing it by some separably identifiable cause (because the only thing which could fill this function, the purpose, is not separably identifiable). One of the roots of this doctrine plainly is Aristotle's thesis of the inseparability of form and matter, and we can see that in contrast to Cartesianism and empiricism, it it plainly antidualist. This is not to say that proponents of the first view are necessarily dualist—at least not simply so; just that their conception permits of dualism, whereas the qualitative distinction thesis does not.

One of the issues that is thus bound up with that about the nature of action is the question of dualism. Another that I want briefly to mention here is the place of the subject. It is clear that the distinction between action and nonaction is one that occurs to us as agents. Indeed, one can argue plausibly that a basic, not further reducible distinction between action and what just happens is indispensable and ineradicable from our self-understanding as agents.[2] That is, it is impossible to function as an agent at all unless one marks a distinction of this kind.

In this context, we can understand part of the motivation for the first, or causal theory of action, as lying in the aspiration to go beyond the subjective standpoint of the agent, and come to an understanding of things that is objective. An objective understanding in this sense would be one that was no longer tied to a particular viewpoint, imprisoned in the categories that a certain viewpoint imposes. If agency seems to impose the qualitative conception of action, then the causal one can appear as a superior analysis, an objective portrayal of the way things really stand, of the real components of action *an sich*. This drive for objectivity, or what Bernard Williams has called "absolute" descriptions,[3] was one of the animating motives of both Cartesianism and empiricism.

Now Hegel is clearly a proponent of the second, qualitative conception of action. And indeed he emerges out of a climate in which this conception was staging a comeback after the ascendancy of Cartesian and empiricist views. In one sense, the comeback can be seen to start with Leibniz, but the tenor of much late eighteenth century thought in Germany was of this stamp. The reaction against dualism, the recovery of the subject, the conception of the aesthetic object in Kant's third critique—all these pushed towards, and indeed, articulated themselves through this understanding of action. I now want to develop its ramifications to show how central it is to Hegel's thought.

II

The first important ramification of the qualitative theory is that it allows for what I shall call agent's knowledge. The notion is that we are capable of grasping our own action in a way that we cannot come to know external objects and events. In other words, there is a knowledge we are capable of, concerning our own action, that we can attain as the doers of this action; and this is different from the knowledge we may gain of objects we observe or scrutinize.

This qualitative distinction in kinds of knowledge is grounded on the qualitative view of action. Action is distinct in that it is directed, aimed to encompass ends or purposes. And this notion of directedness is part of our conception of agency: the agent is the being responsible for the direction of action, the being for whom and through whom action is directed as it is. The notion of action is normally correlative to that of an agent.

Now if we think of this agent as identical with the subject of knowledge, then we can see how there can be different kinds of knowledge. One kind is gained by making articulate what we are doing, the direction we are already imprinting on events in our action. As agents, we will already have some sense, however dim, inarticulate, or subliminal, of what we are doing; otherwise, we could not speak of directing at all. So agent's knowledge is a matter of bringing this sense to formulation, articulation or full consciousness. It is a matter of making articulate something we already have an inarticulate sense of.

This evidently contrasts with knowledge of other objects, the things we observe and deal with in the world. Here we are learning about things external to our action, which we may indeed act with or on, but that stand over against action.

Now the first, or causal view, cannot draw this contrast. To begin with, we can see why it wasn't concerned to: because the contrast is one that is evident from the agent's standpoint; agent's knowledge is available to the knower only qua agent, and thus from this standpoint. It cannot be recognized as knowledge from the absolute standpoint. Thus for the causal view, my action is an external event like any other, only distinct in having a certain kind of cause. I cannot claim to know it in some special way.

Of course, what I can claim "privileged access" to is my desire, or intention—the cause of my action. And here we come to the closest thing to an analogous distinction within the causal view to that between agent's and observer's knowledge. In the original formulations of Cartesianism and empiricism, I am transparently or immediately aware of the contents of my mind. It may be accorded that I intend to eat this apple. But of the consequences of this desire or intention, viz., my consuming the apple, I have knowledge like that of any other external event; I observe it.

We might then contrast the two views by noting that the causal view too recognizes two kinds of knowledge, but it draws the boundaries quite different-ly, between "inner" and "outer" reality. But we would have to add that this dif-ference of location of the boundary goes along with a quite different view of what the knowledge consists in. The notion of immediate or incorrigible know-ledge makes sense in the context of dualism, of a separate domain of inner, men-tal space, of which we can say at least that its *esse* entails its *percipi*. The contrast will be something like that between immediate and inferential know-ledge, or the incorrigible and the revisable.

Once we draw the boundary the way the qualitative theory does, there is no question of incorrigibility. We may never be without some sense of what we are doing, but coming to have knowledge is coming to formulate that correctly, and we may only do this in a partial or distorted fashion. Nor is this knowledge ever immediate; it is, on the contrary, mediated by our efforts at formulation. We have indeed a different mode of access to what we are doing, but it is question-able whether we should tub this access 'privileged'. Neither immediacy nor incorrigibility are marks of agent's knowledge.

Now, in a sense, this idea of agent's knowledge originates in modern thought with Vico. But since his work didn't have the influence it deserved in the eighteenth century, we should perhaps see Kant as the important seminal figure. Not that Kant allowed a full-blooded notion of agent's knowledge. Indeed, he shied away from using the word 'knowledge' in this context. But he made the crucial distinction between our empirical knowledge of objects on one hand, and the synthetic a priori truths that we can establish on the other, about the mathematical and physical structure of things. In Kant's mind it is clear that we can only establish the latter with certainty because they are in an important sense our own doing.

Perceiving the world involved not just the reception of information, but crucially also our own conceptual activity, and we can know for certain the framework of empirical reality, because we ourselves provide it.

Moreover, in Kant's procedure of proof of these synthetic a priori truths, he shows them to be essential conditions of undeniable features of experience, such as, for example, that we mark a distinction between the objective and the subjective in experience, or that the 'I think' must be able to accompany all our representations. Later he will show the postulates of freedom, God and immor-tality as essential conditions of the practice of determining our action by moral precepts. If we ask what makes these starting points allegedly undeniable, I think the answer can only be that we can be sure of them because they are what we are *doing,* when we perceive the world, or determine our action on moral grounds.[4].

Kant thus brings back into the center of modern epistemological debate the notion of activity and hence of agent's knowledge. Cartesian incorrigibility, the immediate knowledge I have of myself as a thinking substance, is set aside. In its place come the certainties that we don't have immediately, but can gain, concerning not some substance, or any object of knowledge whatever, but the structures of our own activity. What we learn by this route is only accessible by this route. It is something quite different from the knowledge of objects.

This has been an immensely influential idea in modern philosophy. One line of development from Kant lies through Schopenhauer, who distinguished our grasp of ourselves as representation and as will, and from this through Wittgenstein into modern British analytic philosophy, for example, in Miss Anscombe's notion of 'non-observational knowledge'.[5]

But the line that interests us here passes through Fichte. Fichte's attempt to define subject-object identity is grounded on the view that agent's knowledge is the only genuine form of knowledge. Both Fichte and Schelling take up Kant's notion of an 'intellectual intuition', which for Kant was the kind of agent's knowledge that could only be attributed to God, one through which the existence of the object itself was given (B72, *Critique of Pure Reason*) or one in which the manifold is given by the activity of self (*selbstthatig,* B68). But they make this the basis of genuine self-knowledge by the ego; and then of all genuine knowledge in so far as object and subject are shown to be identical.

The category of agent's knowledge has obviously taken on a central role, has exploded beyond the limits that Kant set for it; and is indeed, the principal instrument by which these limits are breached and the realm of inaccessible *noumena* denied. But the extension of agent's knowledge obviously goes along with a redefinition of the subject. He is no longer simply the finite subject in general that figures in the *Critiques,* but is related in some way to a single infinite or cosmic subject.

Hegel is obviously the heir to this development. He takes up the task of demonstrating subject-object identity, and believes himself to be alone capable of demonstrating this properly. What is first seen as other is shown to be identical with the self. It is crucial to this demonstration that the self cease to understand itself as merely finite, but see itself as part of spirit.

But the recognition of identity takes the form of grasping that everything emanates from spirit's activity. To understand reality aright is to understand it as 'actuality' (translating *Wirklichkeit*), i.e., as what has been actualized. We see it as not just given, but produced or 'posited' by spirit's action. This is the crucial prerequisite of the final state, which comes when we see that the agent of this activity is not foreign to us, but that we are identical to (in our non-identity with) spirit. The highest categories of Logic, those that provide the entry into the absolute Idea, are thus those linked with agency and activity. We move from the teleology into the categories of life, and then from knowledge to the good.

The recognition thus requires that we understand reality as activity, but it requires as well that we come to understand in a fuller way what we are doing, up to the point of seeing what spirit is doing through us. Coming to this point, we see the identity of the world-activity with ours.

Thought thus culminates in a form of agent's knowledge. Only this is not just a department of what we know alongside observer's knowledge, as it is for our ordinary understanding. Rather observer's knowledge is ultimately super-ceded. But the distinction is none the less essential to the system, since its crucial claim is that we only rise to the higher kind of knowledge through a supersession of the lower kind.

And this higher knowledge is far from immediate. On the contrary, it is only possible as mediated through forms of expression, among which the only adequate medium is conceptual thought. And this brings us to another ramification of the qualitative view, which is also of central importance for Hegel.

III

On the qualitative view, action may be totally unreflecting; it may be something we carry out without awareness. We may then become aware of what we are doing, formulate our ends. So following on a conscious desire or intention is not an inescapable feature of action. On the contrary, this degree of awareness in our action is something we come to achieve.

In achieving this, we also transform our activity. The quality of consciously directed activity is different from that of our unreflected, semi-conscious performance. This flows naturally from the second view on action: if action is qualitatively different from nonaction, and this difference consists in the fact that action is directed; then action is also different when this direction takes on a crucially different character. And this it does when we move from unreflecting response, where we act in much the same manner as animals do, to conscious formulation of our purposes. Our action becomes directed in a different and stronger sense. To become conscious is to be able to act in a new way.

Now the causal theory doesn't allow for this kind of qualitative shift. Indeed in its original, dualist variant, it couldn't even allow for unreflecting action. Action is essentially caused by desire or intention, and on the original Cartesian-empiricist model, our desires were essentially features of inner experience. To have a desire was to feel a desire. Hence on this view, action was essentially preceded by a cause of which the agent was aware. This amounted in fact to making conscious action, where we are aware of our ends, the only kind of action. It left no place at all for totally unmonitored, unconscious activity, the kind of action animals engage in all the time, and we do much of the time.

And even when the causal theory is disengaged from its dualist or mentalist formulation, where the causes of action are seen as material, and hence quite conceivably largely unconscious, the theory still has no place for the notion that action is qualitatively transformed in becoming conscious. Awareness may allow us to intervene more effectively to control what comes about, but action remains essentially an undifferentiated external event with a certain kind of cause.

Now this offshoot of the qualitative view: that action is not essentially or originally conscious, that to make it so is an achievement, and that this achievement transforms it; this also is crucial to the central doctrines of Hegel. I want to look at two of them here.

1. The first is what I have called elsewhere the 'principle of embodiment'.[6] This is the principle that the subject and all his functions, however 'spiritual' they may appear, are inescapably embodied. The embodiment is in two related dimensions: first, as a 'rational animal', i.e., as a living being who thinks; and secondly, as an expressive being, that is, a being whose thinking is always and necessarily in a medium.

The basic notion here is that what passes in modern philosophy for the 'mental' is the inward reflection of what was originally external activity. Self-conscious understanding is the fruit of an interiorization of what was originally external. The seeming self-coincidence of thought in which I am apparently immediately aware of my desires, aims, and ideas, that is foundational to Cartesianism, is understood rather as an achievement, the overcoming of the externality of an unconscious, merely instinctive life. It is the fruit of a negation of what negates thought, not itself a positive datum.

This understanding of conscious self-possession as the negation of the negation is grounded on the conception of action I have just been outlining. In effect, it involves seeing our mental life fundamentally in the category of action. If we think of the constituents of mental life, our desires, feelings, ideas, as merely given, as the objects that surround us in the world are given, then it is plausible to think of our knowledge of them as privileged. They appear to be objects that we cannot but be aware of, if we are aware at all. Our awareness of them is something basic, assured from the start, since it is essentially involved in our being aware at all.

In order to understand mental life as something we have to achieve understanding of, so that self-transparency is a goal we must work towards, we have to abandon the view of it as constituted of data. We have to understand it as action, on at least one of two levels, if not both.

On one level, we have to see self-perception as something we do, something we can bring off, or fail to bring off, rather than a feature of our basic predicament. This means that we see it as the fruit of an activity of formulating how things are with us, what we desire, feel, think, etc. In this way, grasping what we desire or feel is something we can altogether fail to do, or do in a distorting or partial, or censored fashion. If we think through the consequences of this, I believe we see that it requires that we conceive self-understanding as something that is brought off in a medium, through symbols or concepts, and formulating things in this medium as one of our fundamental activities.

We can see this if we leap out of the Hegelian context and look at the quite different case of Freud. Here we have the most notorious doctrine of the non-self-transparency of the human psyche. But this is mediated through a doctrine of self-understanding through symbols, and of our (more or less distorted and screened) formulation of our desires, fears, etc. as something we do. For although these formulations occur without our willful and conscious intent, they are nevertheless motivated. Displacements, condensations, etc., occur where we are strongly motivated to bring them off.

But on a second level, we may also see the features of ourselves that self-perception grasps not as simply givens but as themselves bound up with activity. Thus desires, feelings may not be understood as just mental givens, but as the inner reflection of the life-process that we are. Our ideas may not be conceived as simple mental concepts, but as the precipitates of thinking. And so on.

Hegel understands mental life as activity on both these levels. In a sense, the first can be thought to represent the influence of Kant. It was Kant who defended the principle that there is not perception of any kind that is not constituted by our conceptual activity. Thus there is no self-awareness, as there is no awareness of anything else, without the active contribution of the 'I think'. It was the contribution of the new richer theory of meaning that arose in the wake of romanticism to see that this constitutive thought required an expressive medium. Freud is, of course, via Schopenhauer, the inheritor both of this Kantian doctrine and of the expressivist climate of thought, and hence also through Schopenhauer of the idea that our self-understanding can be very different in different media, as well as distorted in the interests of deeper impulses that we barely comprehend.

The making activity central on the second level is also the fruit of what I want to call the expressivist climate of thought, which refused the distinctions between mind and body, reason and instinct, intellect and feeling, that earlier

Enlightenment thought had made central. Thought and reason were to be understood as having their seat in the single life process from which feeling also arose. Hence the new vogue for Aristotelian inseparability doctrine, of form and matter, of thought and expression, of soul and body.

Hegel's theory is built on both these streams. Our self-understanding is conceived as the inner self-reflection of a life process, which at the outset fails to grasp what it is about. We learn through a painful and slow process to formulate ourselves less and less inadequately. At the beginning, desire is unreflected, and in that condition aims simply for the incorporation of the desired object. But this is inherently unsatisfactory, because the aims of spirit are to recognize the self in the other, and not simply to abolish otherness. And so we proceed to a higher form of desire, the desire for desire, the demand for recognition. This too starts off in a barely self-conscious form, which needs to be further transformed.

In this theory, activity is made central on both levels: (a) on the second, more fundamental level, what is to be understood here, the desire, is not seen as a mere psychic given, a datum of mental life. On the contrary, it is a reflection (and at first an inadequate one) of the goals of a life process that is now embodied and in train in the world. Properly understood, this is the life process of spirit, but we are, at the outset, far from seeing that. So the active life process is primary, even in defining the object of knowledge.

Then: (b) on the first level, the achievement of more and more adequate understandings is something that comes about through our activity of formulating. This takes place for Hegel, as we shall see later, not only in concepts and symbols, but also in common institutions and practices. For example, the institution of the master-slave relationship is one "formulation" (and still an inadequate one) of the search for recognition. Grasping things through symbols, establishing and maintaining practices, are things we do, are to be understood as activities, in Hegel's theory.

And so we have two related activities. There is a fundamental activity of Spirit, which it tries to grasp through the various levels of self-formulation. These two mutually conditioning activities are at first out of phase but are destined in the end to coincide perfectly. That is because it will come clear at the end that the goal of the whole life process was that Spirit Come to understand itself, and at the same time the life process itself will be entirely transparent as an embodiment of this purpose.

But this perfect coincidence comes only at the end. And it only comes through the overcoming of noncoincidence, where what the pattern of activity is differs from what this pattern says. And so the distinction between these two dimensions is essential for the Hegelian philosophy: we could call them the *effective* and the *expressive*. Each life form in history is both the effective realization of a certain pattern, and at the same time is the expression of a certain self-understanding of man, and hence also of spirit. The gap between these two is the historical contradiction that moves us on.

And so for Hegel, the principle of embodiment is central. What we focus on as the mental can only be understood in the first place as the inner reflection of an embodied life process; and this inner reflection is itself mediated by our formulations in an expressive medium. So that all spiritual life is embodied in the two dimensions just described: it is the life of a living being who thinks; and his thinking is essentially expression. This double shift from Cartesianism, from a psychology of immediate self-transparency, to one of achieved interiority, of the negation of the negation, is obviously grounded on the qualitative understanding of action, and the central role it plays here.

The mental life has a depth that defies all immediate self-transparency, just because it is not merely self-contained, but is the reflection of a larger life process; while plumbing this depth is in turn seen as something we do, as the fruit of the activity of self-formulation.

Once again, we see that the Hegelian understanding of things involves our seeing activity as all-pervasive. But the activity concerned is as it is conceived on the qualitative view.

2. We can thus see that this offshoot of the qualitative view, which sees action as first unreflecting, and reflective understanding as an achievement, underpins what I call the principle of embodiment in Hegel's thought. But we saw above that for this conception reflective consciousness transforms action. And this aspect too is crucial to Hegel's theory.

His conception is of an activity that is at first uncertain or self-defeating because its purposes are barely understood. The search for recognition is, properly understood, a demand for reciprocal recognition within the life of a community. This is what our activity is in fact groping towards, but at first we do not understand it in this way. In a still confused and inarticulate fashion, we identify the goal as attaining one-sided recognition for ourselves from others. It follows that our practice will be confused in it purposes and self-defeating. For the essential nature of the activity is not altered by our inadequate understanding of it; the true goal of the search for recognition remains community. Our inadequacy of understanding only means that our action itself is confused, and that means that its quality as directed activity is impaired.

We can see this kind of confusion, for instance, at the stage where we seek to answer our need for recognition through an institution like that of slavery. We are already involved here with what will turn out to be the only possible solution to this quest, viz., community; because even the institution of the master-slave relation will typically be defined and mediated by law, a law that binds all parties, and that implicitly recognizes them as subjects of right. Within this framework, the relations of domination, of ownership of man by man, contradict the basic nature of law. If we think of our building and maintaining these institutions as an activity we are engaged in together, which is how Hegel sees it, then we can see that our activity itself is confused and contradictory. This is indeed, why it will be self-defeating, and why this institutional complex will eventually undermine and destroy itself.

A new form of society then will arise out of the ruins of this one. But the practices of this new society will only be higher than previous ones to the extent that we have learned from the previous error, and now have a more satisfactory understanding of what we are engaged in. And indeed, it is only possible to accede eventually to a practice that has fully overcome confusion and is no longer self-defeating if we finally come to an understanding that is fully adequate.

But throughout this whole development we can see the close relation that exist between the level of our understanding and the quality of our practice. On this view, our action itself can be more or less firmly guided, more or less coherent and self-consistent. And its being one or the other is related to the level of our self-understanding.

We are reminded here of a common conception of the romantics, well expressed in a story by Kleist, that fully coherent action must either be totally unreflecting, or the fruit of full understanding. The birth of self-consciousness on this view disrupts our activity, and we can only compensate for this disruption by a self-awareness which it total. Hegel takes up this conception with an important difference. The crucial activity is that of Spirit, and it aims for self-recognition. As a consequence, there is no such thing as the perfection of totally unreflecting activity. The earlies phases of human life are even there phases of Spirit, and the contradiction is present between their unconsciousness and what they implicitly seek.

In sum, we can see that this ramification of the qualitative theory of action involves a basic reversal in the order of explanation from the philosophy that Cartesianism and empiricism bequeathed to us. It amounts to another one of those shifts in what is taken as primitive in explanation, similar and related to the one we mentioned at the outset.

There I pointed out that in the Cartesian-empiricist view, action was something to be further explained, compounded out of undifferentiated event and a certain kind of cause. The cause here was a desire, or intention, a "mental" event; and these mental occurrences are taken as primitives by this kind of theory, and part of the explanatory background of action.

But the qualitative view turns out to reverse this order. The "mental" is not a primitive datum, but is rather something achieved. But more, we explain its genesis from action, as the reflective understanding we eventually attain of what we are doing. So the status of primitive and derived in explanation is reversed. One theory explains action in terms of the supposedly more basic datum of the mental; the other accounts for the mental as a development out of our primitive capacity for action.

IV

The qualitative view also brings about another reversal, this time in the theory of meaning, which is worth examining for its own sake, as well as for its importance to Hegel.

I said above that for this view, becoming aware of ourselves, coming to self-consciousness, is something we do. We come to be able to formulate properly what we are about. But this notion of formulation refers to that of an expressive medium.

One way to trace the connection is this: if we think of self-consciousness as the fruit of action, and we think of action as first of all unreflecting bodily practice, which only later comes to be self-understood; then the activity of formulating must itself conform to this model. That is, our formulating ourselves would be at first a relatively unreflective bodily practice, and would attain only later to the self-clarity required for full self-consciousness.

But this is just what we see in the new expressive theories of meaning, which arose in the late eighteenth centruy, and which Hegel took over. First, the very notion of expression is that of self-revelation as a special kind of bodily practice. The Enlightenment theory of signs, born of the epistemological theories of the 17th century, made no fundamental distinction between expressing and any other form of self-revelation. You can see that I am afraid of a recession by the fact that I'm selling short; you can see that I'm afraid of you by the expression on my face; you can see that it's going to rain because the barometer is falling. Each of these was seen as a 'sign' which points beyond to something it designates or reveals. Enlightenment theorists marked distinctions between signs: some were by nature, some by convention. For Condillac, there were three kinds: accidental and natural signs, and signs by institution.

But the distinction they quite overlooked was the crucial one for an expressivist, that between 'signs' that allow you to infer to their 'designatum', like the barometer does to rain, and true signs, which express something. When we make something plain in expression, we reveal it in public space in a way that has no parallel in cases of inference. The barometer "reveals" rain indirectly. This contrasts with our perceiving rain directly. But when I make plain my anger or my joy, in facial or verbal expression, there is no such contrast. This is not a second best, the dropping of clues that enable you to infer. This is what manifesting anger or joy *is*. They are made evident not by or through the expression but in it.

The new theories of meaning, which start perhaps with Herder's critique of Condillac, involved a fundamental shift. They recognize the special nature of those human activities that reveal things in this special way. Let us call them expressive activities. These are bodily activities. They involve using signs, gestures, spoken or written words. Moreover, their first uses are relatively unreflecting. They aim to make plain in public space how we feel, or how we stand with each other, or where things stand for us. It is a long slow process that makes us able to get things in clearer focus, describe them more exactly, and above all, become more knowledgeable about ourselves.

To do this requires that we develop finer and more discriminating media. We can speak of an embodiment that reveals in this expressive way as a "medium." Then the struggle for deeper and more accurate reflective self-understanding can be understood as the attempt to discover or coin more adequate media. Facial expressions do much to make us present to each other in our feelings and desires, but for self-understanding, we need a refined and subtle vocabulary.

This amounts to another major reversal in theory. The Enlightenment account explained meaning in terms of the link of designation or 'signifying' between word and object. This was a link set up in thought. In Locke's theory, it was even seen as a link set up through thought, since the word strictly speaking, signified the idea of the object. Meaning is explained here by thought, which once again is seen in the role of explanatory primitive. In this conception, expression is seen as just one case of the signifying relation, which is seen as constituted in thought.

But for the expressive theory, it is expression that is the primitive. Thought, that is, the clear, explicit kind of thought we need to establish new coinages, new relations of 'signifying', is itself explained from expression. Both ontogenetically and in the history of culture, our first expressions are in public space, and are the vehicles of a quite unreflective awareness. Later we both develop more refined media, in concepts and images, and become more and more capable of carrying out some part of our expressive activity monologically; that is, we become capable of formulating some things just for ourselves, and hence of thinking privately. We then develop the capacity to frame some things clearly to ourselves, and thus even to coin new expressions for our own use. But this capacity, which the Enlightenment theory takes as a primitive, is seen here as a late achievement, a change we ultimately come to be able to ring on our expressive capacity. The latter is what is now seen as basic in the order of explanation.

In our day, a similar radical reversal was carried out in the thoery of meaning by Ludwig Wittgenstein, who took as his target the theory that emerges out of modern epistemological theory, to which he himself had partly subscribed earlier. What I have called the Herderian theory is very reminiscent therefore of Wittgenstein's.

But Hegel wrote in the wake of the earlier expressive revolution. And one can see its importance for his thought by the crucial place in it of what I have called the notion of medium. The goal of Spirit is clear, self-conscious understanding. But the struggle to attain this is just the struggle to formulate it in an adequate medium.

Thus Hegel distinguishes art, religion and philosophy as media, in ascending order of adequacy. The perception of the absolute is embodied in the work of art, it is presented there (*dargestellt*). But this is in a form that is still relatively inarticulate and unreflecting. Religious doctrine and cult bring us closer to adequacy, but are still clouded by images and 'representations' (*Vorstellungen*). The only fully adequate form is conceptual thought, which allows both transparency and full reflective awareness. But attaining our formulation in this medium is the result of a long struggle. It is an achievement; and one that builds on, and required the formulations in the other, less adequate media. Philosophy doesn't only build on its own past. For in earlier ages, the truth is more adequately presented in religion (for example, the early ages of Christianity), or art-religion (at the height of the Greek polis). In coming to its adequate form, philosophy, as it were, catches up. True speculative philosophy has to say clearly what has been there already in the images of Christian theology.

Thus for Hegel too thought is the achievement whereby our expression is made more inward and clear. The attainment of self-understanding is the fruit of an activity that itself conforms to the basic model of action, in that it is at first unreflecting bodily practice and only later attains self-clarity. This is the activity of expressing.

V

I have been looking at how the qualitative theory of action and its ramifications underlie Hegel's philosophy, for which in the end everything is to be understood in terms of the all-pervasive activity of Spirit. I have been arguing that we can only understand the kind of activity here involved if we have in mind the qualitative view.

But there are also some important features of human historical action on Hegel's view which only make sense against this conception. I want to mention two here.

1. The first is this: all action is not, in the last analysis, action of individuals; there are irreducibly collective actions. The causal view was inherently atomist. An action was such because it was caused by desire, intention, some 'mental' state. But these mental states could only be understood as states of individuals. The mental is what is 'inner', which means within each one of us. And so action is ultimately individual. That is to say, collective actions ultimately amount to

the convergent action of many individuals and nothing more. To say "the X church did so-and-so," or "the Y party did such and such" must amount to attributing converging action to clumps of individuals in each case. For what makes these events actions in each case is their having inner mental causes, and these have to occur or not occur discretely within individuals.

By contrast, the qualitative view does not tie action only to the individual agent. The nature of the agency becomes clear to us only when we have a clear understanding of the nature of the action. This can be individual; but it can also be the action of a community, and in a fashion that is irreducible to individual action. It can even conceivably be the action of an agent who is not simply identical with human agency.

Hegel, of course, avails himself of both of these latter possibilities. In his conception of public life, as it exists in a properly established system of objective ethics (*Sittlichkeit*), the common practices or institutions that embody this life are seen as our doing. But they constitute an activity that is genuinely common to us, it is ours in a sense that cannot be analyzed into a convergence of *mines's*.

But for Hegel, there is a crucial level of activity, which is not only more than individual, but even more than merely human. Some of what we do we can understand also and more deeply as the action of Spirit through us. In order to arrive at a proper understanding, we thus have to transcend our ordinary self-understanding; and to the extent that our common sense is atomist, we have to make two big transpositions; in the first, we come to see that some of our actions are those of communities; in the second, we see that some are the work of Spirit. It is in the *Phenomenology of Spirit* that we see these transitions being made. The first corresponds to the step from chapter V to chapter VI (here Hegel speaks of the community action by using the term 'Spirit'). The second is made as we move through the discussion in the third part of chapter VI into the chapter on religion.

2. Following what I have said in earlier sections, human action is to be understood in two dimensions, the effective and the expressive. This latter dimension makes it even clearer how action is not necessarily that of the individual. An expression in public space may turn out to be the expression essentially of a common sentiment or purpose. That is, it may be essential to this sentiment or purpose that it be shared, and the expression may be the vehicle of this sharing.

These two features together—that action can be that of a community, and that it also exists in the expressive dimension—form the crucial background to Hegel's philosophy of society and history. The *Sittlichkeit* of a given society not only is to be seen as the action of a community, or of individuals only so far as they identify themselves as members of a community (an 'I' that is 'We', and a 'We' that is 'I', *Phänomenologie des Geistes* 140); it also embodies and gives expression to a certain understanding of the agent, his community and their relation to the divine. It is this latter that gives us the key to the fate of the society. For it is here that the basic incoherence underlying social practice will appear as contradiction, as we saw with the case of the slave-owning society above. Hegel's notion of historical development can only be properly stated if we understand social institutions in this way, as transindividual action that also has an expressive dimension. By contrast, the causal view and its accompanying atomist outlook induces us to explain institutions in purely instrumental terms. And in these terms, Hegel's theory becomes completely unformulable. We cannot even begin to state what it is all about.[7]

VI

I have been arguing that we can understand Hegel against the background of a long-standing and very basic issue in modern philosophy about the nature of action. Hegel's philosophy can be understood as firmly grounded on an option in favor of what I have been calling the qualitative view of action and against the causal view.

I have tried to follow the different ramifications of this qualitative view to show their importance to Hegel's thought. I looked first at the notion of agent's knowledge, and we saw that the system of philosophy itself can be seen as the integration of everything into a form of all-embracing agent's knowledge. I then followed another development of the qualitative view, which shows us action as primordially unreflecting bodily practice, which later can be transformed by the agent's achievement of reflective awareness. We saw that Hegel's conceptions of subjectivity and its development are rooted in this understanding. I then argued that the expressive revolution in the theory of meaning could be seen as an offshoot of this same view of action; and that Hegel is clearly operating within the expressive conception. Finally we can see that his theory of history supposes not just the expressive dimension but also the idea of irreducibly common actions, which only the qualitative view can allow.

One part of my case is thus that Hegel's philosophy can be illuminated by making this issue explicit in all its ramifications. This is just in the way that we make any philosophy clearer by spelling out more fully some of its deepest assumptions. The illumination will be the greater the more fundamental and pervasive the assumptions in question are for the theory under study. Now my claim is that for Hegel the qualitative theory of action is very basic and all-pervasive, and the above pages have attempted to show this.

Perhaps out of deference to Hegel's shade, in this anniversary year, I shouldn't use the word 'assumption', since for Hegel everything is ultimately demon-strated. But my claim stands that the thesis about action I have been describing here is quite central to his philosophy.

But this is only one side of the gain that one can hope for in a study of this kind. The other, as I said at the outset, is that we should attain some greater under-standing of the historical debate itself by situating Hegel in it. I think this is so as well, but I haven't got space to argue it here.

What does emerge from the above is that Hegel is one of the important and seminal figures in the long and hard-fought emergence of a counter-theory to the long-dominant epistemologically based view that the seventeenth century bequeathed us. This can help explain why he has been an influential figure in the whole countermovement where this has been the case. But what remains to be understood is why has also often been ignored or rejected by major figures who have shared somewhat the same notions of action, starting with Schopen-hauer but by no means ending there.

Perhaps what separates Hegel most obviously and most profoundly from those today who take the same side on the issue about action is their profoundly different reading of the same genetic view. For Heidegger, for example, the notion that action is first of all unreflected practice seems to rule out altogether as chimerical the goal of a fully explicit and self-authenticating understanding of what we are about. Disclosure is invariably accompanied by hiddenness; the explicit depends on the horizon of the implicit. The difference here is fun-damental, but I believe that it too can be illuminated if we relate it to radically different readings of the qualitative view of action, which both espoused in opposition to the epistemological rationalism of the seventeenth century. But I cannot even attempt to show this here.

NOTES

1. Cf. his "Actions, Reasons and Causes," *The Journal of Philosophy,* LX, no 23, "Freedom to Act," in Ted Honderich ed., *Essays on Freedom of Action* (London, 1973).
2. I have tried to do this in my "Action as Expression," in C. Diamond and J. Teichman, eds., *Intention and Intentionality* (London, 1979).
3. Cf. his *Descartes* (London, 1978).
4. I have argued this further in my "The Validity of Transcendental Arguments," *Proceedings of the Aristotelian Society, 1978–1979,* pp. 151–165.
5. Cf. *Intention* (Oxford, 1957), 13–15.
6. *Hegel and Modern Society* (Cambridge, 1979), p. 18.
7. I have developed this further in my "Hegel's *Sittlichkeit* and the Crisis of Representative Institutions," in Yirmiahu Yovel, ed., *Philosophy of History and Action* (London and Jerusalem, 1978).

HEGEL'S CONCEPT OF ACTION
AS UNITY OF POIESIS (ποίησις) AND PRAXIS (πρᾶξις)

by

GUY PLANTY-BONJOUR

Your Hegelian Society has chosen a subject as important for the philosophy of Hegel as for contemporary philosophy. Since I am not a specialist in analytical philosophy, I am looking forward greatly to learning the connection between Hegel and the Anglo-Saxon philosophy of action. My paper will deal exclusively with Hegel's point of view. It must be granted that Hegel himself never examined the question of action in its entirety. A cursory examination of this notion is sufficient to understand it. Hegel uses many concepts whose meaning is not strictly defined. It is well known that *Tatigkeit, Tat, Handlung, Hervorbringung* and *praktisch* may all designate what we mean by action. It seems clear that each of these terms can be distinguished from the others. But one term is often exployed instead of another.

There is an ambiguity in Hegel's language because the notion of action is very complex, Hegel being under the influence of three great thinkers: Aristotle, Kant, and Adam Smith. During this conference I will, first, summarize this triple heritage. Then, we shall see how the concept of 'making' and afterward the concept of 'action' are understood by Hegel. Last, we shall try to understand what is the kind of unity between poiesis and praxis and in this way what is the deep meaning of the Hegelian theory of Action in general.

19

I

Heritage

Aristotle

Hegel was not eighteen years old when he read the *Nichomachean Ethics*. It was thus very early that he discovered the famous distinction between θεωρεῖν - ποιεῖν - πράττειν[1] Let me remind you briefly of Aristotle's position:

θεωρεῖν consists in realizing the thought, that is to say in knowing the universality and the eternal. It is contemplation, and this contemplation is the activity par excellence. Thus contemplation is opposed to the discursive activity that is found in meditation and in practical behavior. Theoretical activity is so excellent that it belongs to God. In so far as Hegel retains this aspect of the Aristotelian heritage, an onto-theological theory of action will be worked out by him.

ποιεῖν is action as it changes the external world. Seen from that point of view, it implies the idea of an effort, of a struggle to transform resistant matter. In order to explain the notion of *poiesis,* Aristotle uses the schema of the technique of production in ancient society. It is the essence of *poiesis* that the end must be in the things made (ποιητον) and that the agent does not benefit from his own action. I quote Aristotle: "Making has an end other than itself."[2] Hence the scholastic adage: *"Actio est in passo."* Doing is here opposed to Idea or Reason.

πράττειν is a very different kind of action. Indeed praxis consists in changing the agent himself. It is no longer the transformation of anything in the external world. By acting, the agent spiritualizes in himself his animal life and develops his intellectual life. Therefore action as *praxis* stays inside the agent himself. Aristotle writes:

> For good action itself is its end.[3]
> εστι γαρ αυτη η ευπραξια

Hence the scholastic adage: *"Actio est perfectio agentis."*
Here action, being an act, is opposed to purpose and intention.

Aristotle distinguishes clearly between *poiesis* and *praxis* whose characteristics are opposite. He will say they are totally distinct (ἐπει διαφέρει ἡ ποίσις εἴδη καί ἡ πρᾶξις). Finally he adds that poiesis is ranked second to *praxis* because *poiesis* is an action whose end is merely outside itself.

Opposite influence of Kant and Smith

Paton, in *The Categorical Imperative,* regrets that Kant did not compose a general theory of action.[5] Kant dealt abundantly, however, with the problem of practical philosophy. Hegel considers Kant the modern philosopher who was able to apply to philosophy the great discovery of Christianity: infinity of subjectivity. Kant was the first indeed to understand that practical philosophy is based on the notion of freedom and on the autonomy of will. The subject becomes the agent of his own actions through the spontaneity of will. Hegel was the most implacable critic of Kant and therefore the influence of Kant on the *Philosophy of Right* has been greatly underestimated.

At the same time that, under Kant's decisive influence, the notion of action was tending to be reduced to the ethical act, Adam Smith demonstrated the importance of the activity of production in the life of modern societies. Hegel found in *The Wealth of Nations* the deeper meaning of work for industrial society. On the other hand, Smith helped Hegel to perceive that work (Aristotle's *poiesis*) is not simply an activity whose sole effect is to change the external world. Work is first and foremost an economic activity: both transformation of a thing and intersubjective action.

On the other hand, Smith emphasizes the Aristotelian difference between *poiesis* and *praxis* by distinguishing between two kinds of work: productive and unproductive. Unproductive work is work that does not produce anything permanent. Smith's teaching leads to something like this: neither the menial servant nor the politician nor the lawyer are true workers. Thus action par excellence has become the only work activity capable of increasing the wealth of a nation.[6]

The interpreters of the Hegelian theory of action can be divided into two groups. For some, Hegel is the first philosopher who has understood that the economic problems of work are very important. That is the reason why his philosophy of action is fundamentally a philosophy of work. And the theme of Master and Servant is the vital lead that sheds light on the other questions.

For others, on the other hand, Hegel's originality was that he saw that the highest activity resulted from infinite subjectivity and infinite freedom of the will.

The conflict consists in knowing whether the action is a problem of connection between man and nature or between man and history. The question then arises whether either of these interpretations is convincing. Hegel's concept of action consists neither in making nor in moral action.

II

Hegel's Meaning of Action as poiesis

In his book *Platos Lehre von der Wahrheit*, Martin Heidegger writes: *Das neuzeitlich - metaphysische Wesen der Arbeit ist in Hegels Phänaomenologie des Geistes vorgedacht als der sich selbst einrichtende Vorgang der unbedingten Herstellung, das ist Vergegenständlichung des Wirlichen durch den als Subjektivität erfahrenen Menschen.* Kojéve, Marcuse and Lukács agree with Heidegger's view and they take his idea to extreme lengths. We can emphasize, that even if many Marxists are satisfied with Hegel's theory of work, Marx himself was very critical of his theory.[8]

Professor Riedel writes that work, in Hegel's view, has become *"ein zentrales Moment."*[9] Of course, under the influence of English economists, Hegel had a better understanding of the meaning of work in human activity. His reading of Smith allowed Hegel to understand that, in industrial societies, work or labor was completely different from what it was in the age of the Greeks when production was still carried on very much in the style of a cottage industry. Hegel discovered that the Aristotelian notion of *poiesis* was not quite adequate. He was to work out carefully a new *poietics*. Aristotle thought that "making" was only a transitive action whose end consisted in an external thing. Certainly, to work is still to produce something. But what is new is that, besides the thing that is made, work is the act of a subject and this act is acting on the agent himself. There is a close connection between the worker (as agent), the working (as action) and the thing made (as work). Every one of them reacts upon the others.

Hegel has given a very precise illustration of this fact at Jena, in these books on the *Philosophy of Mind* (1803 and 1805). All activity, whatever Aristotle may think, is dialetical: all action produces a reaction. There is no action that is merely transitive. Already, about the end of Middle Ages, in this very place, at Oxford, a subtle mind, Duns Scotus had brought up the question. Scotus asserted against Aristotle's and Thomas Aquinas' authority, that every act of making produces an effect in the agent.[10] By making something, the agent makes himself. Hegel writes: *"Die Arbeit bildet."*

Hegel's *poiesis* acquires another dimension because it has an another definition. In Aristotle's view, the act of making was the result of a technique: a rule known by the mind made possible the production of an external thing. For this schema of $\tau\acute{\epsilon}\chi\nu\eta$, Hegel substitutes a new category of his own devising, the category of *Entausserung* (alienation). It's really the making subject who becomes himself the external world. The texts of Jena express it very clearly:

Arbeit ist sich-zum-Dinge-machen des Bewusstseins.[11]

This exteriorizing of the working person is caused by his desire. The making is not separate from the wish. We may discuss a possible misconception of the meaning of Hegel's notion of wish. Kant's definition of this notion was still that of Aristotle:

Begierde ist Selbstbestimmung der Kraft eines Subjektes durch die Vorstellung von etwas kunftigen als, einer Wirkung derselben.[2]

This rationalistic definition of *wish* is still employed by the thinkers of the Wittgenstein school. For A.I. Melden, in *Free Action,* there is a complete equivalence between the expressions: wanting and wanting to do, because wanting and to do are mutually implicit. The mind goes from wanting to do to trying to do and from trying to do to doing. Professor Ricoeur, who examines Melden's position, is convinced that linguistic philosophy is more apt to find the meaning of an action than to discover that there is not making without the force of wish. Ricoeur writes:

I will not say that this analysis is wrong, but it is incomplete --- Our authors emphasize too strongly theoretical reason which tends to objectivize all things and consequently to recognize only facts and causes, but not actions, agents and their motives.[13]

Hegel's explanation will consist in showing that the wish is necessarily a tendency towards acting. It is through desire that a man becomes a thing. The necessary means for Hegel to describe this process is the dialectical category of Negativity .There is a negative relation between man and nature. Making is this negative which has its origin in the negativity of wish and tends to change the external thing. According to Hegel, work consisted much less in the result (product) of the work than in the subject's activity itself. For the Aristotelian tradition, it was the external end, the thing made ($\pi o\iota\eta\tau o\nu$) that made it possible to define the *poiesis.* For Hegel's new interpretation, the $\pi o\iota\eta\sigma\iota\varsigma$ is rather characterized by it origin, the agent himself, and, we should say, by the activity itself of the agent.

By emphasizing activity, Hegel is led to examine the source of energy. That shuttles should move themselves was for Aristotle only a dream, no doubt an impossibility. Now industry, which was springing up, had just discovered the machine. Hegel asks if it would not be possible to find a source of energy outside man and to make the machine work in place of man. The answer of the texts of Jena is well known. This cunning by which man entrusts machines with the task of producing objects, changes significantly the nature of making. Production for the ancient world was: the shaping of materials. Industrial production is now: to tame the nature. However, the activity of the machine remains a limited activity. I quote the *Philosophy of Mind:*

Although man has forced the machine to exploit nature, man is still obliged to work. He merely changes the kind of work he does removes it from nature, and in this way man does not turn in a living way towards nature as living nature.[14]

The machine, Hegel says, does not come back inwardly to itself; thus its action does not exempt man from remaining the main agent. Therefore the making is and will always remain a human making. It is insofar as Hegel pays close attention to the new kind of production of his age and therefore insofar as he departs from the theory of Aristotle's *poiesis,* that Hegel was suddenly aware that the action that produces external things will still be the action of the subject.

We can conclude briefly our analysis of the change in the meaning of ποίησις. Hegel found out that making is that kind of activity by which an agent by producing something produces himself. Making is not only a transitive action, but has all the characteristics of an immanent action. Hegel assigns to *poiesis* what Aristotle assigns only to *praxis:* to be an end in itself. Insofar as, by making, the subject made himself a thing, it follows that action is not a mere *Entausserung* but it is also a true *Entfremdung.* Hegel means by that the great ambiguity of the nature of making, also of work in the modern economy. If making is no longer as Aristotle believed, the activity of an unfree man, it is nevertheless not that of a free man either, the activity by which man may realize himself entirely.

III

Hegel's meaning of action as praxis

We have seen that making was not only an activity that had its end in itself. Now, Aristotle will change the Aristotelian meaning of *praxis,* but in the opposite way: *praxis* is no longer exclusively an activity that has its end in the agent himself. Indeed, Hegel says a moral action produces an external work that has a definite connection with the action itself. This affirmation may seem paradoxical if we remember that the true moral action is one that has its origins in the subject's act of will. Hegel becomes aware that neither Socrates, nor Plato nor Aristotle succeeded in seeing that man is endowed with infinite freedom. It falls to the Christian religion to have been the first to assert the infinite dignity of man. We know the famous passage of the Jena's manscripts that I will quote briefly:

> Dies ist das hohere Prinzip der neueren Zeit, das die Alten, das Plato nicht kannet . . . Das sich-selbst absolut wissen der Einzelheit, dieses absolute Insichsein war nicht vorhanden. Durch dies Prinzip ist die aussere wirkliche Freiheit der Individuen in ihrem unmittelbaren Dasein verloren, aber ihre innere, die Freiheit des Gedankens erhalten.[15]

This category of liberty plays a great role in moral activity. Paragraph 124 of the *Philosophy of Right* made clear that the rights of subjective freedom are the break between antiquity and modern times. And it is Kant who is the philosopher par excellence of those modern times, since he based his thoery of action on the autonomy of the will. Indeed, Hegel accepts fully Kant's starting point on the greatness of the human subjectivity:

> Die Handlung ist die klarste Enthullung des Individuum, seiner Gesinnung sowohl als auch seiner Zwecke; was der Mensch im innersten Grunde ist, bringt sich erst durch sein Handeln zur Wirklichkeit.[16]

The end of this text shows that the fault of Kant's philosophy is that he achieves the inner subjectivity at the expense of external things. Hegel will not admit, as Kant has done, the maxim that the subjective principle of a volition may be separated from the concrete circumstances of the action. Hegel loses sight neither of the subjective principle of action: purpose and intention, nor of the objective result of action: morality in the family, the civil society, and the state. Hegel would not say, as Aristotle has said, that the end of moral action stays inside the agent, as if nothing could be more justified than to ignore the concrete outcomes. But, on the other hand, Hegel refuses to judge the quality of the moral action only by the outcomes. Hegel's doctrine is not the ethic of the consciousness concerned only with the intention of the acting subject. It is not a pragmatic ethic concerned only with external actions. The Hegelian doctrine is an ethic of responsibility. Hence, the complexity of his theory. The moral agent is responsible for his actions, but he is not responsible for all that he is doing. Such is the paradox of Hegel's theory. If man were responsible for all that he is making, there would no longer be any distinction between making and moral action. Hegel maintains the distinction between both kinds of activity:

> Die subjektive moralische Qualitat bezieht sich auf den hoheren Unterschied, inwiefern ein Ereignis und Tat uberhaupt eine Handlung ist.[17]

On this point, Hegel could be, perhaps, compared with the linguistic philosophy of action. This latter distinguishes clearly between the notions of agency and action. Agency is a more basic notion than that of action. Agency implies neither imputation nor ascription. Agency is only: man has done this. It is therefore somebody's act without any moral qualification. Is that not what Hegel meant when he criticized the ancient notion of responsibility as it was exemplified in the Greek tragedy by Oedipus?

The difference between the ancient action and the modern one is based on the notion of subjectivity of which the Greeks were unaware. If subjectivity is not recognized, each *Tat* is a *Handlung* and agency is no longer distinguished from action.

IV
Unity of poiesis and praxis

We have seen that Hegel has deeply changed the traditional categories of making and of action. This change has particularly consisted in bringing together two notions Aristotle considered as specifically distinct. So the action is the unity of *poesis* and *praxis*. But what is the meaning of this unity?

Unity is not identity. The man who makes the confusion misjudges Hegel's philosophy of action. And in fact, in his book *Theorie und Praxis im Denken Hegels,* Professor Riedel maintains that Hegel has suppressed the distinction between *poiesis* and *praxis*. He thinks that the connection between man and nature and more especially between subject and object is so close that the distinction between these two notions disappears.[18]

Of course, Hegelian philosophy, because it is a dialectical philosophy, it less able than a philosophy of understanding to distinguish clearly between things. However Hegel, because he fought long enough against the philosophy of Identity, which dismisses all differences, cannot have made the same mistake.

The distinction or the nondistinction of *poiesis* and *praxis is not an academic debate. If you adopt this thesis of identity between the two notions, you must conclude quite naturally that practical technical philosophy is identical to practical moral philosophy. The blending of making and action is realized at the expense of moral action. The thinkers who tend to think that action is no more than production use the famous text of the Master and the Servant. Kojeve, Lukacs, Marcuse find out that action as work is the cause of liberation for men. In their view, Hegel so much changed the Aristotelian notion that praxis* would be reduced to meaning the transforming activity.

This interpretation is wrong because no text of Hegel allows us to say that action is this "*menschliche, sinnliche Tatigkeit*" of which Marx speaks in *Thesis on Feuerbach*. Hegel had never thought that man can be realized through work, because of an alienation is always bound up with the nature of work. Of course, Hegel foresaw that the use of machines would deeply modify the ancient theory of *poiesis*. And he has taken it into account, but did not think that the action as a whole can be reduced to the transforming action.

He continues even to think, as Aristotle said, that ethical action has a greater value than work. And accordinly I do not believe that ethical action can be assigned a secondary role. It is, perhaps, difficult to subscribe to what Professor W.H. Walsh has written:

> Where Hegel is unsatisfying is that he apparently leaves no room for personal morality of any kind.[19]

It's on the contrary, the room that is left for personal morality that permits Hegel to dinstinguish between technical making and ethical action.

The study of the connection between ποίησιζ and πρᾶξις cannot end with examining the inner nexus of these two categories. Traditional philosophy soon changed Aristotle's triple division: θεωρεῖν - ποιεῖν - πράττειν into the following dichotomy: theoretical-practical. This is an unfortunate simplification because it follows that the justified opposition between the world of the technical and the world of the moral disappeared, combining them in an undifferentiated way under the term *practical*. This is especially an unfortunate simplification because it places action outside the theoretical sphere and thus the opposition between the theoretical and the practical becomes the opposition between knowledge and action.

But if Hegel distinguishes between ποιεῖν and πράττειν he retains also θεωρεῖν. In order to be able to understand what Hegel's doctrine about action is, we must not forget that neither *poiesis* nor *praxis* nor even the unity of both represents perfectly the concept of action. What Hegel calls *Tatigkeit* is deeper, more essential than these two kinds of action. We know that this notion is Aristotle's heritage: it is the *energeia*. Here Hegel accepts the ancient heritage, but by changing it. The mind, Aristotle says, is, but does not produce itself. According to this concept, the highest activity will be an activity of pure contemplation, the θεωρειν. Instead of this ontology of the substance, Hegel substitutes a theology of the subject's activity. God is not, He is eternal becoming. This activity is really, like making and action, the principle of a self-objectification. But it is so perfect a self-objectification, that the mind realizes itself without undergoing the least alienation. Hegel writes in the *Philosophy of Religion:*

> Die Natur des Geistes selbst ist es, sich zu manifestiren, sich gegenstandlich zu machen; dies ist seine That, seine Lebendigkeit, seine einzige That (und er ist nur seine That).[19]

By comparison with this supreme activity, all other kinds of activity—whether the activity of making or whether the activity of ethical action—are deficient, finite, limited. In order to compensate for this finiteness, Hegel has introduced the notion of the *Cunning of Man* for technical production and of the *Cunning of Reason* for the ethical action. Since what I have foreseen in purpose is only a part of what I have really produced into the external world, it follows that what I have done has produced something over than what I have foreseen. Really, Hegel does not succeed in eliminating the notion of destiny. He only changes it. It has often been said that *Cunning of Reason* has taken the place of the ancient *Fatum.*

This thesis has been often criticized. Theodor Litt, for example, thought he could trap Hegel in the following dilemma: the *Cunning of Reason* is either a making without knowledge or a knowledge without acting. It is easy to answer that for Hegel: the ethical action is never completely unconscious nor ever completely inactive.

Professor Charles Taylor, in his remarkable work, reproaches Hegel for having ruined his promising thesis about "situated freedom" by adding the questionable theory of the *Cunning of Reason*. And, thus, Hegel is said to have had recourse to the old ontology of a cosmic spirit. Perhaps we may say that it is not a cosmic spirit but it is a historical spirit, which takes on the role of the *Cunning of Reason*. Besides we oversimplify Hegel's teaching if this cunning is attributed only to the divine spirit, be he cosmic or historical. Indeed, the *Cunning of Reason* has in Hegel's philosophy a wider meaning. I believe that, by this expression, Hegel means all that works towards producing the universal, therefore bringing together the behavior or action of the individual with the universality of law. Thus it is not only the cosmic spirit or Providence that is the agent, the principle of the *Cunning of Reason,* but it is also all the many intermediaries like the family, the mechanism of economics in civil socity, the laws of the State, that are the means by which our actions may obtain or realize finally an aim we have not foreseen. Through these considerations we understand that the serious objection against this thesis is a misconception of the meaning of Hegel's analysis. It is no longer possible to support the view that man is duped as soon as the *Cunning of Reason* intervenes. Man's action is not valueless under the pretext that man is not fully aware of his action. Through this *Cunning of Reason,* the human ethical agent is not like a puppet on a string.

To conclude, I can say man's action, both technical and moral, contributes each for its part, to creating the historical world of culture. But it is evident that the true activity is the activity that is only activity, that of God. One cannot deny that Hegel is a "Theologian." The dialectical process obliges us to consider the sphere of the absolute spirit if we will understand the meaning of Hegel's philosophy of action.

NOTES

1.   Aristotle *Metaphysics* E, 1, 1025b21–25.
2.   Aristotle *Nichomachean Ethics* 5, 4, 1140b6.
3.   *Ibis.,* 1140b7.
4.   Aristotle *Politics* I, 4, 1254a5.
5.   H.J. Paton, *The Categorical Imperative* (Philadelphia: University of Pennsylvania Press, 1971), p. 28.
6.   A. Smith, *The Wealth of Nations,* ed. Andrew Skinner (Pelican Classics, 1973), p. 430. *er sieht nur die positive Seite der Arbeit, nicht ihre negative . . . Die Arbeit, welche Hegel allein kennt und anerkennt, ist die abstrakt geistige" (K. Marx, Nationalökonomie und Philosophie, in Die Frühschriften, Kröner Verlag,* Stuttgart, 1953, p. 270).

er sieht nur die positive seite der Arbeit, nicht ihre negative . . . Die Arbeit welche Hegel allein kennt und anerkennt, ist die abstrakt geistige" (K. Marx, Nationalökonomie und Philosophie, in Die Frühschriften, Kröner Verlag, Stuttgart, 1953, p. 270).

9. M. Riedel, *Theorie und Praxis im Denken Hegels* (Stuttgart: Kohlhammer, 1965), p. 286.

10. Dun Scotus, Op. ox., IV, de. 13 q. 1, § *Ex dictis.*

11. Hegel, *Jenaer Realphilosophie* (Meiner edition, 1967), p. 214.

12. Kant, *Anthropologie in pragmatischer Hinsicht,* § 70, A K, VII, p. 251. Cf. Aristotle *de Anima* 3 10, 433a15.

13. P. Ricoeur, *La semantique de l'action,* (C.N.R.S. edition, 1977).

14. Hegel, *Philosophie des Geistes,* in *Jenenser Realphilosophie* I, p. 237.

15. Hegel, *Jenaer Realphilosophie* (Meiner edition, 1967), p. 251.

16. Hegel, *Aesthetik,* t.I, (Bassenge edition, p. 216).

17. Hegel, *Grundlinien der Philosophie des Rechtes,* § 96.

18. M. Riedel, *Theorie and Praxis im Denken Hegels,* p. 108.

19. W.H. Walsh, *Hegelian Ethics,* p. 18.

20. Hegel, *Religionsphilosophie,* Bd. 1, (Napoli, Bibliopolis, 1978), p. 495.

HEGEL'S LAST YEAR IN BERLIN

by

WALTER JAESCHKE

Hegel's last year in Berlin, the last year of his life, shows the philosopher at the height of his literary output and his influence. Since his summoning from Heidelberg to the newly established University of Berlin, his philosophical system had received detailed elaboration in the course of his intensive lecturing activity. Parallel to this inner development of Hegel's philosophy ran a growth of its external influence. The first of Hegel's Heidelberg and even Berlin students were already lecturing at Berlin and other Prussian universities. In 1827 the journal *Jahrbcher für wissenschaftliche Kritik* was founded, and, precisely because it did not present itself as a mere organ of the school, it provided Hegel's philosophy with an influence that reached beyond the subject borders of philosophy as well as beyond the borders of the Prussian state. At the threshold of his last year, Hegel also reached the formal climax of his academic career: he was elected Rector. Not just Rector of any university, but of that university that stood at the center of the newly constituted Prussian state and that, on the basis of a conception impressed upon it by Wilhelm von Humboldt, had already gained an outstanding position among German universities. This is especially remarkable if one considers that Germany in those years, as in most years of its history, did not constitute a united nation, but was divided into several independent states. It has been said, not without justification, that in those years the German universities were the only link between the German states; cultural unity was a substitute for political unity.

In July, 1830, on the three hundredth anniversary of the "Confessio Augustana," the written creed of the Lutherans, Hegel delivered an extremely skillful lecture

The author expresses deepest thanks to Norbert Waszek M.A., Christ's College, Cambridge, for translating the German manuscript into English and to Dr. Z.A. Pelczynski for revising the translation.

to an audience at this key university.[1] This was a difficult task, as the writing divided the Lutherans from members of the Reformed Church and thus stood in the way of Prussian ecclesiastical policy, which in those years attempted to overcome that difference within the Church of the Prussian Union. Neglecting such differences within Protestantism, Hegel used the opportunity to recommend Protestantism in general as a political principle. He outlined an alliance between Prussian politics, Protestant religion and speculative philosophy, a union of state, religion, and philosophy that stood in obvious contrast to the contemporary restoration efforts of the Holy Alliance. This conception was well suited to justify the high esteem that Hegel's philosophy enjoyed—not at the Prussian Court, not even in the Prussian state in general, but among certain sections of Prussia's government and administration at that time.

Although Hegel's philosophy grew in influence during the later Berlin years, it also came under increasing criticism. Whereas in the early 1820s criticism had been directed against the conservative position of Hegel's *Philosophy of Right,* it was now voiced in the name of the opposite side, and also on behalf of Christian religion. The aim of those attacks was to undermine the position of Hegel's philosophy by denouncing its principles as incompatible with the basic elements of the Prussian state. This was done directly, with regard to the foundation of the Prussian monarchy, as well as indirectly, by calling Hegel's philosophy pantheistic and even atheistic. This meant nothing less than criticizing Hegel's philosophy for its alleged weakening of the religious and ethical foundations of the Prussian state. The weight of these attacks—conservative in religious and political respect—was so great that Hegel himself had to go to his own defense.[2]

The increase of such attacks might appear to be linked, both inevitably and proportionately, with the success of a philosophical school. But Hegel's last year was overshadowed not only by such attacks but by political events that seemed capable of endangering the political order. In the past fifteen years, after the revolutionary and Napoleonic wars, this political order had for the first time enjoyed, externally at least, a period of stability, though partly at the expense of a climate of home politics that was hard to bear. It is therefore not surprising that we find in Hegel, who always kept a watchful eye on political events, signs of a growing concern about political developments. Only a few days after he had presented his views on the union of state, religion, and philosophy on the anniversary of the "Confessio Augustana," the news of the July revolution in Paris reached Berlin. In the course of the following months news followed about the revolutionary movements in Belgium, Luxemburg, and Poland. Finally, news came from England about the parliamentary disputes over the Reform Bill.

Hegel's biographers, Rosenkranz and Haym, reported that these news had shaken him "most dreadfully";[3] "an unlimited discomfort" seized the reactionary politicians of the Vienna Congress as well as Hegel, the philosopher of the restoration.[4] According to both men, this shock and discomfort did not seem to be the expression of a sudden political reorientation, but rather a consequence of the development of Hegel's political thought in the Berlin years, that only became manifest as a result of the revolutionary movements during Hegel's last year. For Haym, a later liberal, the Berlin Hegel is in any case the philosopher of the restoration. But Rosenkranz, too, reports that Hegel's thought became more and more conservative; he had given up constitutionalism and idolized power as such.[5] The assumption of such a development is of special interest as it clashes with another view, nowadays more commonly held, that Hegel's later Berlin lectures are more outspoken than his *Philosophy of Right* of 1821 on such issues as the necessity of the constitution and the restricted role of the monarch in a constitutional state. However, Rosenkranz and, following him, Rosenzweig concede that Hegel's intense immediate shock gradually gave way to a more balanced assessment of the justification of the July Revolution.[6]

Of course the assumption of such a breathtaking series of changes in Hegel's political position rests less on documentary evidence than on the dramatic talents of Hegel's biographers, just as the circumstances of the publishing of the *Philosophy of Right* sustained a host of interpreters. Direct references to Hegel's view are unfortunately scarce. Rosenkranz's report on Hegel's dreadful shock is based only upon one letter of Varnhagen, dated 1840.[7] As far as Hegel's own statements are concerned we do have a number of letters in which he comments on the political events.[8] But, first, these comments do not take more space than is reserved for other topics such as his illness, a "cold fever," his wine deliveries, and particularly the royalties for the third edition of the *Encyclopedia*. Second, the phrases in which he expresses his concern about political circumstances are literally identical with those he used a few days before the battle of Jena in 1806. He writes now that the political interest swallows up all the others;[9] he wrote then that one concern swallowed everything else, the concern "may God be with us, should the war break out," that affected the scholars most strongly.[10] These words, written while he was completing the *Phenomenology of Spirit,* are nearly identical with the words he used while completing the second edition of the *Science of Logic,* twenty five years later. Third, and most important, Hegel's comments cannot be interpreted as a general fear of revolutions. He was concerned about new war entanglements that came within the realm of possibility with France's renewed claim to the Rhine border as well as the Polish revolt against Russia on the eastern borders of Prussia.

It is a sign of embarrassment caused by lack of direct evidence that Rosenkranz quotes from one of Niebuhr's letters and concludes that Hegel must have thought similarly.[11] This misconception was later corrected by Hegel's son Karl. He conceded that his father had viewed the July revolution "with horror" and saw it as a catastrophe" which would shake the firm basis of the rational state; however, unlike Niebuhr, he did not think that the revolution would lead to despotism.[12] The later historian Droysen, too, charged Hegel with sympathy for the restoration regime in France. In a letter to a friend he "insisted on the pleasure of presenting Hegel as the philosopher of the restoration and, if possible, accompany him to Cherbourg"—the place from which Charles X went into his English exile.[13] Whether the harboring of such sympathy can be based upon Hegel's statements is no longer possible to determine.

The first direct evidence of Hegel's position, toward the July revolution comes from the winter term 1830–1831 and the summer term 1831, hence from a time when Hegel, according to his biographers, had come back to a more balanced view and even to the recognition of the justification of the revolution. Nothing invalidates the assumption that Hegel ever thought otherwise about the revolution than this evidence warrants. Similarly his views on the Reform Bill should be derived exclusively from his own article and his own last lectures on the philosophy of history.

These statements by Hegel not only bear witness to his personal views on the revolutionary developments. They should also be seen as a test of the principles of Hegel's philosophy of right in general, and they must here be interpreted as such. It is true that Hegel's article on the Reform Bill may be considered simply as an outstanding example of political journalism without regard to Hegel's philosophy. The same holds true of Hegel's other political writings. But the evaluation of the political situation in these writings agrees with the respective level in the development of this political philosophy in its systematic context— in this case with the philosophy of right and the lectures on the philosophy of history and religion. It is also true that Hegel's political writings in general, not only the Reform Bill article, would be misinterpreted if they were only seen as an application of general principles to special circumstances. But the reason for this is not that these writings are just political journalism detached from Hegel's philosophy. The political writings cannot be seen as an application of abstract principles because the principal positions of the philosophy of right were themselves arrived through Hegel's criticism of the natural law tradition and contemporary law as well as through a constant analysis of the political events of his time. This holds true for the first political tract against the Bern oligarchy, the first Württemberg article, the pamphlet on the constitution of the German Empire, the second Württemberg article, up to the Reform Bill article.[14] From his analysis of contemporary political developments Hegel first gained the positions that found their final formulation in his *Philosophy of Right,* without

reference to concrete political relations. These apparently abstract formulations only *seem* less saturated with reality than some of the other parts of
his philosophical system or the political writings. And therefore there remains
the important question whether the political developments during Hegel's last
year may be understood within the framework of Hegel's already developed
positions or whether they go beyond that framework.

II

In his lectures, Hegel deal with the July revolution in France twice—at the
end of his lectures on the philosophy of history, and in a passage of the lectures
on the philosophy religion.[15] The latter has scarcely been used for interpretation although it is the most extensive account of the events in France. The picture that Hegel draws of the July revolution has little in common with the
famous painting by Eugène Delacroix. It lacks enthusiasm for the revolutionary
masses and, in particular, it lacks confidence that the liberty leading the people
is a properly conceived liberty. On the other hand, his comments do not support
the reports about the total shock of the philosopher of restoration. On several
important points he remains critical of the restoration regime. But this criticism
cannot be supported by the frequency quoted statement that "a fifteen years"
farce had been played in France."[16] This quotation does not imply that the rule
of the Bourbons was a farce, but that a farce had been played about the restoration of monarchy—a criticism that also applies to the people who participated
in this farce.

Hegel's exposition shows that he is not concerned with weighing up the pros
and cons, but much more with an analysis of the political background of this
new "rupture." Hegel's analysis is so fundamental that only rarely does he refer
to the course of revolutionary events. This makes it difficult to find a clear statement as to which political group bears responsibility for the revolution. In particular, he is not interested in the question of whether in July, 1830 the constitution was first broken by the king or the people. Nor is he interested in the alternatives of restoration and liberalism or reaction and progress. He interprets the
events in the light of the relationship between religion and state, and especially
the relationship of religious conviction and the constitution of the state.

The stringency of this issue, his assumption that the decisive problem lies
here, was not made clear enough in the *Philosophy of Right* of 1821, although
Hegel did concern himself with the question of the individual's state of mind in
the state. In that work Hegel speaks of "conviction" (or "disposition," "Gesinnung") in a double sense,[17] because he had not yet achieved a complete mediation or religion, philosophy, and the ethical life of the state. It therefore seems as
if there were two forms of ethical life: a secular and a religious one. On the one

hand he states that the supreme test of conviction lies in the realm of religion, on the other that conviction forms an essential moment of the secular state. This creates the possibility of a conflict between the religious ethical and the secular ethical conviction. And Hegel leaves no doubt that when it comes to a conflict, the religious conviction must be subordinated to the ethical life of the state. The reason for this is that the secular ethical disposition in the state is not restricted, like the religious one, to the sphere of personal subjectivity, but extends to the world of ethical life, laws, and institutions. Moreover, the secular ethical disposition leads to philosophical insight, whereas the religious ethical disposition remains limited to the realm of authority and subjective conviction.

The state represents the objective form of ethical life, of reason objectified in constitutions and institutions, and independ of any specific religious foundation. The state is therefore free to let other groups do what they want, to shun the state for different reasons. Especially a strong state may be tolerant of the conviction of individuals and whole groups that do not support it. The state may well demand that its citizens belong to a religious community, but it does not have to prescribe to which one. This is due to two reasons. First, the state cannot be expected to settle specific points and differences of religious doctrine. Second, Hegel implicitly assumes that the political function of religious communities is basically the same, even if there are isolated points of difference between them as, say, between the Anabaptists and the Quakers.

This is the assumption that changed in Hegel's late Berlin years. The change results from his revised conception of the relationship between religious and state. In his late Berlin years, Hegel sketches a union of philosophy, religion, and state, that is not to be confused with a union of church and state.[18] The new conception overcomes the lack of balance found in the competition between secular and religious ethical life in his philosophy of right. This leads to a shift of emphasis, which is decisive for Hegel's evaluation of the July revolution.

On the one hand, Hegel recognized that the central problem of the political unrest of his time lay in the relation of conviction to the formal constitution, institutions, and laws. The demand for a written constitution is thus not at the center of Hegel's political thought although, as the *Philosophy of Right* shows, this demand is not without importance. The political experience of the French revolution and Europe's history since the Vienna Congress taught him that even where written constitutions did exist, as in France, the deeper problem emerged when conviction and constitution did not coincide. Therefore the cardinal political problem of the time is not to secure written constitutions but to produce a unity of conviction and the existing constitution. This is a problem that clearly emerges only with the French revolution, but for Hegel it is also a problem of world-historical dimension. For he distinguishes two forms of guaranteeing the functioning of the state. One form bases everything on conviction; it is represented by Plato's state. The other form bases everything on the formal constitution without considering disposition. In the *Philosophy of Right*, this contrast had not been presented so clearly. One may assume that Hegel's observation of the July revolution at least contributed to the formulation of this sharp opposition between conviction and formal constitution. As this problem had become central, the previous assertion of indifference towards religious communities could no longer be upheld. Such indifference can only exist when the formal constitution alone is decisive for the welfare of the state. As soon as the element of conviction is recognized as a decisive factor in the survival of the state, beside the element of constitution, it becomes clear that Hegel has to reconsider his previous assumption that the political function of all religion is fundamentally the same.

Although the contrast between formal constitution and conviction has not been stressed in the *Philosophy of Right,* Hegel frequently criticizes the attempt to decide what the best constitution is on the basis of religious conviction and intuitive knowledge: "Those who 'seek guidance from the Lord' and are assured that the whole truth is directly present in their unschooled opinions, fail to apply themselves to the task of exalting their subjectivity to consciousness of the truth and to knowledge of duty and objective right."[19] Hegel even mentions atrocities that try to legitimate themselves by claiming to be based on religion. Hegel's choice of words in these passages makes it obvious that he is primarily thinking of his old opponent Jacob Friedrich Fries, even though he does not mention him explicitly as he did in the preface of the *Philosophy of Right*; besides Fries himself, Hegel thinks of his spiritual companions in Protestant circles who stressed immediacy, feeling, and presentiment. As far as the contradiction between conviction and formal constitution is anticipated here, it is implicitly described with regard to a special variety of romantic Protestantism. In the course of the 1820s the importance of confessional opposition becomes clearer in Hegel's thought. According to his later position, a rational constitution can be found only in connection with the Protestant religion. This does not mean that it is impossible to enact such a constitution in other countries. The contradiction of conviction and constitution, however, is for Hegel only overcome in Protestant countries. Therefore, these are the only countries where constitutions can last. It has to be underlined that Hegel bases his thought on a very special understanding of Protestantism. So much is clear from the fact that Hegel in 1821, in the same context, sharply criticized the Protestant theology of feeling.[20] But in his later years it is the special form of piety found in Catholicism that he primarily considers to contradict the rationality of formal constitutions. The experiences of 1830 were not the source of his new position; it appears for the first time in the second edition of the *Encyclopedia* in 1827. However, this new conception forms the framework of Hegel's assessment of the revolutionary events in France. He may have considered these events as a test of his newly acquired opinion on the relationship of conviction and constitution as well as of his belief in the different political function of the two denominations.

When this function is so contrastingly defined, the state can no longer regard the religious community of its citizens with indifference. One might now fear that Hegel would therefore give up his demand for tolerance, which he makes in the *Philosophy of Right*. For reasons that are clear this is not the case. On the one hand, a strong state, which rests on a unity of conviction and constitution, can still exercise tolerance. On the other hand, it would be absurd for the French state to demand of its citizens that they should convert to Protestantism just for the sake of preserving the formal constitution. Hegel's new conception does not have the character of a political action recommendation; it is merely an analysis of the fact that in the Latin countries he observed—France, Spain, Italy—no political stabilization had occurred, although rational constitutions had already been enacted partly by Napoleon and partly after the Napoleonic wars.

Hegel's elevation of Protestantism to a political principle has mostly been misinterpreted. He is not in the least trying, as Rosenzweig insinuates, to base the state on Protestant piety rather than on reason, or even to make Protestantism into state religion.[21] Such a contrast between intellect and piety would be wholly misleading. Hegel did not change his views on the state; it is his views on the function of religion within the state that had changed as he now differently conceived the relationship of religion and the ethical life of the state. Hegel's thought is merely this: Protestantism achieved the reconciliation of secularity and religiosity in the Reformation. This point of view he expounded particularly in the already mentioned lecture on the "Confessio Augustana" a few days before the outbreak of the July revolution. Hegel could find the reconciliation of secularity and religiosity in Protestanism because Protestantism had overcome those religious claims that did not agree with ethical life in general. And as this contradiction of religiosity and secularity was overcome in Protestantism, Hegel believed that a basis had been prepared for the supersession of a specific type of religious subjectivity that elsewhere persisted in abstract opposition to actualized reason and ethical life. This basis would recognize that the whole structure of the spiritual world arose out of the free, self-determined will. In Catholicism, however, Hegel saw an understanding of freedom based on specifically religious convictions that had not yet reached an equilibrium with the objectified reason of the ethical world. Accordingly, the Catholic disposition either submits to authority or develops into a mere religion negation of secular ethical life. Hegel's understanding and criticism of the coalition of clericalism and liberalism in Belgium would have followed from such inter-

pretation. The disposition stamped by Protestantism is based on a reconciliation of secularity and religiosity; it is neither a mere abstract negation of the
secular life of the state nor a disposition to support the state in the form of blind
acceptance of oppression and authority. For Hegel, such recognition of mere
authority is an indication of a religiosity that has not yet been reconciled with
the secular world. In his view, the boundless injustice of the clerical power
interfering with secular affairs matches the equally great injustice of the legitimacy of the monarch derived from divine grace alone.[22] The truly religious
foundation of the state lies in the mediating conviction that there is nothing
higher than a rational system of law. In such a conviction, personal subjectivity
and the objectivity of the formal constitution of the state are reconciled. For
Hegel it is just this condition that had not been achieved in France. If one views
his evaluation of the revolutionary events in the light of this thesis, it also
becomes clear why he could not take sides in the quarrel. It was a political constellation in which both sides, the king and the government on one hand, and the
people on the other, were, from a Hegelian viewpoint, acting in an unethical
way. He himself states: "We have seen a religious sentiment or conviction taking its place at the head of the French Government, a conviction for which the
State generally was something illegitimate and devoid of rights, while it itself
took up an antagonistic attitude to all that was actually established, to justice
and morality."[23] On the other hand, the people's disposition had turned against
the constitution. Hegel did not discuss the fact that the constitution had first
been broken by Charles X as this was irrelevant to the political test of the cor-
rectness of his position. The crucial point was that here a conflict between conviction and constitution had erupted. Both sides to the struggle were
responsible for it. "The last revolution was thus the result of the dictates of a
religious conscience, which contradicted the principles of the constitution, and
yet, according to that same constitution, it is not of any importance what
religion individuals may profess."[24] Therefore the problem could not be solved
by a change of the constitution and still less by replacing the government. It
could only be solved by a change of conviction. If this change did not take place,
new manifestations of the contradiction were always to be expected. This concern has clearly been expressed in Michelet's report on Hegel's position: Hegel
fears that the new political conditions in France cannot be stable as they are not
based upon a mediation of conviction and constitution.[25] The solution by a merely
political change does not go far enough. It does not get to the root of evil.

   A look at later history shows that Hegel's fear of the instability of political
conditions in France after the July revolution was not unjustified. In spite of his
impression as a good bourgeois, Louis-Philippe tried to convert the kingdom set
up by democratic forces into a form of personal rule. The inner tensions
increased again; the followers of Bonaparte tried to revolt; and finally the

February Revolution of 1848 swept away the bourgeois monarchy. Thus Hegel's assessment of the results of the revolution was more realistic than that of his students who, in their analysis and their expectation, exaggerated the political effects of the revolution. They considered the 1830 revolution to have the same world historical importance as the 1789 revolution. Of course even if Hegel's anticipation of future development was correct, it does not follow that his analysis proved true. Nevertheless, he emphasized one crucial element of the problem when he stressed the contradiction of conviction and constitution. His cautious reaction and the traces of resignation in his analysis may have been due to the fact that he could see the fundamental problems of the political development, but was unable to provide recipes for the prevention of future revolutions. A solution could only be found through a reform of conviction and the establishment of law and constitution on this new basis. His conception necessitated a new Reformation. But no plausible political proposal could be derived from this general conclusion. Hegel thus restricted his task to an analysis of political developments and their deeper causes. Those who agree with his analysis of the causes will accept his result: to believe in a revolution without a prior reformation is a shortsighted political view. Hence Hegel understood his task not as the advocacy of one or the other side or as a direct instruction on political action, but as an analysis of prevailing ignorance about the real causes of revolution. Philosophy cannot do anything else.

III

The main aspect of Hegel's evaluation of the political development in France may finally be summarized as follows: the cause of the July revolution was the lack of insight into the fact that the state was the true form of ethical life. Ethical life and freedom depended on a reconciliation between conviction and constitution—a reconciliation that was based upon a unity of religion and secularity, of abstract subjectivity and the ethical life of the state, brought about by the Reformation. Therefore no further revolution was necessary in countries where the Reformation had successfully been completed.

This evaluation, however, contrasts with Hegel's fear as regards contemporary English events, viz., that the enactment of the Reform Bill might lead to a revolution. If one wants to avoid a radical contradiction among Hegel's statements during his last year, one must assume that "revolution" in the English context does not have the meaning of a world-historical break. One reason for his usage of the term "revolution" could lie in his countering the argument of English reform-minded politicians. They demanded the Reform Bill in order to prevent a violent revolution, while Hegel tried to show that a Reform Bill could increase the risk of a revolution.[26] However, Hegel did not oppose the reformers' argument, but insisted that the Reform Bill was not a suitable answer to the danger of the revolution. While the alleged incapacity of Catholicism to obtain the benefit of a free constitution might have been one of the causes of a revolution, social tensions, unrelieved in time, might easily be another cause in both Catholic and Protestant countries.

Hegel's criticism of the Reform Bill cannot be repeated here in detail. Nor is it our task here to judge the validity of his criticism of social relations in the England of the nineteenth century. One point that can justly be made is that Hegel primarily emphasized only those grievances that he saw and neglected to give a fair overall assessment of English conditions. In the framework of a newspaper article, however, this could not have been his task. He had to restrict himself to analyzing the causes that had led to the Reform Bill and estimating the probable results of the Bill. This analysis cannot be disposed of in the manner of Rudolf Haym, the liberal critic, who saw in Hegel's Reform Bill article nothing but an expression of the supercleverness of a theorist and the conceit of a Prussian civil servant, or alternatively as the reasoning of a complacent and frightened bureaucrat.[27] It would also be too easy to condemn Hegel's criticism of the Reform Bill by the simple rule that everyone who opposes an intended reform is a reactionary. Finally, it is permissible to stress that Hegel's article cannot be regarded as an expression of a new, exaggerated nationalism, although he did strongly criticize the English conditions. On the one hand, Hegel was more opposed to nationalism than were contemporary liberal circles. On the other hand, Hegel here used arguments which had not originally been developed with regard to England. Many of the arguments, in part more elaborate, can be found in his earlier political writings, especially in his second Württemberg work of 1816, but also in his very first publication, the commentary on Cart's pamphlet.

Already Rosenzweig had indicated that in Hegel's view the intended reform went in some ways too far and in other ways not far enough.[28] Although Hegel conceded that privileges ought to be reduced, that injustices in the election of MPs and the determination of electoral districts ought to be prevented, he rejected the Reform Bill simply because he did not believe in its efficacy. If any change came about, it would be a reduction in the homogeneity of the ruling class, which could, in extreme circumstances, provide a starting point for a revolution. This might come about when the numerically small parliamentary opposition joined forces with the popular masses against the privileged classes. In any case the argument is so general that it could also be used against Hegel's own proposal of estate representation. It seems more likely, however, that no change whatever would occur. Hegel suspected that the ruling landowning class would find it easy in a short while to restore and even extend the old power relations, in spite of the intended suffrage reform, under a merely external facade of liberalization.

Hegel rejected the Reform Bill as unsuitable for the solution of the existing social conflicts. For a real solution, a different method was needed. The social grievances had first to be overcome, and only then could a reform of the electoral system be successful. One might well be suspicious that the intention of Hegel's argument was to postpone the reform. But the same argument had already been used in his first Württemberg pamphlet, in which Hegel certainly tried to get rid of abuses. If social conditions are not reformed before the electoral system is changed, the result can only be the continuation of social tensions in the new representative assembly. Mentioning the first Württemberg pamphlet, we are also reminded of its failure. There Hegel demanded that a material change in the social conditions should precede any change in the formal constitution of the state. With regard to Württemberg, however, Hegel was unable to indicate how the material conditions could be changed. As far as England is concerned, the same dilemma emerges. Changes within the old institutional conditions could only come about by appealing to the insight of the political leadership to sacrifice its privileges. Such a deliberate sacrifice, as Hegel was well aware, seems highly unrealistic. However, the institutions would not change by themselves. They could be changed either in consequence of a new electoral system, resulting in turn from a new distribution of political power and implying the risk of a revolution, or in response to an appeal to the possessing classes's sense of justice.

In this difficult situation, Hegel considers the form of the English representative constitution to pose the greatest difficulty. His reservations are not directed against representation in general. Representative constitutions are unavoidable in modern states, as opposed to the ancient Greek *Polis,* due to the mere size of the former. But his insight into the necessity of representative constitutions does not imply Hegel's acceptance of national representation. Hegel considered the idea of popular representation, as well as sovereignty of the people, to be a liberal error. On the contrary, he is in favor of the principle of class or estate representation ("ständische Repräsentation"),especially for England. For he finds that the traditional English claim that the major interests of the nation are represented in parliament could be far better realized through his own proposal than through national representation. National representation is based on the atomized individual will. The abstract individual opposes the universality of the state. He is not mediated by institutions, classes, or corporations, nor is he organically integrated into the structured whole of the ethical state. Thus Hegel presents his arguments with all his rhetoric in order to prove the ineffectiveness of universal franchise. His case for class or estate representation doubtlessly bears conservative traits although the "estates" in his theories ought not to be confused with the unchangeable estates of the Middle

Ages. The use of the idea of organism also reminds us of the conservative theory of the state. The special institutions must not be understood as particular in a pejorative sense. They have to be perceived as members of the universal, the ethical state. Moreover, Hegel's rejection of national or popular representation does have a second, justifiable side, which contains a progressive, socially critical element. National representation does not necessarily promote greater liberty, as in general the idea of representation is not in itself a guarantee of freedom. It is not uncommon to find in representative systems that, in the name of freedom, the interests of some are not represented but suppressed. (Hegel here uses the pun: not "ver*treten*," but "zer*treten*.") And this danger of abusing the idea of freedom merely to promote the private interests of the possessing classes is, according to Hegel, especially marked in the English type of national representation. The "people" that is represented there is in itself an abstraction, an abstraction of concrete individual interests that, however, do not just disappear by themselves. As long as there are opposing interests, even class antagonisms in a people—and especially in this context Hegel uses the term *class* (*Klasse*) frequently — the idea of national representation will remain an illusion that only serves to hide class interests, based on property relationships. This effect could presumably be avoided if elections to the assembly were not regulated by an electoral system based on a property census. Hegel was always amused by the idea that political insight was connected with a ground rent of ten pounds. However, should the electoral system based on census be abolished, the revolutionary tendencies might well gain ground. The inevitable outcome would be the destruction of the state. In Hegel's view, the representation of classes was better suited to express the actual relations in the structured whole of the ethical state. The given articulation of the state, the differences of classes and of property relations, are far better expressed and more rationally balanced in Hegel's proposal than in a scheme of national representation.

It was characteristic of England, in Hegel's view, that interests of different groups, e.g. the landowning and trading classes, were represented in Parliament, but only by chance or, more correctly, as a result of the actual power of these interests. It was really a representation of classes disguised as national representation. What Hegel wanted was a consistent development towards a representation of classes, but this did not happen in England. Moreover, one could doubt whether the change of representation from nation to classes would be sufficient to abolish social conflicts by reducing existing privileges. This seems all the more improbable as, according to Hegel, the English Parliament was in reality closer to class than to popular representation without any reforms taking place. Therefore the peculiar character of the English representative system is not the fundamental cause of the problems that Hegel analysed.

In Hegel's view the basic problem, which England had to solve before it could solve other problems, consisted in the private law character of public law, i.e. constitutional relations. England's political conditions were generally based on positive law. The political institutions based on positive law bore the traces of their private law origin. What England needed was the transformation of these positive, private law conditions into public law institutions—a development that had occurred on the Continent in the recent past.

Hegel's lectures on the philosophy of history contain interesting references to the historical origin and fate of institutions based on private law.[29] Hegel shows there that England and France, however different their development had been since the Middle Ages, nevertheless arrived at the same result. When the king deprived the nobility of power, as in France, he did not interfere with the private law relations between nobility and peasants. On the other hand, when the barons gained power from the king, as in England, their private law links with their dependents were not touched either. Even the contemporary private law institutions in political life still bore the traces of their origin in the feudal system. Private law institutions naturally express private interests, and where they continue into the modern state, their positive character blocks the rational development of public law relations, the transformation of law into the universal ethical life of the state. This private law character of what are really public law institutions goes so far in England (Hegel continues) that the country lacks the "universal class" of the *Philosophy of Right*—an independent civil service based not on privilege but on ability.

The analysis clarifies the problem that Hegel considered to be England's crucial one. How can legal structures, based on positive private law, be transformed into public law institutions based on rational principles? Again, this is not a specifically English problem. In France one can also see a private law origin of its modern political conditions, and the same holds true for the German states. Hegel discovered this problem constantly in his political writings. It stood at the center of his second Württemberg work. In Württemberg, this problem had split King and Estates as early as 1815, after the Vienna Congress. The king had granted a new constitution to his country. But the Württemberg Provincial Diet insisted on its old right, the private law foundation of the representative assembly of the old Estates. For several reasons, however, the solution that was found in Württemberg could not be adopted by England. The solution was primarily a political, not a philosophico-legal one. It consisted of the private law basis of the old Estates being abolished as a consequence of the complete change in Württemberg's political structure during the Napoleonic times. The foundation of the kingdom of Württemberg was based on this change. By the de facto establishment of new political structures, new legal conditions were also created, and the followers of the old system lost their former privileges. When they wanted to reclaim their privileges, Hegel criticized them for having slept through the political development of the last decades.

The solution, however, was not exclusively dependent on political power. With the constitutional disintegration of the German Empire in 1806 the basis of the private law character of the old privileges had disappeared. When the League of the Rhine was founded, all the laws of the previous German Empire were declared null and void. At the same time the continuity of traditional privileges was abolished, at first in those states that had joined the League of the Rhine, but soon in all other states. This abolition of rights concerned not only constitutional law, but also the validity of private law. The right of creating new legal relations belonged to the princes. Although an attempt was made to preserve some unity of the German states in the field of private law, the overall constitutional order was unquestionably broken up, and the private law foundation of political structures and authorities disappeared with it. It is strange that the ideology of political restoration, with its intention of reerecting prerevolutionary legal structures, was opposed to the princes' competence to grant new constitutions in newly established states as, e.g., the kingdom of Württemberg. Such constitutions were in accordance with the decisions of the Vienna Congress and the acts of the German League. In a material sense, however, they were not in line with political restoration, as they did by no means imply a return to prerevolutionary legal structures and the private law foundations of the previous representative system. In this respect, the so-called restoration policy of the German princes was a product of the Revolution. There was a hint of this problem also in Prussia, but it became strikingly evident in the struggle for a Württemberg constitution, in which Hegel opposed both the liberals and the old Estates. In his article on the Württemberg Estates he supported the position of the king who wished to create new constitutional conditions after the continuity of the old private law had been destroyed.

The problem that England had to solve had been settled on the Continent by political developments that entailed consequences for the validity of the old legal system. A comparable political and legal development had not taken place in England. This reveals a dilemma for Hegel's analysis. He analyses a condition that had been overcome on the Continent by a unique political and legal development and had led to a result that Hegel welcomed as a rational outcome. This solution—the political and subsequent constitutional development—could not be imported by countries such as England. Therefore in spite of identical starting points, the developments were so different that the Continental prescription could not be applied to England. These difficulties were intensified by a second element in Hegel's analysis—the role of the monarchy—that led to the prohibition of the last installment of Hegel's article in the *Preussische Staatszeitung,* and afterwards gave rise to a number of criticisms directed against its prorestoration character. The criticisms were based on a lack of historical knowledge. The institution that in Württemberg had achieved the establishment of new constitutional conditions, the monarchy, was too weak in England to play a similar role. Hegel may have misjudged the political and legal position of the English king, considering that he dissolved Parliament just at the time Hegel complained about the complete lack of royal power. However, it cannot be doubted that the king had neither the political power nor the legal position to transform the character of constitutional structures from private law into public law.

When one compares England's political situation criticized by Hegel with the Continental development, the central problem of Hegel's Reform Bill article becomes evident. The only solution, political as well as legal, that occurred to him was the one that the Continental states had achieved. Other than that, he had no prescription to offer England. Hence Hegel's embarrassment, which is much more obvious in the article than any fear of revolution. Hegel opposed rational law to the old positive and private law conditions and also recognized rational law arguments behind the changes contemplated in the Reform Bill. But it was not easy to say, especially for Hegel, how rational law arguments could overcome the legal character of privileges based on positive law and create a system of real rights. Apart from the voluntary sacrifice of privileges by the ruling classes, there was only one way left: the revolution. But such an abstract destruction of positive by rational law would mean the destruction of both law and reality. The only answer left was to hope for a historical development that replaced privileges by rational constitutional structures, and to wait for a thorough scientific revision of law and for the enlightened consent of the privileged to abolish their own privileges. The alternative was a revolution.

IV

The result of Hegel's analysis of the political events in England and France during his last year was that developments in both countries as well as the conditions that they were trying to overcome, missed the idea of the state as the objectivity of reason, the idea of the ethical state. In France this happened because of an abstract contradiction between conviction and constitution, a contradiction that remained the same in postrevolutionary as in prerevolutionary France; in England the trouble was the misconception of public affairs as private affairs, a confusion of the *res publica* and the *res privata*, that would not be affected by the enactment of the Reform Bill. For this reason Hegel declined to take sides in either of the two conflicts. The new conditions were as unacceptable as the old ones. The role of the philosopher was restricted to an analysis of the conditions, on a level that was not accessible to everbody. Philosophy cannot give concrete advice on action; it can only remove the prevailing ignorance of the true causes of problems that are only superficially discussed. By doing so, philosophy contributes implicitly towards their final solution. But the solution itself Hegel expected to come not from philosophical recognition, but from another power: history. As regards the problems that Hegel considered with England as an example, history found a better solution that Hegel dared to hope. Unfortunately this cannot be said about the opposition of conviction and constitution. Although the problem of the relation of the individual to the state, the integration of the individual into the universal ethical life, is nowadays separated from the confessional issue and from the concrete case of France with which Hegel had connected it, his words with regard to it remain timely and relevant: "This collision, this nodus, this problem is that with which history is now occupied, and whose solution is has to work out in the future."[30]

NOTES

1.   Hegel, *Berliner Schriften 1818-1831*, ed. by J. Hoffmeister (Hamburg, 1956), pp. 30–55.

2.   Cf. Hegel's review of the writings of Hülsemann and Schubarth-Carganico in *Berliner Schriften*, pp. 330–402.

3.   K. Rosenkranz, *G.W.F. Hegels Leben (*Berlin 1844), p. 414.

4.   R. Haym, *Hegel und seine Zeit* (Berlin, 1857), p. 455.

5.   K. Rosenkranz, *G.W.F. Hegels Leben*, p. 414.

6.   *Ibid.*, p. 417; F. Rosenzweig, *Hegel und der Staat* (München-Berlin, 1920), vol. 2 p. 224.

7.   *Hegel in Berichten and seiner Zeitgenossen*, ed. by F. Nicolin (Hamburg, 1970), pp. 332–333.

8.   *Briefe von und an Hegel*, vol. 3, ed. by J. Hoffmeister, p. 333; H. Schneider, "Dokumente zu Hegels politischem Denken 1930/31," in *Hegel-Studien* 11 (Bonn, 1976), pp. 81–84.

9.   *Briefe*, vol. 3, pp. 323, 337.

10.   *Briefe*, vol. 1, p. 116.

11.   K. Rosenkranz, *G.W.F. Hegels Leben*, pp. 414–415.

12.   *Hegel in Berichten seiner Zeitgenossen*, p. 415.

13.   *Ibid.*, p. 431.

14.   For the English texts of most of the writings see: T.M. Knox and Z.A. Pelczynski, eds., *Hegel's Political Writings* (Oxford, 1964).

15.   Hegel, *The Philosophy of History*, trans. by J. Sibree (New York, 1956), pp. 451–452; Hegel, *Lectures on the Philosophy of Religion*, trans. by E.B. Speirs and J.B. Sanderson (London, 1962), pp. 246–257.

16.   Hegel, *The Philosophy of History*, p. 451. Cf. W.R. Beyer, "Der Stellenwert der französichen Juli-Revolution von 1830 im Denken Hegels," in *Deutsche Zeitschrift für Philosophie* 19, (Berlin, 1971), pp. 628–643.

17. *Hegel's Philosophy of Right*, trans. by T.M. Knox (Oxford, 1967), § 270.

18. Hegel, *Encyclopedia of Philosophy*, trans. by G.E. Mueller (New York, 1959), § 552.

19. Hegel, *The Philosophy of Right*, § 270.

20. *Ibid.*, § 272.

21. F. Rosenzweig, *Hegel und der Staat*, vol. 2, p. 218.

22. Hegel, *Vorlesungen über die Philosophie der Weltgeschichte*, vol. 4, ed. by G. Lasson (Hamburg, 1923), p. 917.

23. Hegel, *Lectures on the Philosophy of Religion*, p. 256.

24. *Ibid.*

25. *Hegel in Berichten seiner Zeitgenossen*, p. 415.

26. Cf. M. Brock, *The Great Reform Act* (London, 1973); M.J. Petry, "Hegel and the 'Morning Chronicle,'" in *Hegel-Studien 11*, (Bonn, 1976), pp. 11–14.

27. R. Haym, *Hegel und seine Zeit*, pp. 456, 459.

28. F. Rosenzweig, *Hegel und der Staat*, vol. 2, pp. 232–233.

29. Hegel, *The Philosophy of History*, pp. 429–430.

30. *Ibid.*, p. 452.

THE SOCIAL IDEAL OF HEGEL'S ECONOMIC THEORY

by
H.S. HARRIS

Readers of Shlomo Avineri's *Hegel's Theory of the Modern State* will know that the manuscripts of Hegel's Jena period contain some remarkable anticipations of the Marxian analysis of the economic dialectic of factory capitalism. Avineri cited most of the more startling passages, but I shall content myself with just three that illustrate the essential aspect of Hegel's proto-Marxism.

In the first place Hegel saw that the rationalization of labor, and the substitution of the formal task of machine minding for the material burdens of physical effort, both reduces the value of individual labor and impoverishes the activity of labor, itself regarded as the life occupation of the worker:

> in the MACHINE man supersedes just this formal activity of his own, and lets it do all the work for him. But this deceit that he practices against nature, and through which he abides stably within its singularity, takes its revenge upon him; what he gains from nature, the more he subdues it, the lower he sinks himself. When he lets nature be worked over by a variety of machines, he does not cancel the necessity for his own laboring but only postpones it, and makes it more distant from nature; and living labor is not directed on nature as alive, but this negative vitality evaporates from it, and the laboring that remains to man becomes itself more machinelike; man diminishes labor only for the whole, not for the single [laborer]; for him it is increased rather; for the more machinelike labor becomes, the less it is worth, and the more one must work in that mode.[1]

The main thesis of this paper sprang from a critical reaction to the claim of D.E.S. Macgregor (in an unpublished manuscript) that Hegel's ideal of society was already a form of communism. The acknowledgment is all the more necessary because in the revised version of Macgregor's work, which will be published by the University of Toronto Press, this claim appears only in a very muted form.

In the second place, Hegel saw that the operation of a free market upon laborers subject to this process of rationalization, as also its effect upon artisans whose "formal" activity with tools was superseded by the machine, must turn them into a revolutionary force of the kind that he called "barbaric." (We need to know that in his view the historical function of the "barbarians" was to be the "broom of God"—to overrun and sweep away the complex social institutions of civilized life whose existence they did not even recognize):

> great wealth, which is similarly bound up with the deepest poverty (for in the separation [between rich and poor] labor on both sides is universal and objective), produces on the one side in ideal [ideel] universality, on the other side in real [reell] universality, mechanically. This purely quantitative element, the inorganic aspect of labor, which is parcelled out even in its concept, is the unmitigated extreme of barbarism. The original character of the acquisitive estate, namely, its being capable of an organic absolute intuition and respect for something divine, even though posited outside it, disappears, and the bestiality of contempt for all higher things enters. The mass of wealth, the pure universal, the absence of wisdom, is the implicit essence (das Ansich). The absolute bond of the people, namely ethical principle, has vanished, and the people is dissolved. The government has to work as hard as possible against this inequality and the destruction of private and public life wrought by it. It can do this directly in an external way by making high gain more difficult, and if it sacrifices one part of this estate to mechanical and factory labor and abandons it to barbarism, it must keep the whole without question in the life possible for it. But this happens most necessarily, or rather immediately, through the inner constitution of the estate.[2]

This second quotation contains some puzzles. What is the "universality and objectivity" of labor? And how and what does labor produce in "ideal" and "real universality" respectively? What is the "capacity for an organic absolute intuition" that disappears, and why does it do so? To the last question we shall have to return. About the others, let me say, briefly—and for the present dogmatically—that the "*universality* of labor" is its reduction to the bare form of machine minding, so that any single laborer is easily replaced by another, just as any tiller of the soil is; and its "objectivity" consists in the fact that the energy source derives from the order of nature, not from living effort; thus "great wealth" produces, on the one side, in the ideal universality of understanding, the engineering problem, on the other side, in real universality, by making, linking together, and minding the engines.

I will concede that other interpretations of "objectivity" and "ideal universality" are possible, but this one is consistent with the context here (and with a number of others); and, in any case it is indisputable that Hegel is talking about the industrial rationalization and mechanization of labor, and that he claims that it reduces one part of the "acquisitive estate" (*Erwerbsstand*) to "barbarism."

My interpretation of what "barbarism" means can be justified from the analysis of barbarian "havoc" in the *System of Ethical Life* (the work from which the quotation itself is taken).[3] But since there can at best be no more than a very imperfect analogy between the "barbarism" of Genghis Khan (or even of Attila) and that produced by the economic class war, I will add finally a third quotation from the last and plainest of Hegel's early lecture manuscripts, which states the social effects of the economic dialectic in more familiar terms:

> The antithesis of great wealth and great poverty emerges—the poverty for which it becomes impossible to come up with something on its own account;—wealth like every [physical] mass makes itself into force—accumulation of wealth [is] partly by chance, partly through the universal [economy] by way of its apportioning. [It is] a centre of attraction. [i.e. one] of a kind which casts its glance more widely over the universal, gathers [it] around itself—just as a great mass draws the lesser one to it;—he that hath, to him shall be given.—Acquisition becomes a many sides system, bringing in income on all sides, on sides which a smaller business cannot make use of; or the abstraction of labor reaches out to embrace ever more singular types, and achieves an ever wider scope. This inequality of wealth and poverty, this need [*Not*] and necessity becomes the most extremem disruption [*Zerrissenheit*] of the general will-inward insurrection and hatred.[4]

When Avineri drew attention to this proto-Marxist analysis of factory capitalism for the first time (at the Marquette Hegel Symposium in 1970), Otto Pöggeler commented gently, but, as I thought then, very cogently, that he had not taken any account of the extremely different character of the three different "systems" to which the manuscripts he had lumped together belonged. When I arrived at the "Real Philosophy" of 1805/6 in my own snail–like progress through the Jena papers, I felt that my conviction was justified; for it seemed to me that I could make out a plausible case the Hegel has an *answer* in 1805 for what was only a *problem* in the manuscript of 1802. But when I came to gather the threads together, I found that this was almost certainly a mistake. Hegel's social philosophy and ideals are constant, I am now prepared to maintain, not only throughout the Jena period, but in all probability throughout the earlier Frankfurt period as well. There is one concept of "political justice" implicit in all of his social writings, theoretical and practical, from his first venture into print as an anonymous pamphleteer in 1797 to the emergence of his great theoretical casting of accounts with his time in the *Phenomenology of Spirit* a decade later. And his firm grasp of this criterion of "justice" fairly surely guarantees that he already knew what was implied in 1802 when he wrote that the "keeping of the whole in the life possible for it . . . happens most necessarily, or rather immediately, through the inner constitution of the estate"[5] as definitely as he did in 1805 (when he made the implication as clear as his philosophical obligation to stick to the rational recognition of the actual would allow).

It would seem therefore that in the end I must concur with Avineri's cheerful indifference about the lost systematic contexts to which the fragmentary and long unpublished remains originally belonged. This is not the case, however, for the supposition of coherence to which I have *returned* differs from the one that Avineri spontaneously adopted in a predictably Hegelian way. By taking the papers in their order, and seeking to understand each statement in its full context, so far as that context can be reconstructed, I believe that we can discover more about Hegel's unchanging concept of social justice than would ever be apparent to an observer who lumps all the statements together at the start.

Thus although I do not dissent, and I hold that no one rationally can dissent from, Avineri's claim that

> the major difference [between Marx and Hegel] has, however, already been pointed out by Lukács: while Hegel sees alienation as a necessary aspect of objectification, Marx maintains that alienation does not reside immanently in the process of production itself, but only in its concrete historical conditions. For Marx, therefore, there exists the possibility of ultimate salvation, whereas the Hegel one will never be able to dissociate the cross from the rose of the present.[6]

I think that this "difference" between them is not mainly a matter of their different social situations and sympathies, but of differing speculative analyses of natural and spiritual necessity, applied to moral ideals of human life that are virtually identical. Of the two speculative analyses, I take Hegel's to be quite demonstrably the sounder. Hence I can sum up the difference within identity by saying that while both Hegel and Marx are Christian socialists, Hegel is less of a *believer* and for that very reason, a better philosopher. (The Marxist ideal of a coming social millenium does, however, do more adequate justice to some aspects of the gospel of universal brotherhood, which Hegel can now be seen to have slighted unnecessarily. So the advantage is not quite *all* on Hegel's side; and perhaps the philosopher ought to take "belief"—or what Ernst Bloch called "the principle of hope"—a little more seriously than Hegel, with his violent antipathy to the optimisitic moralism of Fichte, would ever allow.)

Turning now to the task of making out my case in due order, I must concede at once that we cannot be *sure* about Hegel's socio-economic philosophy in the Frankfurt period, because all of the *primary* documents are lost to us. It was the great merit of Lukács that, although he conceded far too much to the romantic image of Hegel in this period established by Wilhelm Dilthey, he grasped the significance of all the political and economic papers, of which we have only the most inadequate secondary accounts; and he made everyone see how different our view of the so-called "early theological writings" is bound to be when they are restored to the context of revolutionary political and economic theorizing in which they wer born. When we read what remains to us with the proper awareness of what Hegel was trying to do, out inadequate reports about what is lost sometimes yield a more concrete significance than they appear to have on the surface. Thus, in the *Spirit of Christianity,* Hegel comments on the ideal communism of the Sermon on the Mount:

> About the command . . . to cast aside care for one's life and to despise riches, as also about Matthew XIX, 23: 'How hard it is for the rich man to enter the Kingdom of Heaven,' there is nothing to be said; it is a litany pardonable only in sermons and rhymes, for such a comment is without truth for us. The fate of property has become too powerful for us to tolerate reflections on it, as if its abolition were thinkable for us.[7]

That "property" was regarded by Hegel as a "fate" is instructive. On the one hand it is an impediment to the freedom of the spirit (as we can learn from the fragment on "Love");[8] on the other hand, it is unavoidable. This is the fundamental disagreement between Hegel and Marx. Property, upon Hegel's view of it, quite simply *cannot* be abolished. But "fate" is a power with which we must be *reconciled;* the basic problem of Hegel's ethics (then and later) is to achieve a properly *reverent* attitude towards it.[9] So when Rosenkranz tells us that in his notes on Steuart's *Principles of Political Economy* (February— May, 1799): "Hegel fought against what was dead [in the mercantile system] with noble feeling, with a wealth of interesting examples, as he strove to save the *Gemüt* of man amidst the competition and mechanical interaction of labor and commerce,"[10] we must assume that although Hegel found many faults in Steuart's mercantilist doctrine, he regarded it as preferable to the *irreconcilable* form in which man's economic fate appears in Adam Smith's *Wealth of Nations.*

The general view has been that Hegel was not, at this date, familiar with *The Wealth of Nations* at all. But this view is almost certainly wrong. It is plausible enough, as long as we can assume, as I used to, that Hegel depended on the German translation of Smith that appeared between 1796 and 1798 in Frankfurt and Leipzig. But the fact is that at the time of his death, he *owned* the Basel edition of the English text (1791); and in his earliest explicit reference to Smith (1804) he confuses the calculations in Smith's opening example of the pinfactory in his own way (not in the way that Garve, the German translator, confused them). So there is every reason to think that he was using his English text in 1804. Once we put it in his library at *that* date, the question why he acquired it, rather than the translation that had appeared in his local bookshops while he was in Frankfurt (at a time when he was deeply concerned about political economy and more comfortable for money than at any time in the next decade) can have only one likely answer. The only plausible assumption is that he bought the Basel edition for himself while he was a house-tutor in Switzerland (1793–1796). Thus he had Smith's *Wealth of Nations* at hand all the time he was working over Steuart, and he had probably read it long before he read Steuart (though we cannot be sure of that).[11]

So we must ask why Hegel preferred the economic theory of Steuart to that of Smith. It was Steuart's fate to be a pioneer, completely overshadowed even in his own time by a younger contemporary better attuned to the mind of the time. His *Principles* appeared in 1767 just nine years before the *Wealth of Nations*. Smith made no reference to it (though he probably profited from studying it). The reason why Hegel did not follow the fashion is simple; and it had already been remarked on by Steuart's reviewers. Steuart sought to advance the old science of "political economy" as first conceived and established by Plato and Aristotle. Smith, on the other hand, was inventing a new *natural* science of "economics." "Political economy," as Steuart conceived it, was vital part of the great armory of rational statesmanship; the statesman must understand economic life and policy, in order to secure the best life possible for his citizens. Smith's "economics," however, is founded on natural laws that operate to maximize wealth; so that for a political authority to have an economic *policy* (of a positive directive kind) can only inhibit what is generally desirable; political interference should be limited to the care and maintenance (and occasional repair) of the natural machinery of economic life. The thoughtful English merchants of the time did not need Smith to tell them that Steuart's "statesman" must be kept out of the engine shed. As soon as the *Principles* appeared one of the them declared in an authoritative review:

> We have no idea of a statesman having any connection with the affair, and we believe that the superiority which England has at present over all the world, in point of commerce, is owing to her excluding statesmen from the executive part of all commercial concerns.[12]

But Steuart's *political* conception of economics was, of course, just what attracted Hegel. For Hegel too, was from the first, a *political* economist. For him Adam Smith was the *Newton* of human affairs, analysing the life of the social whole as a dead mechanism, just as Newton had already analysed the solar system as a marvellous clockwork model operated by occult forces that must be rationally postulated, instead of recognizing it as a model of organic *life*. That Newton's model *could* be adapted to the study of human society was one of the most disastrous aspects of the *Principia* as "natural philosophy." To study society as a mechanism driven by the forces of human need is to learn only about the *needs* of life, which bring the mechanism into existence, not about the potentialities of the good life, which the mechanism brings into existence. The mechanism of needs certainly exists, and the needs that drive it must be appreciated. They must even be *"reverenced as fate,"* i.e., as the ineluctably necessary structure of life itself. But we reverence fate in order to enjoy our freedom. The object of studying economics is not just to understand how we are *fated,* but to comprehend society as an *organism,* and so "save the *Gemüt of man"* from the blind operation of the social mechanism. It was natural, therefore, for Hegel to *begin* with Steuart, who understood that the forces driving the economic mechanism were alive, and therefore plastic and subject to some degree of rational control; and to see Smith's theory only as the formulation of the essential *problem* that our nature poses for us, not as a triumphant demonstration that the problem will solve itself in the best possible way if we leave the natural forces to find their own spontaneous equilibrium. The natural forces of social life will not, in fact, do that. The natural dynamism that produces the wealth of nations is social dynamite. If we wish to *maintain* prosperity, we must not merely work industriously as individuals, we must think intelligently as a community.

The object of this communal labor of thought is the achievement of social justice. "Social Justice" is the focal concept in Hegel's practical philosophy just as it is in that of Plato. The justice of fairness, which is the *individual* virtue that is vital in social relations, must derive its essential criteria of what *is* "fair" from the ideal harmony of the whole. What is fair is not generally or abstractly what is equal, but what is proportioned to the harmony of that whole, or what is required by and for the "living bond" that holds the whole together.

In every society, the sense of what is socially "right" (as what is requisite for its peaceful and effective maintenance) is necessarily present. The duty to do what is "right" in this sense does not rest on me simply as a rational individual. Not everyone has the same social duty, and no one has a duty that is uniquely his; one's social duty derives from one's social role, from one's being one of a group of individuals distinguished by their having the same determinate function or status in society (one which they all share, and which others do not have). Thus the problem of defining social justice is the problem of securing a *satisfied* consensus about the duties (functions) and rights (rewards) of each determinate status.

A considerable degree of consensus about what the actual status system is, must exist or there would not be a community at all. But the consensus is never a fully satisfied one. There are always *prima facie* grounds of some sort for protesting against being assigned to a certain status, or against the way that that status is itself socially defined; indeed, a human society must contain some statuses that are *dissatisfying* by definition. It is an axiom of the theory of social health, for example, that a child ought to want to change his status for that of a grown-up. It is no part of my present concern to expound the general theory of society as an organism, but this elementary example is important to my theme, because the greatest thinker of the generation before Hegel had defined the ideal of rational enlightenment as *man's coming of age*. The child perceives his own coming of age as desirable, because grown-ups at least *appear* to possess the freedom to choose between statuses, or to define for themselves what status and duties they will accept, whereas his own child status is defined for him partly by nature, and partly by arbitrary social authority. In the same way the status system of the unenlightened world was determined by the divine author of nature (and father of the human family) or by the arbitrary authority of long established custom. A social world that had come of age must naturally want to throw off religion's parental control and work out ways of defining the standards of social justice for itself, instead of accepting what is customary. "Justice" for the future, must depend on a consensus reached by rational deliberation, not on an unthinking acceptance of the "will of God" or the way of our fathers.

This is the black-and-white silhouette of the thought context in terms of which the appeal to "justice" in Hegel's earliest social writings must be interpreted. He has not theory of what the *justified* social structure will look like (or at least no theory is stated in the surviving manuscripts). He only knows that every customary structure must be submitted to criticism, and the the necessary process of justification is one of communal deliberation. That society consists of different "estates" he takes for granted. But the "estates" have to be redefined, and whatever customary rights are not acceptable to the community as a deliberative council must be surrendered. Unless this is accepted, the forces of newly adult human self-consciousness will sweep *everything* away (as the Revolution has already done in France) and begin again with a clean slate. Thus in his very first (anonymous) publication, he introduces his translation of Cart's *Confidential Letters* by citing the words of a Titan swept down into the Underworld by the Olympians in the very first political revolution of our western tradition; "Learn *justice*, being warned [not to have contempt for the Gods].[11] Upon those who are deaf to this cry for justice, he adds, "their fate will smite hard."[13] He did not agree with Cart's Jacobin view that social stratification could and should be swept away.[14] But he did hold that "Justice is the unique criterion for deciding" what is untenable in the existing social structure; and he was quite prepared to terrorize all traditionalists into accepting this criterion, by directing attention to the great slate-cleaning operation that filled the first years of the Revolution in France.[15]

This Girondin revolutionary commitment created an instructive contradiction in Hegel's practical programme. The "justice" that he appealed to could only be achieved by a representative assembly of all estates in which Rousseau's "General Will" was genuinely dominant. But the general will could only emerge in its requisite *enlightened* form in an assembly of representatives for whom the traditional foundations of social justice were no longer valid. They must all alike know that they were there to formulate the judgment of the community, not to reaffirm the will of God or of their ancestors. For on either of these latter bases every social privilege that ought to be surrendered in the interest of "justice" would have an entrenched position. Because of this, Hegel's projected pamphlet, which announced the principle of enlightened "justice" on its title page: "That the magistrates should be chosen by the citizens," came to the uncomfortable conclusion that "the essential thing is that the right of election should be placed in the hands of a body of enlightened and upright men independent of the court," since it was not "advisable to hand over the choice of its defender suddenly to an unenlightened mass of men, accustomed to blind obedience, and dependent on the impression of the moment.[16] On this view of things, the new social order could be established only under the aegis of a revolutionary army; Hegel's proposal was practically relevant to the situation in Mainz, but not to the summoning of the Estates in Württemberg (even after a lapse of twenty-seven years). So his friends advised him not to publish his pamphlet, and he very sensibly accepted their advice.

Practical politics was never Hegel's forte. But the creation of "enlightenment" in the minds of "upright men independent of the court" was his lifelong concern. The whole subsequent evolution of his theory of the social estates is one long effort to articulate the concept of "justice" as a harmony of these estates. The classical model was, of course, Plato; and Plato is the most important influence on Hegel's theory of the social organism. But Plato produced only the undeveloped concept of the authority of Reason.[17] In the developed or free social organism, there is nothing authoritarian. Every proper part of the organism governs itself. "The organic principle is freedom, the fact that the ruler is himself the rules."[18] Thus the identification and living organization of the "estates" as society's proper parts—which (in peace time at least) must have a large measure of self-regulating autonomy—is vital to Hegel's theory. For these are the unit constituencies that must choose their own "magistrates" in the rationalized constitution of the new age that is dawning.

The "estate" is an *economic* entity. This is *must* be, for it is the essential mediating term between the private interests that can only be aggregated into a "will of all," and the public interest that can only be expressed in a truly "general will." Without this mediation, the "general will" can only have a negative, authoritarian or repressive, relation toward all private interests. If we attempt to realize the "general will" according to Rousseau's own recipe for its expression, we are bound to create the very "factions" whose elimination he regarded as essential, and thus to generate a climate of universal suspicion. The political expression of this is the Terror.[19] Before it can be reconciled into the positive universality of a community at peace with itself private interest must be generalized into its proper *species*. If this can be done, the individual will and intellect will never directly appear in the arena of political deliberation at all. The general will gets formulated by a body of legislators who represent their "estates"; and since each estate is itself a community united by a *specific* social interest, it would be absurd for a Hegelian legislator to claim, as Burke did in his famous speech to the electors of Bristol, that "your representative . . . betrays instead of serving you if he sacrifices his judgment to your opinion." For his judgement is supposed to express as well as possible a consensus of interest, or a "will of all."

From this mediating function the essential character of a properly con-stituted estate necessarily follows. Hegel agreed almost completely with some-thing else that Burke said in that same speech: "Parliament is not a *congress* of ambassadors from different and hostile interests . . . but . . . a *deliberative* assembly of *one* nation, with *one* interest that of the whole." Hegel almost agreed, but not quite; for his own concept of the "estate" was designed to pro-duce a congress of interests that were different without being essentially and necessarily hostile. Only through a congress of this kind is the transition from a "will of all" to a "general will" possible. If the interests to be summed are diametrically opposed, and hence necessarily hostile, because whatever is con-ceded to one side must be directly denied to (or subtraced from) the other, the birth of "fraction" is unavoidable. We can only pass from a "will of all" that is implicitly general (because in each "faction" the members share the same interest distributively) to one that is *explicitly* tyrannical (because it arises from a preponderance of factions on one side of a balance).

Because he means to ensure the *Aufhebung* of faction—i.e., not to eliminate it but to guarantee that it will not break the "absolute bend" of the *Volk*— Hegel's "estates" are radically different from the "three orders" of society that we find in Adam Smith (or again in Marx) or from most of the "interest groups" of more recent democratic political theory. Hegel's "estates" are different because they must already have resolved "class" conflict before the political process can properly begin. This is the primary reason why each estate needs its own internal "government." It must regulate not only the conditions of entry into its particular sphere of activity, and the conditions of the activity itself, but also the distribution of its rewards—and it must achieve a general consensus of support in all this. Then when the estates come together in their assembly they will be directly conscious of their interdependence and complementarity. For the economic "estates" that Hegel distinguishes are the primary producers (agriculture), the secondary producers (manufactures and trade) and the non-producers (public service of all kinds).

The way in which a class of secondary producers naturally develops in a pro-sperous agricultural economy was remarked on already by Steuart (whose evolutionary or phenomenological approach to economic theory was another important ground for Hegel's natural predilection for his work). Steuart calls his two classes "farmers" and "free hands" initially; and generally "labourers" and "free hands" thereafter.[20] He subsequently distinguishes the "consumers" from these two types of producers;[21] and finally he adds the necessary though unproductive class of social defenders (i.e. soldiers).[22] The influence of his distinctions on the *System of Ethical Life* will be apparent to anyone who compares the texts carefully.

Adam Smith, by contrast, analyses only the fully developed society; and he distinguishes his classes according to the type of monetary income that they live on. There are "those who live by rent , . . . those who live by wages,and . . . those who live by profit."[23] The universal concept specified by division in Smith's theory is "wealth"; in that of Steuart and Hegel it is "industry." Thus for Smith the continuing *growth* of an economy is vital to its health:

> The wages of the labourer, it has already been shown, are never so high as when the demand for labour is continually rising, or when the quantity employed is every year increasing considerably. When this real wealth of the society becomes stationary, his wages are soon reduced to what is barely enough to enable him to bring up a family, or to continue the race of labourers. When the society declines, they fall even below this. The order of the proprietors may, perhaps, gain more by the prosperity of the society than that of labourers: but there is no order that suffers so cruelly from its decline.

For Steuart, on the other hand, the ideal condition of society is that of a stable economy with full employment: *"That number of husbandmen, therefore, is the best, which can provide food for all the state; and that number of inhabitants is the best, which is compatible with the full employment of every one of them."*[24] Steuart's whole science is directed toward the regulation of population and its stabilization at the optimal level.[25] This goal is nowhere stated explicitly in Hegel's social theory; but it is implicit in everything he says about the government's responsibility for economic planning.

In Hegel's theory of the estates, it is the *ethos*—the virtue, or spirit—of the three modes of social life that is of primary importance.[26] The primary producers exhibit human virtue "raw" and undeveloped. The mediation of private and public interest is hardly possible for them, because it is hardly necessary. The conflict has not properly arisen. The peasant is aware only of the interest of the natural community, the family. He has no purely private interest of his very own, and his relationship with the public interest is one of "trust" (*Vertrauen*). The peasant is—or should be—a free man, but he accepts the existing order of society as naturally given. Hegel seems to think of the peasant as essentially a *tenant*. He must go to his landowner for justice in peacetime; and he exhibits his "solid" virtue—his essential manliness—as a common soldier (with his noble lord as his officer) in war. Hegel's distinction between the primary level of finite "feeling" or reality, and the reflective level of "infinity and ideality" (in the *System of Ethical Life*) shows that he fully appreciated "the difference between agriculture exercised *as a trade* and *as a direct means of subsisting"* that Steuart emphasized.[27] And since that distinction is introduced by Hegel within the sphere of natural ethics, it is evident that he conceives the peasants as "traders" even before the transition to properly political society. But peasants never develop a properly commercial attitude toward their own patrimony; and the communal sharing of labor—which is basic to its rational *division*—is alien to the natural mode of life of peasants, and is only imposed on them by force (in the institution of serfdom.)[28] But because they *do* identify with their land, they will fight for it; so that serfdom can never be more than a transitional phase in the evolution of political society.[29] And because of his basic manliness, and his distrust of the civil world, which he does not properly understand, and whose values he can never completely share, the peasant remains as the maker of *violent* revolution, when the dialectic of bourgeois society finally drives him to it.[30] After his revolution, the peasant's situation cannot, with respect to *Bildung,* remain as undeveloped as it is in Hegel's logical analysis. But just how the peasant is to become a fully self-conscious participant in the expressing of the General Will, is for history, not for philosophy, to decide. All that can be said about it, in terms of conceptual necessity is that the political incorporation of agriculture is bound to be *regional;* the development of representative democracy on the basis of local residential constituencies since 1776 and 1789 reflects the aristocratic bias of the American and the peasant bias of the French revolutions. This agrarian regionalism is quite inappropriate for articulating the voice of Steuart's "industry"—as any observer of the struggles of central and local governments for control of a nation's industrial resources is soon forced to recognize.

The absolute or universal estate is less interesting because it is identical with the concept in its full development. This is the final cause in Hegel's system. So far as we can all be brought to see that social justice is a regulative ideal, and is *not finally* achievable, since the perpetual awareness of *injustice* in some shape is a rational necessity of free self-conscious existence (so that not justice as Plato thought, but injustice, is itself "just")—so far as *Bildung* can be universalized as this philosophical insight, we shall *all* be members of the universal class. The dawn of the atomic age makes it necessary to believe in the possibility of this philosophical millenium since the *instinctive* (violent) reaction of absolute freedom against perceived social injustice could now lead to a Terror that would be the Armageddon of eschatological prophecy.

The universal estate contains in itself no principle of further dialectical development or *revolutionary* change. But this estate is self-transforming—it develops from an "absolute" estate of soldiers into a "universal" estate of philosophers. The absolute estate is, to begin with, the military aristrocracy who are the masters in the "natural" relation of lordship and bondage. But as soon as this natural nobility begin to govern a differentiated society (one that contains Steuart's "free hands") they must absorb the "priests and elders" who are the organic governing body of the "free hands." (They are, of course, themselves "priests and elders" for the undifferentiated or "natural" society).[31] Thus as the "absolute government" they cease to be a distinct "estate"[32] and become the "universal estate"—which will *be* completely "universal" if and when, the "general will" ever is perfectly articulated and self-conscious.[33] and when Hegel offers his *systematic* analysis of the structure of the "universal estate"—as distinct from the evolutionary or phenomenological view of it that is dominant earlier—the professional soldiers (*Soldatenstand*) come not at the beginning but at the end of its *logical* development. With their devotion unto death, they show us the way into the "kingdom of heaven," the realm of "absolute" (or *free*) *Bildung* in Art, Religion, and Philosophy. In spite of his bourgeois prejudice about the naturally given limits of peasant educability, or for that matter his distinctively personal prejudice about the natural limits of female educability, I take it to be clear beyond doubt that Hegel conceived of that world of Absolute Spirit as a universal democracy. His conviction that the *Volk* must possess Homer (at the hands of Voss) and philosophy (at his own hands) along with the Bible (at Luther's) *in its own tongue,* native and unadulterated is quite inexplicable on any other basis (however quaint his conviction may appear in view of the form in which he actually bequeathed "philosophy" as a "possession" to his people). The "noble" warriors lay the foundations of constitutional government; and they are the seedbed of the *Gemeingeist* because they display for us the *totality* of self-commitment that "life in the *Volk*" is. But in the truly *free* constitution each of us "lives in the *Volk*" as a member of his own *Stand.*[34] Hegel thought that this noble seedbed was a permanent part of the order of things, because the sense of "life in the Volk" could not be maintained against the divisive tendencies of bourgeois distributive justice (and injustice) without periodic wars. It seems rather that the evolution of Reason as Understanding has taken the security of this pendulum of Nature away from us; either Art, Religion, and Philosophy must suffice to teach us what political justice is in the universal community, or we shall perish.

This brings us finally to distributive justice, the virtuous concern of the bourgeoisie. This is the moment of judgement, the middle between the conceptual "solidarity" (or substance) of the peasantry, and the syllogistic return to dynamic equilibrium in the universal class. Instead of wanting to *die* justly, as the absolute (military) or universal (cultured) estate does, this estate has *living* justly (or "righteously") as its distinctive virtue. Now we are in the world of recognized or legal status, in which all agents are persons with defined or definable rights. The highest public function of this estate is the administration of justice, and the legal profession is just that part of it that belongs immediately and necessarily to the universal class (others do so, of course, through being selected to bear communal responsibilities or make communal decisions and regulations).

This is the world for which the *Wealth of Nations* is a sort of bible, for the God of this world is Wealth; the maintenance of formal righteousness in all dealings (or honesty in word and deed) is also the appointed form of worship of the "Mammon of Unrighteousness." Even Adam Smith recognizes the danger that his perfect mechanism of natural competition may be prevented from producing general prosperity by selfish conspiracies to monopolize trade; and he also recognizes that the same mechanism that produces general prosperity distributes it in an essentially unfair way.[35]

So far as Hegel found inspiration in *any* economic source for his analysis of the evils of industrial capitalism it has to have come from Adam Smith.[36] For Steuart, with his ideal of full employment, does not think of the labor market simply as a competitive one; and he is quite oblivious of the impending effects of the technological revolution.[37] His long residence abroad and his interest in social policy, freed Steuart from the Anglo-Saxon obsession with private profit; but, by the same token, Smith's close observation of the world of those merchants who were so resolutely determined to keep all "statesmen" out of their affairs, together with an extra decade of industrial development in their methods of production, gave him a crucial advantage in the task of identifying what was logically distinctive in modern industry. His book opens with a famous chapter "Of the Division of Labour," and with an equally famous example (which he says "has been very often taken notice of") taken from "a very trifling manufacture . . . the trade of the pin-maker." This example made an immense impression upon Hegel. He refers to it in his first analysis of how the mechanization of labor diminishes both its economic and its experiential value;[38] and again in the margin of his discussion of the rationalization of labor as "actual spirit" in 1805.[39]

The context of this second reference confirms—if any confirmation is thought to be necessary—the hypothesis that Smith's recognition of the right starting point for economic analysis is what lies behind Hegel's identification of the division of labor as the explicit (though still *formal*) universal in the second *Potenz* of the *System of Ethical Life*.[40] Steuart habitually speaks of agriculture as "labor," and generally refers to the modes of secondary production as "manufacture" or "work."[41] Sometimes he uses "labor" to embrace the whole genus of productive activity (as when he speaks of the "market for goods or labor"), but generally he prefers the term "industry" for this. It is clear that the reason for this distinction is that he regards primary production as essentially *unskilled* (i.e., it involves no skills that were not originally quite general in their distribution), while the secondary producers are artisans with *special* skills. Hegel accepts this distinction likewise in his conception of the natural economy (though he distinguishes the skills of stockbreeding from the mechanical labor of tilling the soil.)[42] But he also recognizes that the *rational* division of labor abolishes this natural distinction, and makes all the special skills of natural society into a universal possession. Anyone can learn, quite rapidly, to mind the machine. This is what makes rationalized labor so deadening. Whether Steuart's insistence that the minimum subsistence that must be *guaranteed* for the unskilled laborer, should also not be allowed to rise beyond that minimum, sharpened Hegel's perception of how the mechanism of a competitive labor market actually tends to push the minimum ever lower, I am not sure. But anyone reading Smith with the memory of Steuart's remark (in the same context) that "The poor slave . . . who gets no more than his subsistence at all times, is in the situation of the poor laboring horse, who is fed with the same provender, let it be dear or cheap" or of his reflection that foot soldiers manage to subsist below the minimal level of the day laborers because they generally do not marry,[43] would be in a good way to recognize that when everyone is equally reduced to the status of the day laborer, the situation of free labor can easily become worse than that of the slave or the horse (whose replacement is an extra cost). At the least it is certain that any student of Steuart's "subsistence level" theory would know why, once the economy was rationalized through the division of labor, Steuart's confidence that "the industrious free-man must share in the profits of him who employs him" was ill founded; Smith's comment would ring a bell here:

> Though the interest of the labourer is strictly connected with that of the society, he is incapable either of comprehending that interest or of understanding its connection with his own. His condition leaves him no time to receive the necessary information, and his education and habits are commonly such as to render him unfit to judge even though he was fully informed.[44]

For, precisely because of the "condition" that it puts him in, the interest of society in the accumulation of wealth is indeed strictly (but *negatively*) connected with the laborer's interest. That is what Hegel sees and says in all of his Jena manuscripts.

For this reason, the intervention of Steuart's "statesman" in the world of civil society is a logical necessity if there is to be a society at all. In any labor market, private interest is essentially antithetic not identical. Thus the bourgeois estate does not naturally or necessarily form an organic whole; it is, rather, *inorganic*, and the "justice" upon which it prides itself is the justice of *death*, or of an inevitable appeal to higher judgement. The peasant estate is a natural whole, which will work out its own salvation, and resolve its own self-alienation or antithesis (serfdom), in the normal course of its existence (as long as we are dealing, with communities small enough to be continually at war with others for survival, the Athenian constitution will emerge, and that of Sparta will perish).[45] The universal estate is a spiritual whole, i.e., by definition it is one that has already worked out its salvation. But the estate of "righteousness" is a life-and-death struggle in which death must triumph, at the last. Out of its own mouth this estate is condemned, for while professing justice, it *does* only what is unjust.

Obviously, if there is to be any stability in our social existence, some human court must take the place of this ultimate "judgement of God." The "absolute government" must be enshrined in a system of constitutional rights, and must maintain a balance of the estates such that the mortally organic estate will stay alive, and not degenerate into the "chemical" polarity of Plato's "two cities" of the rich and the poor. On the one hand, the formal ideal of justice as "honesty," must be linked with the political ideal of self-sacrifice for the preservation of the community. The bourgeoisie must be both patriotic and charitable. It must not think of its taxes as the payment of public servants and mercenaries, but as the subsistence allowance for a form of life that is genuinely higher than its own, because it maintains the *presence* of an ideal of "nobility"; and the favored postulants of Mammon must give generously both for public causes and for private charity. On the other hand, the economic activity of the bourgeoisie, must be so regulated that these formal or symbolic gestures toward the higher values of *political* justice and *living* charity do not appear as a hollow sham. Before the "system of justice" can be left to the "formally universal estate"—the legally constituted authorities of civil society—the universal system of needs must itself "become a government."[46]

The object of governmental economic policy is the same in Hegel as in Steuart: to ensure full employment, and a secure livelihood for everyone. But his ideal is less Spartan, more Athenian than Steuart's (or if you like, it is German Lutheran, rather than Scottish Calvinist). For whereas Steuart advocates the subsidized export of agricultural produce whenever the circumstances of his "day laborers" threaten to become too easy,[47] Hegel is sensitive both to the way in which general social expectations determine what a *decent* livelihood is in every economic status, and to the *barbarizing* tendency of being driven to labor by sheer economic need. "Respectability" is the best name for the organic principle of virtue of his bourgeois estate, and it is respectability (rather than simply money) that every member must be educated to want, and have a fair opportunity to achieve and to enjoy.

In the *System of Ethical Life* this is a problem that the government resolves as well as possible with external means. "Inequality of wealth is absolutely necessary"; "the individual who is tremendously wealthy becomes a *Macht"*; and the relation of mastery and service on the basis of *Lebensmacht* is natural and inevitable. When Hegel says that in the struggle for the means of life the good is forgotten ("The mass of wealth, the pure universal, the absence of wisdom, is the *An sich"*) and "the absolute bond of the people . . . has vanished," he seems to be saying that in spite of the best efforts of wise statesmanship, the social system is *inevitably* mortal.[48]

In the first Philosophy of Spirit this natural standpoint is decisively transcended. That Reason exists in Nature (which serves as the body and instrument of rational and *second* nature) is denied. The human world now embodies Reason only by emerging *out of* nature into spiritual freedom. Thus social history is *not*, as Aristotle assumed, the unfolding of "human nature" as the highest dimension of nature generally; it is the phenomenology of spirit, not as finite, but as *absolute* spirit. For our purposes, this speculative development is significant in two ways. First, the existence of civil society as a system of *natural* recognition, based on differential *Lebensmacht*, is irrelevant. Law, and legal recognition, presuppose the emergence of the consciousness of what rational freedom *is*, through a *struggle* for recognition. In the second place, the development of mechanized industry is analysed in a way that makes the economic struggle evident. The manuscript breaks off with "property" which is the object of that struggle. There is no sign that Hegel intended to draw any explicitly revolutionary conclusions (which would be out of place in his conception of systematic *thoery* at all times). But the working of the economy is now called a "life of the dead body, that moves itself within itself, one which ebbs and flows in its motion blindly, like the elements, *and which requires continual strict dominance and taming like a wild beast.*"[49] Adam Smith is now the *visible* inspiration of the account; but this political *response* accentuates Hegel's commitment to Steuart's ideal of economic policy.

The "life" of the dead body is *gravity*. Hence in the second Philosoophy of Spirit, where the logical structure of concept, judgement, and syllogism, familiar in the mature *Philosophy of Right* is applied to the organization of social theory as a whole for the first time, Hegel displays Smith's world of economic acquisition as Newtonian gravitational system. Once more the revolutionary dialectic of wealth and poverty produced by the rational division of labor is summed up (more briefly than in the lectures of 1803/4 but in the same trenchant terms). Hegel explicitly refers to it as "the extremest shattering (*höchste Zerrissenheit*) of the will—inward outrage and hatred"; but he says nothing now about the "strict dominance and taming (of the economy) like a wild beast." The policies of governmental control that he mentions are all such as would need to be continued in a syndicalist economy (the search for new markets, and for new employment for those thrown out of work by developments in technology, for example).[48] It is clear that he is still wrestling with the lessons of the French Revolution, and that the focal importance of personality in his legal theory represents his formulation of the "rights of man and citizen." I shall argue now, finally, that he actually looked forward to a world in which labor power itself would no longer be marketed.

This supposed world of his hopes will not have a centralized socialist economy, for that would not be "organic" (self-governing). Far from using the language of "dominance and taming," he now says that government interference—even the taxation system—should be as slight as possible.[51] The economic sphere is one in which personal freedom and initiative must be allowed to display itself. The commonwealth should not own property, but be supported by taxes—because (however insignificant it manages to make them) its expenses must be accounted for.

The protection of property and securing of contracts is the primary function of state authority in the judicial system—which Hegel now treats as an extension of the state's economic functions. The state-authority must look first to the problem of general social health, and advance from that to the task of securing what Aristotle called distributive justice. But Hegel once more acknowledges the difficulties of intepreting contracts and applying laws, the endlessness of occasions for dispute and of distinction in judgement. Also, the larger the body of applied law grows, the more difficult it is for anyone except a specialist to acquire the requisite knowledge of it. For this reason the spirit loses its *presence*.[51]

Both the fate of the *ancien régime* and the decadence of the German Empire come to mind here. How are we to choose between these possible outcomes? The answer is that we do not need to choose, since the human community does not really die, either naturally or violently. Its death, like that of the phoenix, is a rebirth. Thus the crucial point is that Hegel goes on at once to say that the *procedure* of justice is "almost more essential than the law itself." And in this connection he reverts to the revolutionary dialectic of rich and poor in what seems to me to be a conclusive way. For he points out that the more complex the law becomes, the more expensive it is to go to law. So there comes to be one law for the rich and another for the poor, simply because the rich have access to legal remedies while the poor, whose need is greater, do not. It is difficult now, not to believe that Hegel's criticism of the acquisitive society rests on a concept of human *economic* independence, which he has consciously formulated. In other words, he is expecting a social revolution, and his economic and judicial "syllogisms" require a conclusion that he knows how to write, but must be enacted by the world-spirit before it can become the concern of the philosopher.[53]

That the anonymous pamphleteer of 1797 is still very much alive in Hegel—and that he might speak more plainly about the inevitable need for social reconstruction if it were *safe* to do so—is shown by one remark in his transition from the sphere of civil law to that of political sovereignty. Discussing the "community, the living *Volk*" in its first aspect as the "Common*wealth*," he remarks how it "condemns a mass of men to savagery (*Rohheit*), to being worn out (*Abstumpfung*) in labor—and poverty, in order to let others accumulate wealth, so that it can take this wealth away from them," i.e., in taxes. Heavy taxes, he says, make this situation bearable, but "Aristocrats who pay no taxes stand in the gravest danger of losing it (wealth) by violence."[54]

When we come to the explicit discussion of the "estates," Hegel's silences speak even more eloquently. He first presents the solid world of the comfortable worthies of the city guilds and of commerce, as if their system of recognized status were as stable as it takes itself to be when it walks abroad "outside the City Gate" of Goethe's Frankfurt on the Sabbath.[55] But behind this stable facade is not the soil and the cycle of the seasons, but the labile fluidity of money, and the changes and chances of business. A city worthy is worth just what he owns. We find out what this is in the market, where the commercial class forms the middle between the two great categories of producers, the peasants and the artisans of the guilds.

Logically the factory worker belongs to the bourgeois class. But Hegel delays all mention of him until we come to the *monetary* product of the whole process, and the feedback reaction that the market economy has on the *Gesinnung* of everyone involved.[56] And he speaks then of the *Elend* (misery) of a "class" (*Klasse*) not of an "estate" (*Stand*). There is no mention of mere laborers on the one hand, or of mere financiers on the other in his structural analysis of the system of property-gravitation. From Hegel's discussion of "recognized status," we know that his bourgeois society is a mechanized and factory-based one. The rationalization of labor, culminating in the arrival of machines, marks the end of feudal industry for Hegel. So the class structure he describes: peasants, burghers, and merchants, everyone being by implication an independent proprietor, contains in each case its own internal antithesis. In the case of the peasant proprietors, the antithesis (serfdom) is clearly on its way out. In the other estates the antithesis—the urban proletariat—is waxing rather than waning (as the first Philosophy of Spirit showed). But the implicit destiny is surely the same. For what the work of the "middle" estate brings to light, is that the *object of all this life and work is to make money.* The "disposition" of commerce is not to be as comfortable and self-satisfied as peasants and guildsmen alike, but to be "just" with the grasping honesty of Ebenezer Scrooge. So the "disposition" of the factory worker upon whose misery (*Elend*) the most advanced aspect of the system of production rests needs no elaboration.

The conclusion seems to be obvious. The political revolution that is already in progress is the necessary prelude to a socio-economic one by which the marketing of labor will be halted. Hegel's confidence of this rested on his conviction that the drive toward family independence was part of the order of nature. That this order itself could be distorted by the rational mechanisms of law and economics he did not foresee. But then, he did not foresee the retreat from Moscow or the Battle of Waterloo either.[57]

But if Hegel believed that capitalist accumulation must be brought to an end, because it was the blind movement of a dead machine driven by living energies that ought properly to be rationally self-conscious and self-governing, why did he not say so? The answer is that, so far as it was appropriate for a systematic thinker to say so, he did say so. He did not make his doctrine quite as *explicit* as he might have done, probably out of simple prudence. We should always remember how Fichte, the most important philosopher still alive after 1804, had lost his professorship a few years earlier. We should also remember that Hegel, who was still a virtually unknown thinker struggling to *get* a professorship, heartily abominated Fichte's *utopian* pretensions. It is not the philosopher's function to say how things *ought* to be; his task is to make explicit the rational structure implicit in the way they actually are. This Hegel *did*. He showed what aspects of the social structure were stable in fact, and coherent in consciousness (i.e., the belief structures were consistent with the functioning process); and he showed what aspects of the social structure were not stable, but *in process* and why.

But, of course, it was also part of his concern to show that social life must *always* be in process. "Distributive justice" is in itself *dialectical,* in a way that he analysed brilliantly in the *Phenomenology.*[58] The ideal of *equal* treatment, conflicts with the ideal that everyone should have *what he needs.* Hence in any situation of scarcity there will always be dispute about what distribution is best and fairest. Does it follow therefore that Hegel *as a philosopher* had *no* view about the dialectic of riches and poverty as it existed in his time? My contention is that this is the *wrong* conclusion to draw from his antipathy to utopian thinking, and his convincing analysis of the mistake implicit in the socialism of such thinkers as Fichte and William Godwin. The philosopher cannot tell the statesman *how* to solve the problems of social justice. For what he knows is that to solve it in one form is *always and necessarily* to pose it in another. So "what to do now?" must always be a problem for *moral* decision. Nevertheless the philosopher *can* show all of us, as moral agents, how a problem *must* be posed if it is to receive a *moral* solution at all. This is the point of Hegel's adherence to

Steuart's perspective in political economy. He *knew* Adam Smith's work, and he fully recognized the superiority of the analysis of the mechanized economy that it contains. But he also saw that to regard economics as the natural science of *wealth* is to surrender our human responsibilities.

Herein lies his superiority over Marx. Marx despised utopian socialism too; but in relying on the economic process to produce a "classless" society he fell back himself into the rational moralism of the Enlightenment. What the "classless society" means in practice, Hegel showed negatively in his analysis of the Terror, and postively in the critique of Fichte's "machine state" (in which "the police know pretty well where every citizen is at any time of day and what he is doing").[59] That we *all* now live in this kind of "machine state"—whether "capitalist" or "Marxist" in its orientation—is a direct result of the "trust" we have all shared in "the universal without wisdom." The socialist societies have *made* that "universal without wisdom" "become a government"—but only as a self-*conscious* tyranny. Nonsocialist societies have *let* it become a tyranny, which their social critics have forced into self-consciousness. Hegel's conception of freedom as the *organic* principle, logically requires that every function in the economy should be *self*-governing, and that the "universal government" should emerge from that self-articulation, while the "absolute government" (the sovereign power) is concerned only to maintain the organic principle. What this presupposes it that every effective member in the community is a *proprietor*. The "class" of day-laborers is not an estate because they own nothing on which to work, and must sell their labor *power*. This means that they are *wage slaves*. They are not an estate of realm, any more than the slaves were in the natural communities of old times. *How* the statesman is to incorporate them into society Hegel does not presume to say. But what it means for them to be incorporated, he *does* say. Only a society in which men *own* the means of their subsistence can be a community of moral agents. They must own that means neither as a political community, nor as an assembly of stockholders, but rather in the way in which the artisan is accorded absolute ownership of his tools of trade in Magna Carta. In other words, in a factory economy there must be factory cooperatives. How this is to be brought about, is not the philosopher's business to decide. He can only show why society will not be economically rational until it *is* brought about. Nothing that has happened since 1789 seems to me to have shown that this connection, logically enshrined in the axiomatic roles accorded to "property" and "personality," in the "Real Philosophy" of 1805 (and in the *Philosophy of Right*), is mistaken; on the contrary everything seems to confirm it. The actual has shown itself to be "rational" in the way that Hegel claimed; and in the process our lack of "wisdom" has been demonstrated.

NOTES

1.　*Gesammelte Werke* VI, ed. Rheinisch-Westfaelischen Akademie der Wissenschaften, (F. Meiner, Hamburg, 1968), p. 321; Hegel, *System of Ethical Life*, ed. H.S. Harris and T.M. Knox, (Albany: Suny Press, 1979), p. 247. Avineri (pp. 93–94) has accidentally attached this passage to a quotation from the *second* Philosophy of Spirit of 1805/6).

2.　*System der Sittlichkeit*, ed. G. Lasson in Hegel, *Schriften Zur Politik* (Leipzig: Meiner, 1923), pp. 491–492; Harris and Knox, pp. 170–171.

3.　See Lasson, *System der Sittlichkeit*, pp. 450–451; Harris and Knox, pp. 133–134.

4.　*Gesammelte Werke* VIII, 244, 10–22. My translation is slightly more literal than Avineri's (*Hegel's Theory of the Modern State*, Cambridge, U.P., 1972, p. 97) partly because I have augmented the text only minimally, and partly because I wanted to make the controlling presence of the analogy with Newtonian gravitation as clear as possible.

5.　Lasson, *System of Ethical Life*, p. 452; Harris and Knox, p. 171.

6.　Avineri, p. 94 ng32.

7.　Hegel, *Theologische Jugendschriften*, ed. H. Nohl, Tübingen Mohr, 1907 p. 273; Knox, p. 221.

8.　Nohl, pp. 381–382; Hegel, *Early Theological Writings*, ed. T.M. Knox (Chicago, 1948; reprinted, U. of Penn. Press, Philadelphia, 1971, p.221) Knox, p. 308.

9.　*Thesis IX, Hegel Erste Druckschriften*, ed. G. Lasson, F. Meiner, Leipzig, 1928, p. 404.

10.　K. Rosenkranz, *Leben Hegels*, (Berlin, 1844) repr. Wissenschaftliche Buchgesellschaft, Darmstadt, 1963, p. 86.

11.　For the details on the Basel edition of Smith see *Gesammelte Werke*, VI; 384–385 (note to 323, 10-16). Chamley's plausible reasoning in favor of Hegel's having used the Tübingen translation of Steuart (*Hegel-Studien* III, 1965, 238) must be mistaken if the record of the auction catalogue of Hegel's library at the *Hegel Archiv* is correct. Their listing shows "Hamburg, 1796" [i.e., 1769] for Steuart's *Principles*. This tends to strengthen Chamley's, not very conclusive, arguments that Hegel did not read Steuart's work before 1797. (Tübingen was the obvious place for him to have obtained Steuart's work before he went to Frankfurt; but in Tübingen he would naturally have bought the *Tübingen* translation. In the more cosmopolitan bookshops of Frankfurt he could, presumably, have found either translation. In Bern the Tübingen translation would certainly have been easier to come by).

12.　*Critical Review*, XXIII (1767): 412 (quoted in Sir James D. Stewart, *An Inquiry into the Principles of Political Economy*, abridged ed. by A.S. Skinner, Olivera and Boyd, Edinburgh, 1966, I, XLVI–XLVII).

13.　J. Hoftmeister, (ed.), *Dokumente Zu Hegels Entwicklung*, Frommann, Stuttgart, 1936, p. 348.

14.　Hence he did not translate Cart's first letter in which this Republican ideal is expressed.

15.　See the surviving fragment of the introduction to his pamphlet on the Württemberg Estates Assembly of 1797, Lasson (1923) pp. 150–153; Hegel, *Political Writings* ed. T.M., Knox and Z.A. Pelczynski, Clarendon P., Oxford 1965.

16.　See the summary account given by R. Haym, *Hegel und seine Zeit* (Berlin, 1857); repr. G. Olms, Hildesheim, 1962, p. 66.

17.　In the immediate (or natural) realization of the *bare* concept, there is a *dictatorship* of Reason, because no *middle* term has yet developed. This has obvious relevance to the practical need for a military dictatorship in the establishment of the "new order" that Hegel wanted both for Germany and for his native Württemberg.

18.　Lasson, *System der Sittlichkeit*, p. 496 (Harris and Knox, p. 174).

19.　The first germ of Hegel's famous analysis of the Terror of 1793 is to be found in the theory of "the absolute government" in the *System der Sittlichkeit:* "The absolute government is only not formal [*formell*] because it presupposes the difference of the estates and so is truly the supreme government. *Without this presupposition the whole might of reality* falls into a clump (no matter how the clump might otherwise ramify internally) and this barbarian clump would have at its apex its equally barbarian power undivided and without wisdom. In the clump there cannot be any true and objective difference, and what was to hover over its internal differences is a pure nothing. For the absolute government, in order to be the absolute Idea posits absolutely the endless movement of the absolute concept. In the latter there must be differences and, because they are in the concept, universal and infinite, they must therefore be systems. And in this way alone is an absolute government and absolute living identity possible, but born into appearance and reality." (Lasson, pp. 482–483; Harris and Knox, p. 162–my italics).

20. *Principles,* (ed. Skinner), pp. 43, 47, 58, 93–95, 129–132 (for the designation "farmers" or "husbandmen"); pp. 47, 57, 62, 154–155, 340–341 (for the equally frequent distinction between "labourers" and "free hands"—in the first of these passages the "free hands" are also called "manufacturers").

21. *Principles* (ed. Skinner), pp. 68–70, 300–301.

22. *Principles* (ed. Skinner), p. 301.

23. *Wealth of Nations,* London, Everyman, 1:230.

24. *Principles* (ed. Skinner), p. 93 (the italics are Steuart's).

25. Compare, for instance, *Principles,* pp. 68, 300–302.

26. Steuart talks much of the "spirit" of the people, as that that sets the boundaries of what is possible for the statesman; but he is also concerned in places to point out the social value of the typical ethos of a social class (see, for example, the comparison of the noble ethos of "glory" with the bourgeois ethos of "gain," *Principles,* pp. 70–72). Smith is more concerned about the degree of conscious understanding possessed by his different "orders." But he is suprisingly confident that the interest of the landlord *must* coincide with that of the community. Hence he anticipates Hegel's contrast between the noble and the bourgeois ethos even more completely than Steuart (see *Wealth of Nations*, Everyman, 1:230–232).

27. *Principles,* p. 92.

28. Lasson, *System der Sittlichkeit,* p. 469 (Harris and Knox, p. 150).

29. In the *System of Ethical Life,* the "lordship-bondage" relation is treated as natural, and the "struggle for honor" occurs only between families and tribes that already include servants in bondage. The importance of *universal* bondage in the translation from the natural societies of Greece to the universal community of Christendom, only began to occupy Hegel's attention in 1805. But he always maintained that political freedom depended on the capacity of individuals to identify with their family, hearth, and land. Thus the *distrustfulness* of "trust" (in the *System of Ethical Life*) reappears as absolute *Eigensinn* in the more phenomenological "First Philosophy of Spirit" (see *Gesammelte Werke* 7:296; Harris and Knox, pp. 227–228); and the "struggle for recognition" is there analysed for the first time as necessary for the great transition to the political society as based on the command recognition of legal status (*Gesammelte Werke* 6:307–315; Harris and Knox, pp. 235–242).

30. So far as I can see, Hegel never alludes directly to the role of the peasants in the French Revolution. But his whole theory makes them the natural source of *violent* rebellion. Marx was too much influenced by Hegel's insistence on the primitive and undeveloped character of the peasant consciousness, and did not appreciate (perhaps because most of the documents were not available to him) the essentially *volcanic* character of peasant "solidity" in Hegel's theory. But Lenin and Mao would have done better to study Hegel and the French Revolution, than to try to adapt the Marxist theory of revolution as a *rational* political process to peasant conditions. The *bourgeois* revolution need not come violently at all, but even if it does, it ought not to be followed by an extended period of cultural servitude (or *Bildung*) as a peasant revolution (which must, in the order of nature, come first) has to be. *Bildung* is the *precondition* of a bourgeois revolution; in spite of 1789 we are still undergoing it; in devoting his life to it, Marx was only carrying the same torch that history knocked out of Hegel's hands in 1814.

31. Compare *System der Sittlichkeit,* Lasson (1923), p. 480; Harris and Knox, p. 160.

32. Compare *System der Sittlichkeit,* Lasson, p. 483 (Harris and Knox, p. 162).

33.   That this is the *goal* of social development is first clearly stated in *System der Sittlichkeit,*
        Lasson, p. 496 (Harris and Knox, pp. 174–175); compare the comment about "democracy,"
        Lasson, p. 498 (Harris and Knox, p. 177). The goal does not have to be stated in the later
        systematic presentation, because the standpoint of "nature" is now transcended from the
        start (*Gesammelte Werke* 8:214, 22–27), and Hegel is concerned throughout with the
        order of human society in its self-conscious freedom. In *this* context the goal is directly
        expressed by the designation of what was previously the *"absolute estate"* as the *"universal
        estate,"* and by making the professional soldiers (*Soldatenstand*) the middle term
        between this estate of civil servants, and the realm of free culture (Art, Religion, and
        Philosophy), which provides citizenship with its ultimate meaning (*Gesammelte Werke*
        VIII, 270, 14–277,6).
34.   *Gesammelte Werke* VIII, 276, 1–177, 6. This is the promised elucidation of the "capacity
        for an organic absolute intuition" mentioned in the quotation on page 72 above.
35.   See for instance, *Wealth of Nations,* Everyman, 1:230–232. The essential admission
        of the distributive unfairness of a free-trade economy comes in the quotation given earlier.
        The admission that the god of the capitalist is really Mammon is as follows: "The interest
        of the dealers, however, in any particular branch of trade or manufactures, is always
        in some respects different from, and even opposite to, that of the public. To widen the
        market and to narrow the competition, is always the interest of the dealers."
36.   Raymond Plant has correctly pointed out that the source of Hegel's insight into the life-
        impoverishing effect of mechanization upon human labor is almost certainly Schiller's
        Aesthetic Letters—see "Economic and Social Integration in Hegel's Political Philosophy,"
        in D.P. Verene, ed., *Hegel's Social and Political Thought (*Atlantic Highlands, N.J.:
        Humanities Press, 1980), p. 79 (and *Aesthetic Letters,* VI, 7, ed. by Wilkinson and
        Willoughby, Oxford, Clarendon Press, 1967 pp. 34–35; or by Snell, Routledge and Kegan
        Paul, London, 1959.
37.   Thus about wages he can write:

        Let therefore subsistence be ever so cheap, the free man will insist upon
        wages in proportion to the value of his work, when brought to market.
        Should his employer tell him, that because subsistence is at a low price
        he must therefore work cheaper, he will tell his employer that since on this
        account he sells no cheaper to his *customers*, neither will he work cheaper
        for *him*; and his argument is good . . . .

At the bottom of the scale he admits competitive pressure:

        In every industrious society, the lowest class is frequently found reduced to
        the barely necessary. The competition among themselves obtain employ-
        ment at any rate, produces this effect; and competition must be allowed its
        free course. (*Principles,* p. 401).

But he does not mean to allow competition a free course nevertheless. He is (indirectly) a defender
of the *minimum wage:*

        the best, and indeed the only way to judge of reasonable prices, is to com-
        pare, as I have said, the gains of the lower classes with the price of the
        shortest subsistence. (p. 403).

About machines he says that where there *is* a perfectly balanced economy, their introduction is to
be deprecated because they can only upset it. But

        The present situation of every country in Europe is so widely distant from
        this degree of perfection, that I must consider the introduction of machines,
        and every method of augmenting the produce or assisting the labor, and
        ingenuity of man, as of the greatest utility. Why do people wish to augment

population, but in order to compass these ends? Wherein does the effect
of a machine differ from that of new inhabitants?

As agriculture, exercised as a trade, purges the land of idle mouths, and
pushes them to a new industry which the state may turn to her own advantage; so does a machine introduced into a manufacture, purge off hands
which then become superfluous *in that branch,* and which may quickly be
employed in another. (pp. 123–124).

38. *Gesammelte Werke* VI, 323; Harris and Knox, p. 248.
39. *Gesammelte Werke* VIII, 224, 23–26. (The editors failed to notice the reference here. Consequently they failed to point it out, and "Smith A." does not appear in their index.)
40. Lasson, pp. 432–433; Harris and Knox, pp. 116–118.
41. Compare especially the passages cited in note 19 above.
42. *System der Sittlichkeit,* Lasson, p. 423 (Harris and Knox, p. 108).
43. *Principles,* pp. 400–401. (The following quotation about "the industrious free-man" is in this same context.)
44. *Wealth of Nations,* Everyman 1:230–231 (my italics). (Smith himself, though very conscious of the economic importance of mechanization, is quite oblivious of its conse-quences for his comfortable doctrine that wages must rise steadily as long as the economy can keep growing. Only someone who had learned to distinguish "labor" from "man-ufacture" as Steuart does would see the implications of mechanization clearly.)
45. Note that this is an assertion about the constitution, not about the cities. In the war, Sparta triumphed over an Athens which had become the capital of a commercial empire. But in constitutional history, Thebes liberated the Messenians when she triumphed over Sparta thirty years later. The Greece that went down before Philip and Alexander was Athenian in spirit (and in leadership so far as it had any leadership).
46. Lasson, *System der Sittlichkeit,* p. 489 (Harris and Knox, pp. 167–168). Hegel's language here is a sure sign that he is thinking in terms of the *Wealth of Nations.* For one can speak in this way only after the autonomy of economic life has been asserted. Throughout these pages, he is making Steuart's case *against* Smith, and his way of presenting Steuart's doctrine of state control over the economy only makes sense if we take if for granted that he has read Smith and knows what is fundamentally at issue between them.
47. *Principles,* pp. 403–404.
48. Lasson, *System of Ethical Life,* pp. 491–492 (Harris and Knox, pp. 170–171). Compare also Lasson, pp. 441–442 (Harris and Knox, pp. 125–126).
49. *Gesammelte Werke* VI, 324 (Harris and Knox, p. 249; my italics).
50. Compare *Gesammelte Werke* VIII, 243, 5-245, 5 with VI 321, 1-326; the quotation is from VIII, 244, 21-22.
51. *Gesammelte Werke* VIII, 27–245, 1; and 245, 12–13. We should remember that Fichte's socialist economy was a model of the "machine-state" for Hegel. The success that modern governments have achieved in finding out what their citizens are doing every minute of the day would appall him—compare *Difference, Gesammelte Werke* IV, 23 (Harris and Cerf, pp. 146–147).
52. *Gesammelte Werke* VIII, 248, 8–16. This is the first point in the discussion of the judicial system that is new. Criminal justice has already been discussed in this manuscript itself; and the bad infinity of civil law is a point made in the System of Ethical Life, Lasson, p. 496; (Harris and Knox, p. 174).
53. *Gesammelte Werke* VIII, 248, 17–249, 7. (In this connection, the explicit presence of a revolutionary hope in the *Phenomenology* deserves to be remembered.)
54. *Gesammelte Werke* VIII, 252, 3–9.
55. Compare *Gesammelte Werke* VIII, 268, 15–269, 10 with *Faust,* Part I, 808–1010. (There is no question of a direct influence here, since the scene did not form part of *Faust, Ein Fragment*).
56. *Gessammelte Werke* VIII, 269, 22–270, 13 (especially VIII, 270, 8–9).
57. Not that his social ideals changed at all when these events occurred—only he was made aware how unfathomable and dark the future is.

58.   See *Phenomonology of Spirit*, trans. A.V. Miller, Oxford, Clarendon Press, 1977, section 430.
59.   *Difference between Fichte's and Schelling's Philosophy,* ed. H.S. Harris and W. Cerf, Suny Press, Albany, 1977, p. 147—the quotation comes from Fichte himself and Hegel gives the reference, with a long footnote quoting the context.

HEGEL: INDIVIDUAL AGENCY AND SOCIAL CONTEXT

by
A.S. WALTON

INTRODUCTION

In this essay there are two things that will *not* be done, and it is as well to point these out at the beginning in order to signal the kind of approach to the study of Hegel adopted here. First, no attempt will be made to offer a detailed historical account of the development of Hegel's thought, although some aspects of his intellectual development will not be entirely ignored. This is not because I hold such work to be unhelpful; indeed, the approach offered in this essay is dependent upon the detailed scholarly investigation of Hegel's development carried out by others. However, what follows assumes that it is also worthwhile to take hold of some of Hegel's central concepts with a view to critically assessing their usefulness in the context of social theory generally. Second, no attempt has been made to locate Hegel's social theory within the context of his philosophical system as a whole. That is not to deny that such a project would be worthwhile, but since it is not self-evidently the case that the system holds together as a coherent unity, a case can be made for concentrating on particular parts of it. And in this respect refuge can be taken in Lukàcs' claim that a "really incisive critic would have to conclude that he had to deal, not with an authentically organic and coherent system, but with a number of overlapping systems."[1]

In this essay I want to explore certain features of Hegel's account of the relationship between the individual and the social context. There are several reasons for wishing to do this and for supposing that such a project is worthwhile, both from the point of view of the interpretation of Hegel in particular, and in terms of its importance for social theory generally. First, there is an interpretative

75

problem that requires clarification, particularly in view of some of Hegel's more extravagant claims. That is to say, his individualist critics seem to be on strong ground when confronted with the claim that, for example, the spirit of a nation is an "ego."[2] We get the distinct impression that, for Hegel, the proper object of enquiry is the social whole, and that the individual is but a moment within it. And Karl Popper and others have seized on claims of this kind in order to tease out what they take to be the sinister implications of non-individualist social theories. This is an urgent problem in so far as critics of an individualist persuasion have been disposed to think that, not just that Hegel's view generates the idea of a supraindividual ego, but that any nonindividualist account of social reality necessarily implies such an idea. This view of the matter is to be found in Karl Popper's defence of methodological individualism, where the claim is made that all nonindividualist accounts of social relations, that is to say accounts that do not reduce explanation of social phenomena to the beliefs and actions of individuals, necessarily presuppose arguments about the extent to which the social whole is over and above individuals who are but instances of the whole's own separate development. In this paper, drawing on Hegel's thought, I want to pursue, if only tentatively, the line that nonindividualism does not entail *anti*individualism.

Second, even Hegel's more sympathetic critics have been concerned with what is taken to be his emphasis on community, social integration, and the respects in which personal identity and self-hood are dependent upon coherent and harmonious social relations. In the intepretative work done recently by Plant and Taylor,[3] the emphasis has been on Hegel's concern for the community, with the importance of its integration, and with the individual's identification with his social relations. In this paper I will not attempt to undermine the claim that Hegel is concerned with the ideal of community—it would be silly to deny it. But I do want to suggest that much of some of the essential features of Hegel's social theory is lost by failing to gain a secure interpretative grip on the centrality and importance of the individual as the subject of social action.

This suggests a third reason for looking at Hegel on this issue. Among social theorists recently, the issue of the relationship between the individual and the social context has been much explored, partly I suspect because of a growing dissatisfaction with the major propositions of characteristically individualist theories, and a corresponding interest in exploring in sympathetic terms, the importance of the social as a dimension of individual experience. And in recent years, the parameters of the problem have been identified quite closely, and in a way that does make it possible both to clarify Hegel's position and to assess his contribution to thought about the issue. Recent social theorists have paid particular attention to the social and structural aspects of individual experience, but with a corresponding attempt not to undermine the importance of individual consciousness and agency. Anthony Giddens, for example, has attempted to theorize the concept of structure, but has simultaneously sought to invoke a more active conception of human agency than is to be found in much sociological theory.[4] And Roy Bhaskar, from a broadly Marxist perspective, while insisting on the "material" nature of social relations, has also insisted on the respects in which those relations only hold and are reproduced through the consciousness and agency of social actors.[5] Finally, W.E. Connolly[6] has inferred conclusions about the potentially active role of human agency from a critique of Althusserian structuralism, and from an associated insistence on the extent to which social reality must be understood as at least partly constituted by the concepts and meanings generated by, and available to, social actors. Thus, there is considerable interest in the problem of the individual and society, with demonstrating the limits of individualism, but also in showing that nonindividualist accounts do not need to dispense with the critical importance of consciousness and agency.

It is not possible within the scope of this paper to take on board the general problem of the relationship between the individual and society. As a topic in itself it is a very wide and Hegel's treatment, too, is expansive. So I want to focus on a particular—although nevertheless still formidably wide—issue within the general problem of the relationship between the individual and society, namely the issue of agency and social context; and the problems at issue here revolve around a number of difficult questions of the following kind. Do individuals or groups of individuals determine their own goals and purposes? Or are goals and purposes determined by the social context? Does it make sense to speak of individuals or groups of individuals consciously changing their social environment? What role, if any, does the consciousness and agency of individuals play in the constitution of the social environment? Or does that environment have a dynamic of its own, independent of and elusive to the consciousness and agency of individuals? These questions in turn imply further, more general questions about the very constitution of the social world.

Most typically, questions of this order have been asked within Marxism, and rivalries have been fierce, Althusserian structuralism standing in opposition to, say, Sartrean humanism and Habermassian notion of conscious subjectivity. The question of whether working class movements are made or whether they make themselves remains, for Marxists, a hotly controversial matter. But it should not be inferred from Marxism's widespread interest in these issues that it has a theoretical monopoly, and that only Marxism lends itself to and generates interesting questions about the relationship between human agency and the social context. Indeed, it might be hazarded that Marxism's capacity to generate fruitful debates on the issue derives in part from its *Hegelian* origins, and that the least successful Marxist forays have occurred when it has attempted to deny those origins, as in the case of Althusserian structuralism. I am suggesting, then, that certain features of Hegel's conceptualization of society provide a powerful insertion into this fundamental and important issue.

In exploring these issues in Hegel I shall attempt to relocate the individual at the center of the Hegelian social stage. This is a formidable task because it goes against the grain, somewhat, of the main drift of interpretation, which stresses Hegel's attention to the idea of community and his insistence on the social constitution of the individual. I do not want to suggest that Hegel is a heavily disguised individualist, but will suggest that something of Hegel's attempted synthesis of the individual and the social can be established by redirecting attention towards the individual.

II

Who or what are the agents?

The first problem to be confronted is that it has sometimes been supposed that for Hegel there is some sense in which it is the social whole that is the subject or agent of social action. That is to say, it is the social whole that has purposes and goals, and that the extent of individuals' significance is in virtue of their implication in those goals and purposes.* Hegel's most hostile critics have attributed this view to him, most notably Marx in the 1843 *Critique of Hegel's Philosophy of Right*.[7]

There Marx accuses Hegel of a crude explanatory reductionism, the basis of which is the claim that the social whole is the subject of social action, and individuals the predicates. Marx, in addition, supposes that Hegel arrives at this view through the deployment of a particular kind of metaphysical argument or, as he says, "logical, pantheistic mysticism" according to which the "idea is given the status of a subject . . ."[8] and embodied in a reified and abstract conception of the state. And this deterministic metaphysics, according to Marx, coupled with an extravagantly coercive notion of the state, issues in a dramatic undermining of any viable conception of human agency and the conditions of its realization.

This criticism—as well, of course, as a number of specifically Marxian points—essentially involves the claim that Hegel invokes the idea of a supraindividual subject, or collective mind with goals and purposes of its own that transcend those of ordinary individuals. There are, however, a number of

---

That is not to deny that collectivities can have purposes, for clearly they do. But a minimal claim in respect of the purposes of collectivities needs to be distinguished from the larger claims that (a) collectivities constitute subjects or agents in the sense of having minds, and (b) that individuals are significant only by being implicated in the goals and purposes of the collective subject.

reasons, embedded deeply in Hegel's thought, that indicate the inappropriateness of this interpretation, some of which I shall come to later. But for the moment I want to draw attention to one specific argument used by Hegel, which strongly suggests an alternative reading. In the *Phenomenology*, in a passage referring to classical Greece, Hegel suggest that one feature of Greek society is the unreflective acceptance of the ethical order. It is a mere given and is accepted by its participants as such. The effect of this, so it is argued, is to reify and abstract the social whole such that the "universal spirit itself is a separate, individual spirit, and the customs and laws in their entirety are a *specific* ethical substance . . . ."[9] The essential point about this is that the *appearance* of Geist as having an independent existence is the product of a particular kind of society, namely one in which reflective subjectivity has not broken in. And the view on the part of the participants in Greek society that there is, in some sense, a supraindividual ego constitutes a gigantic misapprehension on their part, a misapprehension issuing from their failure to appreciate their own essential subjectivity and the respects in which the social context is less a subject bearing upon them but rather a *medium* drawn upon by them and reconstituted through their use of it.

The view held by the participants in Greek culture represents, therefore, a kind of "false consciousness." Social actors misunderstand the nature of their own social reality. They reify the social whole and attribute to it characteristics and properties deriving from false beliefs about themselves and the social reality with which they interact. Or if those beliefs are not false, they are at least partial and one-sided. The Greeks, in this view, were correct to attach significance to the community and to place a value on social integration. But they inferred too much from their beliefs about the importance of community and concluded that the community was a supraindividual subject rather than a medium to be drawn upon by individual subjects.

And, most important, the Greek culture lacked a set of concepts with which to critically assess its own beliefs and practices. There is no element of self-criticism in Greek culture, no available set of concepts that individuals can draw upon in order to reflectively engage with their social order. And its reification as a supraindividual ego is in part a consequence of the absence of such concepts. It is a consequence of the absence of such concepts because when individuals do not have the capacity to criticise and reflect upon their social context, they can not recognize it as in some sense an expression of their, albeit collective, attitudes and beliefs, and as maintained and reproduced only through their consciousness and action. In the absence of critical concepts, individuals are disposed to think their social order as something given, and as over and above them, rather than as a medium that is drawn upon in the pursuit of their own goals and projects as the subjects of social action.

III

Social Context and Individual Agency

However, even if it is true, as I have suggested it is, that Hegel treats the social whole as a medium that is drawn upon by individual agents and that, by implication, the goals and projects of individual agents are in some sense primary, this still leaves substantial problems, since by no stretch of the imagination can Hegel be characterised as an individualist in the tradition of, say, John Stuart Mill or Kant. For the purposes of explanation, it is clear that Hegel does not suppose that all descriptions and explanations of individuals are reducible to facts about individuals as such, as methodological individualists hold; and as far as ethical considerations are concerned, it is clear that he believes a person's capacity for moral integrity is bound up with membership of the social context. Thus the social context is both constitutive of the individual and a condition of his capacity for morality.

But a great deal hinges on *precisely* how the relationship between the individual and the social context is formulated. In Hegelian terms, this hinges on what, exactly, is taken to be the relationship between the universal and the particular. How is it that the universal is embodied in the particular, and the particular dependent upon the universal? In what sense are universality and particularity mutually reinforcing moments of the subject's experience?

In relation to the problem of agency and social context, looking at these questions requires a consideration of two opposed theoretical positions.

The first position is the one alluded to in Hegel's critique of Greek philosophy and society. This is the view that individual agents can be explained wholly as the outcome of their social context. In Durkheim, for example, this view issued in a conception of the individual as related to, and as the outcome of, a constraining and external context, which was both a necessary condition for, and a heavily determining force over, individual action. For Althusser, socioeconomic structures throw up individuals as bearers of their structurally determined positions or functions. Thus, in this view, explanations of individual action that make reference to the consciousness and agency of individuals or, indeed, groups of individuals, are to be discounted, for Durkheim as unscientific, and for Althusser as both unscientific and ideological.

At the opposite end of the theoretical polarity stands a second position of a characteristically individualist kind according to which all explanations of both the individual and the social are reducible to accounts of the formation and attempted execution of individual goals and projects. In this view, society is the outcome of, and a means to, the securing of personal goals formulated by rational self-determining agents. This is the view which finds expression in modern liberal pluralist political theory, in neoclassical economics, and in some forms of more individualistically oriented sociological theory, the emphasis being on how individuals make their world as conscious agents rather than it being made for them by the properties and dynamic of the social context. This view is addressed by Hegel, in for example, the *Natural Law* essay where he takes to task the individualism of Kant and theorists of the state of nature, and in the *Philosophy of Right* where the individualist presuppositions of contract theory are criticized.

Both the extreme holistic and individualist views involve a reductionism of a kind that Hegel's own theory attempts to avoid. The first reduces the individual agent to his structural position within society and implies that any description of the individual essentially and exclusively involves reference to his role, function, and position within the societal scheme of things. Individualists, on the other hand, reduce social contexts and the patterns of intersubjectivity to the interaction between an aggregate of asocially construed individuals using one another in the pursuit of their personal goals and projects.

Hegel's theory is, in part, an attempt to get to grips with the inadequacies and abstractness of both positions, and he effects the project of reconceptualising the individual-society relation through a critical examination of, on the one hand, classical Greek society and philosophy, and, on the other, modern individualism. The task he sets himself is that of integrating the social and the individual, of formulating a conception of men and society of a kind that recognizes that individuals are conscious agents determining their own goals and projects and, in some sense, creating and reproducing their social environment, but that they do so as *social* beings whose thought and action is in part constituted by the social context. That is to say, individuals are the subjects and agents of social action, but they are so only in virtue of their social being. But, in addition, their social context undermines their capacities as conscious agents. Thus, no account of what individuals do determining of their personal goals and their interaction with the social context can be exhausted by an account of the social context itself.

This is, of course, a familiar and persistently intractable problem for social theory, and finding a way through the problem involves mapping out cases against *both* the counter-intuitive claims that anything that can be stated about the power of agency is reducible *either* to some account of the social context *or* to alleged properties of individual agents *per se*. Thus, the problem is that of formulating an account of individual agency that recognizes the constitutive importance of the social context without wholly reducing the individual to that context.

This is a deep and perplexing issue touching on a number of major areas of philosophical discourse and I can do very little here either to attack the problem or demonstrate the details of Hegel's attempted solution. But there are some central points that can be made, at least as a basis for further thought, and they hinge on the question of the respects in which social contexts might be thought to be undermining in relation to individual agency.

IV

Conceptual Intersubjectivity

Why, in Hegel's view, do social contexts undermine individual consciousness and agency? And why should we suppose that there are crucial respects in which reference to the consciousness and agency of individuals is a necessary condition for explaining social action? In this respect I want to look at the importance accorded by Hegel to *conceptual intersubjectivity*. This, so it seems to me, is the core of his analysis.

But first it is necessary to see the more general route by which Hegel arrives at a theory of intersubjectivity, and this revolves around his arguments against individualism as such. Among contemporary social theorists, individualism has been heavily criticized. The claims of rational-choice theorists to be able to determine coherent preference orderings and suitably strategic social arrangements as a means to securing optimum satisfaction have been submitted to damaging criticism.* And both the explanatory and ethical implications of individualist theories have been questioned. Hegel thus stands in, and makes an important contribution to, a tradition of thought that has seriously questioned the claim that individuals can be understood in isolation from the social context of which they are a part. Indeed, much of Hegel's thinking is a philosophical extension of the straightforward sociological point that the child is "suckled at the breast of the universal life, lies first in an absolute vision of that life as alien to it, but comprehends it more and more and so passes over into the universal spirit.[10] This is partly what the contemporary sociologist would call the process of "socialisation," and it is an assertion of the view that individuals just cannot be understood in abstraction from their social context, the implication being that ahistorical conceptions of rationality and morality cannot be sustained.

But whatever the limits of individualism, there does remain the important question that I have already posed, namely that of whether what individuals do, the choices they make, and their interaction with their social context is explicable *only* in terms of the impact on them of the social context. That is to say, in what respects, and how, is the social context undermining? What truth is there in the individualist's claim that individual consciousness and agency

---

*For a Hegelian critique of rational choice theory, see my "Hegel and the Common Good," *Ethics* (January, 1983).

are critical for understanding social action? How far do men make themselves as well as being made by society?

In order to get at the roots of Hegel's position on these questions, it is necessary to invoke a basic philosophical distinction, frequently drawn on by Hegel himself, between social actions explicable in terms of their causally determining conditions, and explicable in virtue of the meanings and concepts expressed in them. Hegel disputes the value of the former—causal—account in, for example, his various criticisms of empiricist psychology. That is, individual thought and action cannot be explicated as the outcome of empirically identifiable psychological properties of mind such as the desire for pleasure or natural gregariousness. He holds, rather, the view that social actions are both explicable in terms of, and significant in respect of, the *meanings and concepts* expressed in them. Thus, to explain social action is necessarily to recover the meaning expressed in it.

What is crucial for the present purpose is the implication of the claim about the conceptual character of social action for an account of consciousness and agency. The view that I am trying to put forward, and which I take to be central to Hegel's entire political theory, infers an active conception of the self from arguments about the meaning or conceptual character of social action. That is to say, to recommend a mode of explanation in which reference to concepts is critical is also—necessarily—to place some weight on the anthropological claim that men are self-conscious and reflexive beings capable of determining their own goals and submitting their social environment to reflective judgement. This link between the conceptual character of action and the power of agency is central to Hegel's analysis, and will be returned to in due course.

Hegel delivers his characterisation of the respects in which the conceptual character of action issues is a notion of self-determining subjectivity in the theory of the will. He treats social life as in some sense an embodiment of the will, and the introduction to the *Philosophy of Right* is an extended elucidation of the structure of the will. The will is not determined by empirically given needs and desires, but is, rather, determined by itself. Thus, the fundamental feature of the will is its "pure indeterminacy or that pure reflection of the ego into itself" which involves the dissipation of every restriction and every content immediately presented by nature, by needs, desires and impulses, or given by any means whatever.[11] But the constitution of self-determination is not exclusively individual; it has, rather, a social and universal dimension. It is only in virtue of being a participant in a complex of shared social concepts that the capacity for self-determination is acquired.

The distinction between causal explanations and conceptual or meaning explanations is one that underlies much modern debate between, say, on the one hand, deductive nonomological or positivistic structural explanation and,

on the other, hermeneutic expressivism, the latter invoking a more active conception of the human subject than the former and placing greater explanatory
emphasis on the consciousness of agents. Reference is made to the intersubjective realm of concepts that are constitutive of the social whole, a realm that only
exists in virtue of the consciousness and agency of its participant individuals.

But reference to the consciousness of agents, and to the internal connection
between consciousness and action, still leaves the more than residual problem
of the social context. For clearly, if anti–individualist critiques are right—and
Hegel supplies one—then it follows that explanations of consciousness and
agency must in some way be tied to an account of the role of the social context,
and it is certainly Hegel's contention that we cannot plausibly construe the
social context as an aggregate of individual meanings. The task, therefore, is
that of formulating the relationship between individual agency and the context
within which it is generated, and in such a way that we are left with a coherent
conception of individuals as the subjects of social action. That is to say, we
need, and Hegel goes a long way to providing, a conception of the individual
that recognizes the constitutive importance of the social context, but that does
not regard it as wholly determining.

The link that Hegel forges between the individual and the social consists of an
intersubjective complex of concepts and meanings that are drawn upon, implicated in, and invoked in justification and rationalization for action. That
social contexts are explicable in terms of the particular constellation of concepts and meanings constitutive of them is fundamental to Hegel's theory.
Indeed, all social relationships, whether they are those characteristic of the
general periods of history analyzed in the *Lectures on the Philosophy of History* or phenomenologically recovered in the *Phenomenology of Spirit,* are
constituted by a particular constellation of concepts. Each of those con-
stellations has its own characteristics and properties identifiable as a particular
phase or period of historical development. The 'substance', then, of the social
world is its essentially *conceptual* character.

This argument about the conceptual character of social experience provides
the grounds for a number of further points about human agency which are
implied in what I have already said. First, to speak of human action being constituted and guided by concepts necessarily presupposes that those concepts
can be intelligently known and used. In this view, the, social action is less the
outcome of causally determining forces—psychological or structural—but is,
rather, an *accomplishment* achieved by self-conscious rational agents, and it is
an argument of this kind that is at the heart of Hegel's claim that social actions,
institutions, and practices are in crucial respects expressions of the self-determining will. In this view, particular social actions stand, analogously, in much
the same kind of relationship as language use stands to the rules and conven-

tions of language. That is to say, we cannot conceive of a language user without ascribing to him at least minimal knowledge of how to use language, of what expressions are appropriate or inappropriate, and what utterances are required in particular situations. This is part of the import of Hegel's account of modern *Sittlichkeit* and the contrast with Greek *Sittlichkeit*. *Sittlichkeit* does not consist of a complex of concepts and ideas that externally impose themselves on unreflective subjects; rather it is intelligently drawn upon and used by conscious agents with the power to determine their own goals and purposes and to accept or reject given standards of appropriateness.

A second point follows closely from this. If human beings are capable of using concepts and expressing them in their actions, then it follows that they are, in principle, capable of questioning those concepts, or at least understanding what is involved in doing something different. Obeying the state, for example, expresses a particular set of understanding about what is appropriate. But this also presupposes being able to see that there is an alternative set of understandings in which not obeying the state might be taken to be appropriate.* And, further, to know what is involved in obeying is also to be able to envisage alternative understandings and social practices; it is to be able to submit the social context to criticism. This, I take to be part of what Hegel understands by *subjectivity*. In the modern world, subjectivity is present in a way not experienced in the Greek world. Or if it is present, it can, as in the case of Socrates, only manifest itself in opposition to the social order, and as a destructive force. The difference between Socrates, on the one hand, and, on the other, the modern individual reflecting upon his society in a critical manner, is that the latter draws on and uses a set of generally available critical concepts that are part of the conceptual apparatus of the modern world. Socrates, on the other hand, can only criticize his society by taking a point of reference which, to his contemporaries, seemed private, exclusive, and belonging to an alien political discourse.

Arguments of this kind are explicitly developed by Hegel. First of all, he asserts that "pure subjectivity is the innermost root of the certainty of myself,"[12] and consequently "it no longer satisfies man to obey law as an authority and external necessity, for he desires to satisfy himself in himself, to convince himself, through his reflections, of what is binding upon him and what he has to do for this end."[13] Further, by implication, to recognize why something is binding is, equally, to see why it might not be and why alternative understandings might be appropriate.

We can see now, I think, how these arguments about subjectivity are closely tied to Hegel's arguments about intersubjectivity, and his account of Greek

---

*A similar point to this is made and helpfully formulated by W.E. Connolly in *Appearance and Reality in Politics,* although not in relation to Hegel specifically.

philosophy and society again provides a useful point of insertion into his view. Greek society exhibits a particular constellation of concepts, and an understanding of it involves reference to those concepts rather than to causally determining forces. As Hegel characterizes it, Greek society collapses through the emergence of subjectivity, that is, at the point at which the citizen becomes reflective and no longer unreflectingly accepts the customs of the community as necessarily appropriate in virtue of their mere givenness. Hegel's point about the emergence of subjectivity is not a straightforward empirical observation; it is embedded in a conceptualisation of a fundamental "dialectical" tension within Greek society. The problem with Greek society, in Hegel's view, is that it suppresses the conditions of its own existence, thereby stultifying the human potential generated by its very existence. Thus, Greek society exists as a "spiritual" as opposed to merely "natural" social form, and can *only* exist in virtue of the power of humans to internalise and use shared concepts; that is, the existence of Greek society, despite its lack of reflective subjectivity, is dependent upon human beings using concepts and being able to see some point to their social life. Greek man is not a mere effect of psychological or structural determinations. But at the same time as being dependent upon human beings' conceptual powers, Greek society denies their full realization, and this is the profound contradiction inherent in that social form. It denies their full realization by refusing the right to individual conscience, choice, and criticism, and by demanding the unreflective acceptance of given social rules and customs. Hegel's point, then, is—and it has significant moral and political implications—that man's conceptual powers are only fully realized in a social context where individual criticism of the social order is legitimated, and where the institutional arrangements are such that changes can be brought about as a consequence of the opinions and activities of individuals. The *Philosophy of Right* can, accordingly, be interpreted, although not unambiguously, as a characterization of an open, responsive, and self-critical society deriving from a philosophical anthropology according to which men's conceptual powers are closely linked to their capacities as conscious agents.

There is, however, a problem outstanding that requires clarification. It has been suggested so far that individual thought and agency are in important ways constituted by the social context, in so far as they are dependent upon participation in an intersubjective realm of concepts. But, further, it has also been suggested that individuals are capable of judging existing institutions and practices, criticizing them, and perhaps recommending alternatives. The question that arises, however, is where the criteria of judgement and criticism derive from. One possible answer is that a complex of concepts supplies its own self-criticism. Another, related, possibility is that rival systems of concepts emerge in the womb of dominant sysems and in time, perhaps, displace them. Indeed,

such a view is consistent with Hegel's characterization of historical development as the successive displacement and replacement of modes of self-reflection
embodied in socially generated clusters of meanings and concepts. However,
given the argument of this paper, with its stress on the centrality of individual
agency and freedom, both of these possible answers suggest an uncomfortable
anti–individualism. In both views, the source of criticism is not individual agency, but rather a set of socially constructed meanings and concepts that are
expressed in individual thought. The individual is just the vehicle for the
social.

However, in Hegelian terms, these views embody an excessively premodern,
particularly Greek, conception of the interconnection between individual
agency and the intersubjective system of concepts. They imply a determining
relationship between the individual and society that does not hold in the modern
world where the principle of subjectivity is firmly established. To become a participant in an intersubjective realm of concepts does, of course, involve taking
on and accepting a determinate set of rules, values, and principles. But in the
modern world—and this is the crucial contrast with Greece—it involves the
acquiring of the *capacity* for criticism and reflection. The modern world supplies a set of critical concepts that individuals can draw upon and invoke in the
assessment of their social environment. The manner and extent of criticism is,
of course, bounded and constrained by the critical concepts available to them.
But it is not reducible to them, nor wholly determined by them. Rather, they are
something to be drawn upon by self-conscious and reflective agents.

V

Sittlichkeit

Hegel's political theory has as its kernel the theory of *Sittlichkeit*, and I
should like to gather together some of the points I have already made by offering
some further comments on what I take to be the essential elements of the theory
of *Sittlichkeit.* Since Hegel makes the rather grand claim that "ethical life is the
concept of freedom developed into the existing world and the nature of self-
consciousness."[14] There does seem to be some obligation placed upon us to
consider carefully what this amounts to.

The conventional wisdom of interpretation is that *Sittlichkeit* is Hegel's
point of insertion into the notion of social integration and community. And so it
is. But it is also more than that, and his characterization of it in the *Philosophy
of Right* embodies elements and features missing from the early *System of
Ethics* and *Natural Law* essay. This developmental change in Hegel's thought
reflects the extent of his move beyond the ideal of Greek community as something

to be aspired to. It is a move towards a consideration of how the ideal of community can be realized in societies in which civil society has been established as a distinct moment. The emergence of civil society means the articulation of the principle of private right, the recognition of the validity of contractual relations, and relatively free economic relations among producers and between producers and workers. These developments amount to the powerful and ineluctable assertion of the individual, and the nature and structure of ethical life is heavily determined by them.

I have already suggested that in Hegel's view the social context is to be regarded as a medium rather than a subject, and Hegel's account of modern ethical life with its insistence on the recognition of the interdependence of the universal and the particular, and its inclusion of civil society as one of its moments, is the expression of this notion of a medium rather than a subject. That is to say, modern ethical life, as opposed to Greek ethical life, is explicitly established as a medium that is drawn upon by individuals and reconstituted through their use of it. This shift from subject to medium from classical Greece to modern society, is the accomplishment of the modern world, and it is achieved through the articulation and expression of the various social and cultural forces producing the phenomenon of modern individualism. And this shift substantially alters the relationship between the individual and society.

First this shift accords a primacy and legitimacy to individual goals and projects. Individuals are not required to take the goals of the social whole as their own, but rather to draw on the concepts embedded in the whole as a medium of rationality in the pursuit of their personal goals and projects. That is not to deny that the formation of goals is only possible within a social context, and that there cannot be personal goals and projects understood independently of the background concepts and rules within which they emerge. That is to say, it is central to Hegel's view that there is necessarily a social dimension to the determination of personal goals. But that does not, however, entail the further proposition, that individuals cannot have exclusively personal goals and that there is only available to them the alleged "higher" purposes of the community as a whole. It is in Greek society, to invoke the analogy of language again, that it is as if individuals take the rules and conventions governing the use of language as the purpose of language use. Contemporary society, on the other hand, does not require this of the individual, legitimacy being accorded to the self-determination of personal goals and projects. Thus, the moment of particularity is deeply embedded in the experience of contemporary man, and the social context stands in relation to the individual rather as the rules and conventions of language use stand to individual statements. That is, they do not determine what should be done, but they do provide criteria of intelligibility and mutual understanding.

One consequence of this is that modern *Sittlichkeit* leaves a great deal of scope to the individual determination of personal goals, a major expression of which is modern civil society where, as Hegel says, "the right to launch forth in all directions" is recognized.[15] And in the *Encyclopedia*, Hegel claimed that "the capacity for determining ourselves towards one thing or another is undoubtedly a vital element in the will. . . . "[16] Further, in the essay on the German *Constitution* Hegel had claimed that "one great virtue of the old states of Europe" was "that while the public authority is secure so far as its needs and its progress are concerned, it leaves free scope to its citizens' own activity in details of administration, of law, and customary usages."[17] Indeed, he deplores the "pedantic craving to determine every detail, the illiberal jealousy of any arrangement whereby an estate, a corporation, etc., adjusts and manages its own affairs, this means carping at any independent action by its citizens. . . . "[18]

This leaves us, however, with one final feature of modern *Sittlichkeit* that follows directly from what I have said about the power of agents—as users of concepts—to reflect and to consider alternative sets of self-understandings. This concerns the issue of criticism and social change. In the Griesheim lecture notes, public opinion is described as an "ethical power."[19] By that Hegel means that it is one of the bases of the community, a force out of which its constituent concepts are forged. In the early *Realphilosophie* lectures Hegel had claimed that "one cannot do anything against informed public opinion. . . . From it proceed all changes, and it is nothing less than the progressively developing spirit conscious of its deficiency."[20] In, this view the social context is submitted to criticism and revision through the conscious agency of individuals, expressed in public opinion. And Hegel develops a similar argument concerning the role of representative institutions and the functions of the corporations and estates within them. They are construed as vehicles of change, as the institutional expression of changes in attitudes and beliefs within society as a whole.

What is distinctive about modern—as opposed to Greek—ethical life, is that is supplies both the criteria and the institutional expression for its own self-assessment. This is a point of some importance because one line of criticism of Hegel's position could be its implied relativism and an associated political conservatism. That is, it might be supposed that the criteria of rationality are exclusively relative to a particular, historically given set of norms and values. However, it does not follow from the claim that the criteria of rationality are internal to a particular context that there are no grounds for criticism of that context. Such a conclusion would only follow if the context failed to supply the conditions of its own self-assessment. And as I have argued, it is precisely this that Hegel's modern *Sittlichkeit* does provide.

CONCLUSION

I have claimed that Hegel links a theory of conceptual intersubjectivity with a theory of conscious individual agency. Thus, beings capable of drawing upon and using concepts are also capable of understanding them, assessing their implications, and potentially standing in a critical relationship to them, thereby generating social change.

Second, I have tried to draw attention to what I take to be the political implications of this general view of the constitution of society and the nature of social action, and I concluded that the theory issue is a view of politics in which the articulation and recognition of individual and group opinion are important.

What, I hope, emerges from what I have said is that individualist critics of Hegel have inferred much too much by way of conclusions about political tyranny and the suppression of individual agency from premises asserting the importance of the social dimension of experience. These premises are to be found in Hegel's theory, but they lead to arguments about the potentiality of individuals for exercising their power of agency. That is to say, persons who are capable of subscribing to, and participating in, an intersubjective realm of meanings are, in principle, capable of questioning and changing those meanings, and the most rational society is the one in which full opportunities are provided for this. Indeed, so deep is Hegel's conviction that any reasonable philosophical anthropology must contain detailed reference to the powers of subjectivity and agency, that when, historically, it appears to be absent, this is, in his view, something that requires specific explanation, as in the case of ancient Greece.

Hegel's account of agency provides a powerful lever against both psychological and structural determinist theories. According to both theories, individual action is explicable as the outcome of causally antecedent conditions in which consciousness and agency, if they figure at all, have the status only of being part of the chain of cause and effect. And in view of what I have said about the centrality of conceptual intersubjectivity and the implications of that for reflective subjectivity, this general argument is of particular interest as a counter to various extreme versions of structural theory. It becomes rapidly clear from Hegel's arguments that structuralism's reification of the social context issues from a failure to grasp the intersubjective complex of concepts as the mediation between the individual and society. Structuralism wrongly treats conceptual intersubjectivity as an effort of social structures rather than as constitutive of them. That is to say, it fails to recognize that social practices and institutions are sustained by the interpretations and understandings of social actors who can see the point of what they do because they hold it to be appropriate, or who, alternatively, come to reject their social context because it no longer serves their needs and purposes.

It doesn't, of course, follow from the claim that individuals are capable of understanding themselves and their social context that they always do so, or do so fully. They may be deluded, deliberately duped, or simply mistaken in their beliefs. But once it is asserted that conceptual intersubjectivity is essentially constitutive of the social context, mistaken beliefs, or indeed anything that limits the power of individual agency, becomes something that requires explanation. In addition, it is also something that requires critical analysis of existing social institutions and practices. Do they provide adequate conditions for the expression of individual agency? If not, why not?

This brings me, then, to the final and perhaps most significant question, a question that I can only pose but not discuss here since that would require another paper. Does the Hegelian edifice of recommended social practices and institutions provide an adequate vehicle for the development and expression of the self-determining subjectivity it purports to serve? This is a vast question extending beyond the details of Hegel's institutional and organizational recommendations to the need for an assessment of the nature of contemporary liberal democratic capitalist states. I do not know how, exactly, to go about approaching that particular question, but what can be asserted with some certainty is that Hegel develops a philosophical anthropology that demands the critical assessment of social institutions and practices, and that presses upon us the need to assess institutions and practices as vehicles for the development and expression of essentially human powers and capacities for which the self-determination of the individual is of central importance.

NOTES

1.   G. Lukàcs, *History and Class Consciousness* (Merlin, 1971).
2.   G.W.F. Hegel, *Phenomenology of Spirit* (Oxford, 1977), p. 177.
3.   R. Plant, *Hegel* (Allen and Unwin, 1973); C. Taylor, *Hegel* (CUP, 1975).
4.   A. Giddens, *Central Problems in Social Theory* (1979).
5.   R. Bhaskar, *Possibility of Naturalism* (1979).
6.   W.E. Connolly, *Appearance and Reality in Politics* (CUP, 1980).
7.   K. Marx, *Critique of Hegel's Philosophy of Right* (CUP, 1976).
8.   *Ibid*, p. 7.
9.   Hegel, *Phenomneology of Spirit,* para. 354.
10.   G.W.F. Hegel, *Natural Law* (Pennsylvania, 1975), p. 115.
11.   G.W.F. Hegel, *Philosophy of Right* (Oxford, 1967), para 5.

12. G.W.F. Hegel, *Rechtsphilosophie*, vol. 4 ed. K. H. Ilting, (Fromann Holzboog, 1974), p. 144 (from notes made on Hegel's lectures by von Griesheim).
13. G.W.F. Hegel, *History of Philosophy*, vol. 1 (London, 1896), p. 358.
14. Hegel, *Philosophy of Right*, para. 142.
15. *Ibid.*, para. 182.
16. G.W.F. Hegel, *Enzyklopadie der philosophisches* Wissenschaften im Grundrisse, ed. F. Nicolin and O. Pöggeler (Felix Meiner, 1959), para. 145.
17. G.W.F. Hegel, *Political Writings* (Knox/Pelczynski), (Oxford, 1964), p. 159.
18. *Ibid.*, p. 161.
19. *Rechtsphilosophie*, vol. 4, p. 724.
20. G.W.F. Hegel, *janaer Realphilosophie* (Hamburg, 1967), p. 260.

IS THERE A FUTURE
IN THE PHILOSOPHY OF HISTORY?

by
RAYMOND PLANT

In this paper I shall be concerned with the future of the philosophy of history as a philosophical activity, but I shall approach the question in a rather oblique manner. I shall argue that an examination of the role of the future in Hegel's *Philosophy of History* will throw light upon the epistemological and metaphysical requirements of any substantial nonanalytical philosophy of history.

The topic of the philosophy of history lends itself to a form of expansiveness, an expansiveness that leads to platitudes. I gather that Professor Ayer summed up what he had learned from the subject in the following propositions.

1. We have had a history.
2. We have now had the history that we have had.
3. We cannot now have any other history than the hisotry that we have had.
4. We ought to be grateful.[1]

I hope the paper will be able to say something more substantive than this!

My topic then is the vexed question of the end of history or the foreclosure of the future in Hegel's philosophy of history and what we can learn about the nature of the subject from his work. As we know, Hegel divided the phases of world history into four states:

1. The Oriental World.
2. The Greek World.
3. The Roman World.
4. The German World.

The initial question is whether the German World should be properly seen by Hegel as standing at the *end* of history and what it would mean to say that it does. The argument here usually takes two forms:

93

1. Textual evidence to show the Hegel did *not* regard the German World as the end of history.

2. Arguments to show that Hegel's philosophical presuppositions are inconsistent with the postulate of the end of history. This argument takes two forms: the first in that the notion of the end of history is inconsistent with the negativity of Dialectic; the second is that Hegel's notion of freedom is not compatible with the foreclosure of the future.

In his *Lectures on the Philosophy of World History*, Hegel makes the following point, which is usually taken as repeating his claim that he thought that the German World stood at the end of history:

> America is therefore the land of the future, and its world historical importance has yet to be revealed in the stages which lie ahead—perhaps in a conflict between North and South America. It is a land of desire for all those who are weary of the history of Europe.....It is up to America to abandon the ground on which World History has hitherto been enacted. What has taken place there up to now is but an echo of the Old World and the expression of an alien life and as the country of the future it is of no interest to us here, for prophecy is not the business of the philosopher. In history we are concerned with what has been and what is, in philosophy however we are concerned not with what belongs exclusively to the past or to the future but that which *is* both now and eternally.[2]

On the face of it, an important conclusion can be drawn from this passage. It seems to contain clear evidence that Hegel did not see the German World as the end of history because he seems to be saying not that America will realize in its own way the *Geist* of the German World but will rather realize its own *Geist:* "It will abandon the ground on which World History has hitherto been enacted," and "What has taken place is but an echo of the Old World."

The second set of arguments are not textual in the straightforward sense but rather point to the philosophical contradiction between the ideas of dialectic and freedom and the foreclosure of history.

The first form of this argument has been summarized by G.A. Kelly as follows:

> Hegel has emasculated his own dialectic with its never-ending power of criticism and negation by virtue of his arrogant system which halts at the Rubicon of ideology and partial truth.[3]

Similar types of criticism can be found in the works of Raya Dunayevskya, Raymond Polin, J.N. Findlay and Henri Michel.[4] To arrest the process of dialectical development in history with the German World is itself undialectical in the sense that it is inconsistent with the absolute or infinite negativity of the dialectic. The whole tendency of the dialectic is to dissolve and negate every fixed content and this process applies equally well to Hegel's world as to those whose decline and dissolution is the result of the types of dialectical contradiction he so eloquently describes in *The Philosophy of History* and *The Phenomenology of Spirit.* A parallel but more specific objection is that such a view of history is incompatible with the freedom and self-transcendence with which Hegel credits human nature and the history of which forms the subject matter of *The Phenomenology of Spirit.* Raymond Polin encapsulates this argument quite well when he suggests that:

> To affirm that history has come to an end is an arbitrary postulate and it even contradicts the essential postulate of history that man is free, that he always exists beyond himself in constant self renewal.[5]

In arresting the historical process with the German World, Hegel is constraining in a wholly arbitrary way the self-transcendence of human nature that is the basis of historical change and renewal.

These two arguments seem to me to embody mistakes about the Hegelian notion of dialectic and his conception of freedom. To assume that the impetus of the dialectic means that *all* determinate structures must be overcome neglects the intimate relationship between dialectic and Reason (*Vernunft*). The dialectic is the means whereby Reason is developed and achieved in the world and, as Hegel shows in *The Science of Logic*, essential to the realization of Reason is the relationship between the moments of universality, specificity, and individuality. If these moments can never be reconciled, then the dialectic must be a continuous process because it is the contradictions between these that produces dialectical change. However, to say that the dialectic is a continuous process also implies that Reason can never be achieved.[6] Surely though, it would be a negation of Hegel's philosophy to suggest that Reason cannot be attained. Of course, this is not to say that Hegel is correct in thinking that it is attained in the German World, only that its attainment is inherent in the process of world history, otherwise Reason would be like a Kantian regulative principle, the status of which Hegel always divided as a form of *sollen* of what ought to be. Hegel clearly thought that the German World was in the process of producing an adequate bridge between universal, particular, and individual. This is not to say that it is actually achieved in any particular state, only that we do have intimations of its achievement in the German World. Unless dialectical change comes to an end, the achievement of Reason will always be a mere *ought-to-be*, and consciousness will be 'unhappy' not *zu Hause* not *bei sich Selbst.* The overcoming of these states of mind and being are quite central to Hegel's philosophical position. Without the achievement of Reason in the end of history, the process of history would be a form of bad infinity (*schlechte Unendlichkeit*).[7]

The second objection is that to arrest the process of history and therefore of human development is incompatible with human freedom which, after all, in Hegel's view is at the center of the historical process. Again this objection seems to assume that Hegel holds a sort of unqualified Promethean view of freedom as a *continuing* process of self-transcendence, but this is *not* Hegel's view of the relationship between human freedom and history.

> Freedom discovers its concept in reality and has developed the secular world into the objective system of a specific and internally organized state. . . . This is the goal of World History: the Spirit must create for itself a nature and a world to conform with its own nature so that the subject may discover its own concept and the Spirit in this second nature. . . . and in this objective reality it becomes conscious of its subjective freedom and rationality.[8]

The process of history and dialectic is the working out of this reconciliation between subjective freedom and an internally organized state. The achievement of this reconciliation must be a real possibility. If history were a continued form of existential self-transcendence, freedom would again become a sort of bad infinity. Again, this is not to say that Hegel correctly identified the German World as the one in which this reconciliation is achieved, but a failure to recognize the possibility of its achievement would be inconsistent with Hegel's major philosophical premises. It seems then that we cannot argue that the foreclosure of the future is inconsistent with the particular meaning that Hegel attaches to the notions of dialectic and freedom.

These two points lead on to another observation, that the notion of the end of history is *not* primarily a chronological one. It is rather a logical one concerning the institutional patterns required for the completion or realization of certain concepts—freedom and reason in particular. The end of history is the realization in specific form of these universals. It is the period in which the concepts reveal their truth (to use Hegel's language).

However, this still leaves untouched the textual question posed by the passage cited earlier in which Hegel seemed to endorse the view that the future is in fact open and the present can be transcended. In dealing with this aspect of the argument I want to make two points:

1. We have to say that this passage is an aberration and that there are internal grounds for saying this within *Lectures on the Philosophy of History*.

2. There are central philosophical reasons for thinking that any philosophy of history must recognize the end of history or the foreclosure of the future and that paradoxically empirical history, as Hegel calls it, must also depend upon an idea of an end of history.

To accept the passage about America being the land of the future at its face value seems to reveal a deep inconsistency in Hegel's writing here. An important example of this discrepancy is to be found in the following passages:

> World History travels from East to West, for Europe is the absolute end of history.
>
> In the Christian/Germanic Age the Divine Spirit has come into the world and taken up its abode in the individual who is now completely free and endowed with substantial freedom. This is the reconciliation of the Subjective with the Objective Spirit. The Spirit is reconciled and united with its concept.[9]
>
> This is the goal of World History: the Spirit must create for itself a nature and a world to confirm to its own nature so that the subject may discover its own concept of the Spirit in this second nature, in this reality . . . Such is the progress of the idea in general and this must be an ultimate point of view in history.[10]

Granted that this formal process described in the third passage is in fact achieved in the German World (second passage) it is very difficult to see how Hegel could regard America as capable of breaking new ground in the development of Spirit. It may of course achieve the reconciliation between subjective freedom and the organized state in its own way, but this is not breaking new ground for Spirit—this has already been achieved in the German World. It seems that Hegel is clearly inconsistent in what he says about these issues in *Lectures on the Philosophy of History* but, granted that his notion of dialectic and freedom require the idea of completion, and granted what he actually says about the German World, the balance of interpretation must be that Hegel believed in the end of history and that what he means by this is that his conceptual framework generally will enable us to encompass all human experience in his past and will not require fundamental modification or change in order to enable us to understand the subsequent development of human activity.

If Hegel's philosophy involves this commitment, it might be thought by many to be its own *reductio ad absurdum*. Surely such an assumption is so bizarre and involves such a transcendence of human finitude—that if Hegel's philosophy requires the idea of the end of history, then his philosophy must be basically at fault. However, in what remains of the paper I want to show that a notion of the end of history is a necessary condition for the whole exercise of philosophy of history (understood as more than the analytical treatment of historical concepts and methods) and that an idea of an end of history may well be a condition for the pursuit of history at all, insofar as historical writing seeks to be in the least degree interpretative.

In order to argue this point I shall refer to the work of some analytical philosophers particularly Feinberg, Davidson and Danto.[11]

The thesis that history requires some notion of the end of history is connected to the idea developed by Davidson that action sentences embody what has come to be called the 'accordian effect', that is to say the description that is applied to an action can be developed. This is because of the platitudinous point that by doing certain things we bring about other things and what we bring about becomes incorporated into a more complex description of the original action, e.g.,

> Luther nailed a piece of paper to the door of his church in Wittenberg. Luther started the Reformation.

Unless we limit the description of what Luther did to a conjunction of statements about his physical movements, the effect of his action—the other things his action brings about—will become build into the identification of what Luther did. Historical writing embodies this aspect of action statements to a very high degree, and this, of course, means that typically the historian is in the position of identifying action in the past in the light of events—those things that the action brought about—that are in the future in relation to such actions, although of course they are still in the past for the historian. If this is a central feature of the identification of action—that the description identifying the action can be developed to incorporate future events into the description of the action—then the question clearly arises as to whether there are any objective limits to the extension of descriptions of actions. Davidson himself says that the possibilities of such expansion are "without clear limit," and it could be argued that in the absence of a clearly grounded criterion for limiting the extension of descriptions of action, the identification of historical action is going to be to some extent arbitrary—relative to various sorts of things, for example, the interest of the historian, the assumptions of a particular school of historians, etc.[12] The only possibility of removing this element of relativity and arbitrariness would be if the future were foreclosed so that we could know all the consequences and all the effects of a particular action so that we could have a basis for picking out the most appropriate descriptions of action. The end of history would determine what otherwise seems to be without clear limit according to Davidson and the presence of this clear limit would then remove arbitrariness. This point has been very well made by Danto in *The Analytical Philosophy of History:*

> Completely to describe an event is to locate it in all the right stories, and this we cannot do. We cannot for the same reason that we cannot achieve a speculative philosophy of history.[13]

The ideal of an objective and complete history therefore requires the fulfillment of the same condition that is usually taken to be a necessary condition for speculative philosophy of history, the complete account of the future:

Any account of the past is essentially incomplete. It is essentially incomplete, that is, if its completion would require the fulfillment of a condition which simply cannot be fulfilled. And my thesis will be that a complete account of the past would presuppose a complete account of the future, so that one could not achieve a complete historical account without our achieving a philosophy of history. So that if there cannot be a legitimate philosophy of history, there cannot be a legitimate and complete historical account.[14]

On this view therefore, there is a logical connection between the idea of objective (nonspeculative) empirical history and the necessary condition for the speculative philosophy of history, namely the foreclosure of the future. The logical point here could be compared with the more dramatic but essentially similar point made by Dilthey, Heidegger, and Sartre about the significance of death within the life of the individual. It is only at death, when the possibility of future action for an individual is foreclosed, that we are able to begin to give final significance to what he has done in life.

At the same time the notion of the end of history, while it may be of central importance, as in their very different ways Danto and Hegel have shown, is nevertheless a notion to which it is very difficult to give any concrete sense. It requires a transcendence of human finitude and this is no doubt why Hegel regarded the categorical structure of *The Science of Logis* as the thoughts of God before the foundation of the world. It is unlikely that such a view would today find such favor and we have to deal with the question posed by the end of history in a more modest way.

The obvious way forward is to regard the end of history as provisional and reversible and this is the view taken by the great German theologian, Wolfhart Pannenberg in his *Basic Questions in Theology*, vol. I[15] and in particular in the essay "Hermeneutic and Universal History." The problem as he defines it is:

We must ask how it is possible today to develop a conception of universal history which in contrast to Hegel's would preserve the finitude of human experience.[16]

This is to be achieved in Pannenberg's view in the notion of a provisional end of history. This provisional end would enable us to make determinate judgements about the past and provide a "clear limit," in Davidson's phrase, to the expansion of statements about action while preserving the limited nature of human experience and knowledge. However, Pannenberg's own account of the provisional end of history is complicated by the fact that he is a Christian theologian and the commitments that this naturally embodies about the importance of Jesus in world history and the idea of eschatology. Charles Taylor though has provided some secular examples in support of something like Pannenberg's view.[17] He takes two cases:

1. Certain kinds of social changes—the occurence of which one might regard as contingent (in a way that Hegel would deny)—such as urbanization, industrialization, technology, may seem to be irreversible and provide a limit to the horizon within which we are to understand the past.

2. The development of certain ideas about ourselves, which again may be contingent; for example, the development of a sense of moral individualism may now effectively rule out alternatives, for example, a social system in the West based upon Maoism.[18]

These changes and ideas provide us with limits within which to interpret the past and foreclose alternatives within the future—there can be no wholesale retreat from urbanism, technology, and individualism. Such a view of history would preserve human finitude—it would be arrived at by reflection upon our experience and not by the *a priori* application of logical catergories as in Hegel, but it would provide us with a standpoint, although not an Archemedian one against which to interpret the past.

However, there are difficulties with this view. If the argument is introduced to meet the Hegel/Danto point that history will to some extent be arbitrary and incomplete without the foreclosure of the future, then it is really rather difficult to see how the basis for the provisional foreclosure of the future can be on any other than a subjective basis and a basis that can be wholly parochial. Early Medieval man, for example, might have to say on a Taylorian view that secularization (assuming the concept could be made intelligible to him) was foreclosed just because religious and ecclesiastical conceptions had so entered into notions about the nature of persons and institutions. There is the danger in this view, however appealing it may be, of being in the position of the man who, confronted with a giraffe, said that it was impossible!

Of course an alternative formulation of the view might avoid the problem altogether. Pannenberg, in a sense, points the way to this in his essay "Hermeneutic and Universal History." Hermeneutic history would seek to avoid the problems posed by the extension of the descriptions that are applied to actions by restricting them to those descriptions that the agent performing the action could have entertained. Luther could have described his action as nailing a paper to the door of the church in Wittenberg, but *not* as starting the Reformation. To recover the intentional description of actions, the meaning that they had for agents, rather than the significance that they had for the future in what they brought about is central to this form of Hermeneutical history, and it does bypass the problem of the end of history and the limitations on the descriptions used to identify action. However, this is a large issue which I cannot really deal with here beyond asserting one or two points:

1. The distinction between meaning and significance is very far from being clear-cut. When an agent describes his own action, he is describing a project or an undertaking with consequences and thus, the distinction between these judgements and those about the longer term significance of those projects is unclear.

2. There is, of course, the immense difficulty in seeking to recover the intentions of those who act.

Obviously there are very large issues here, which have been much discussed by historians of political thought recently. This alternative does seem to be the only one to the problem posed by the end of history thesis, but it is not without difficulties of its own.

My conclusion is a modest one. I have argued that Hegel did hold the view that the end of history has been realized and that there are good textual grounds for thinking this and compelling philosophical reasons for thinking that such a view was the only one consistent with the basic presuppositions of his philosophy. However, the notion of the end of history is an important one and repays study by those interested in both speculative philosophy of history and empirical history. It does seem though, that there is no "halfway house" between a view that the future is open and therefore our view of the past always radically capable of revision, and a notion of the end of history that would limit our relationship with the past. The idea of a provisional end of history has an insecure epistemological basis and may well embody a form of temporal parochialism that for all practical purposes will make its role in the understanding of history very much like the 'open future' view.

NOTES

1.   I owe this story to Bernard Crick.
2.   G.W.F. Hegel, *Introduction Lectures on the Philosophy of World History,* trans. H.B. Nisbet (Cambridge, 1975), pp. 170–171.
3.   G.A. Kelly, "Mediation Versus Compromise in Hegel," in *Compromise in Ethics, Law and Politics,* ed. by J.R. Pennock and J.H. Chapman (New York, 1979), p. 88.
4.   R. Dunayeskaya, *Philosophy and Revolution* (New York, 1973); R. Polin, "Farewell to the Philosophy of History," in *Philosophy of History and Action,* ed. by Y. Yovell (Jerusalem and Utrecht, 1970); J.N. Findlay, *Hegel: A Re-Examination* (London, 1959); H. Michel, *L'Idée de l'état* (Paris, 1890).
5.   R. Polin, *Farewell,* p. 205–206.
6.   *Vide* R. Plant, *Hegel* (London, 1973), p. 101.

7.   G.W.F. Hegel, *Introduction Lectures,* p. 208.
8.   *Ibid.,* p. 197.
9.   *Ibid.,* p. 131.
10.   *Ibid.,* p. 208.
11.   J. Feinberg "Action and Responsibility," in *Philosophy in America,* ed. by M. Black (New York, 1968); Donald Davidson, "Agency," in *Agent, Action and Reason,* ed. by R. Binkly, R. Bronagh, and A. Manas (Oxford, 1979); Arthur Danto, *Analytical Philosophy of History* (Cambridge, 1965).
12.   *Vide* Danto, *Analytical Philosophy,* p. 272.
13.   *Ibid.*
14.   *Ibid.*
15.   London, 1970.
16.   *Ibid.,* p. 135.
17.   In the final chapter in *Philosophy of History and Action* (see note 4 above).
18.   See also C. Taylor, *Hegel and Modern Society* (Cambridge, 1979), p. 111.

RELIGION AND CULTURE

by

QUENTIN LAUER, S.J.

There is in Hegel's *Phenomenology of Spirit* a peculiar enigma which, to my knowledge, has received relatively little attention from commentators and interpreters down through the years. As I see it, the concept of *Bildung*, which in this paper I shall translate as "culture"—despite the multiple shades of meaning the term expresses in different contexts—is an unquestionably key concept in coming to grips with the march of human spirit, from the absolutely minimal consciousness of a world of reality, presumed to be "out-there" and immediately available to sense awareness, to the ultimate in human self-knowing, which consciousness tortuously comes to recognize as the only absolutely authentic mode of contact with objective reality, since it is spirit and spirit alone that is the "locus" of reality's objectivity; spirit, so to speak, "makes" the world objective and in so doing makes the world its own. The enigma lies in the fact that the concept of "culture," the process whereby spirit becomes what it is to be through it sown activity of self-integration, is treated explicitly in only one brief section in chapter 6, "Spirit," the section entitled "Culture and Its Realm of Actuality" (25 pages).[1] What is more, the "culture" (or "cultivation") here treated, which looks exclusively to the coming-to-be of a "European" spirit, culminates in a burlesque, typified by the French culture of the Ancien Regime, where *esprit* has replaced spirit, and the only cultivation that counts is the cultivation of clever language, a burlesque that trails off in a series of references to Diderot's brilliant little satire, *Rameau's Nephew.*

Be the enigma what it may, it is not until the *Vorlesungen über die Philosophie der Weltgeschichte* that Hegel speaks at great length of *Bildung* (in the sense of self-cultivation) as the mainspring of all *spiritual* development throughout the course of history. Here it is that the panoramic view of the *Bildung* of the human spirit that pervades the whole of the *Phenomenology*, even though it is made explicitly thematic only with regard to the cultivation of the European spirit, is seen to be characteristic of the human spirit throughout the millennia of its history.[2] It is precisely *Bildung,* as both the activity and the product of spirit, that reconciles the particular, without which spirit would not be concrete, having nothing to build upon, and the universal, without which spirit would not be authentic, having no depth of its own (*WG**, 65–66). Here is unfolded the process of successive integration, disintegration, and reintegration, that characterizes the saga of human progress, and which is recapitulated, so to speak, at higher and higher levels, as one "world-historical people" after another develops its own peculiar culture, each of which crumbles under the weight of its own logic--precisely because each is only partial--thus giving way to another culture, which in the same way blossoms and dies (see *GPR*, no. 343). What is peculiarly significant in all this—and here the theme is common to the *Lectures on the Philosophy of World History* and to the *Phenomenology of Spirit*—is that "culture" is inadequate to the task it has to perform until the human spirit is progressively "alienated" from the merely "natural" in which it is immersed, an alienation that does not take place independently of the religious consciousness from which emerges into reality a progressively more concrete human spirit, aware, precisely, of what it is to be spirit (see *G,* 125, 128, 131–132). In Hegel's view, then, religion and culture can never be separated in the process of man's becoming human, which, to employ an expression that is not Hegel's, can be called *die Menschwerdung des Menschen.* The "modern" age, it is true, beginning with the Enlightenment, has made valiant efforts to effect this separation, but it is precisely in this, as Hegel sees it, that it has failed. It too cannot escape the dialectic of integration, disintegration, and reintegration, and its *Bildung,* like that of the ages that preceded it, will be self-defeating, if the only possible integrator of spirit, Absolute Spirit, initially, at least, revealed in religious consciousness in its orientation of the authenticity of the human, is left out of the picture. Characteristic of the truly human are art, science, morality, law, religion, and philosophy. If any of these is missing, man is less than truly human (see *WG,* 43, 124, 126, 127).

What, then, is "culture," as Hegel understands it? It might be well to note at the beginning of our investigation that, although the term *Kultur* is common enough in German, it is a term that Hegel employs very rarely, and never as signifying culture in the profoundest sense of interior self-cultivation, self-realization. *Kultur* refers exclusively to the external products of an interiorly developed human spirit, and its meaning can range from cultivation of the soil (agri-culture) to the sublimest creations of fine art—the temple of Apollo, the palace of the king, the sculpture of Phidias, or the *Antigone* of Sophocles. It

---

*A guide to the abbreviations used in this paper appears on page 121.

might also be well to note that "culture" in the proper sense, although it can and must be said of individuals—who are *gebildet* or *ausgebildet*—refers primarily to the spirit of a people, all of whose members share, albeit in varying degrees, in a *Bildung* that is common to all. One can speak legitimately of the culture of China, of India, of Persia, of Egypt, of Greece or Rome. It is in this sense that Hegel sees the culture of a people as inextricably bound up with that people's religion. One can also, however, in a rather more limited sense, speak of English, French, Italian, or German culture, where the link with any one identifiable religion (or even "church") is not at all obvious—although Hegel does contend that the Christian religion not only characterizes but also molds the culture of Western (European) man in a unique way (see *WG*, 131), even though, as he makes abundantly clear in his critique of the "theologians" of his own day (e.g., in *PdG, GPR, EpW,* and *VPR*) that philosophy must take up the task which "theology" has abdicated, precisely because philosophy, as Hegel sees it, takes the concrete reality of God more seriously than do either a "pietistic" religion or an "erudite" theology.

The use of the term *Bildung,* however, is not confined to an expression of this rather obvious meaning—obvious to the extent that only if the term can have this meaning does it make sense at all to speak of a "Philosophy of World-History." Hegel has often been accused, most recently by Mr. Bronowski, of having denied—or, at the very least, ignored—the concept of evolution. But this is not quite accurate. Hegel, it is true, does not deal with the theory of evolution—one wonders how he *could* have in 1825—but it is not difficult to understand why he *would* not: his concern is not to trace a "natural" process, whose determining factors are not under the control of man, but rather to interpret a process of humanizing the human through that activity which characterizes the human, spiritual activity (see *WG*, 61–62, 72–73, 530, 554, 576)—man can *become* human only by *making* himself human. If, we might say, *natural* evolution must precede *spiritual* development, so be it! It is still true, as Hegel sees it, that only *spirit* has a history—*evolution is not* history. In Hegel's view, man is most authentically human when man is spirit, and this does not happen all at once—spirit is that unique process that is its own result.

It may very well be that what Hegel has to say about "the spirit of a people—or the spirit of a period in human history—leave much to be desired in terms of preciseness. It is nevertheless true that, if we are to come to grips with the concept of "culture"—in a sense more profound than that of mere *Kultur*—we cannot dispense with a concept of "spirit," which, although it cannot be confined to designating the individual spirit of each individual man, nevertheless does admit of a usage in the plural, the *Geister* of the final chapter in the *Phenomenology,* whose dialectical process of development culminates in the unique integrated and integrating "Absolute Spirit," without which Hegel's philosophy would not be a philosophy at all. Without the concept of *Geister*, in the plural, there would be no concept of "culture" (*Bildungen*), in the plural (see *WG*, 785, 805), which, despite their multiplicity, constitute one continuous dialectical process of *Bildung* that culminates also in the uniquely unifying "Absolute Spirit." It is for this reason that, for Hegel, religious consciousness (religion) is indispensable for the process that is spirit and for *Bildung*, which is the self-developing mode of that process (see *WG*, 172). The *Bildungen* that characterize "world-historical" peoples do not merely follow each other in time, nor do the diverse *Bildungen* that characterize different simultaneously existing peoples (the British, the French, the Italian, the German) merely complement each other in space. They constitute the ongoing dialectical process of integration, disintegration, and reintegration, that is the human history of spiritual growth. To each culture there corresponds an image of man, and that image of man is intimately linked to the manner in which men represent (*vorstellen*) to themselves the overarching Spirit that unites them, from the spirit completely immersed in nature, through the multiple spirits that express the particularities of the human condition, to the unique Absolute Spirit that transcends both the natural and the particular—without at the same time eliminating either the natural or the particular (see *PdG*, VIII).

That the picture of human spiritual development that Hegel paints constitutes, in broad lines at least, an accurate description of a process that has taken place need not be too difficult to accept. That the process links culture and religion in such a way that neither is intelligible without the other may be more difficult to accept. That the whole process is "logical," determined by its own inner "dialectic," may be completely unacceptable. The main point that Hegel is making, however, is a valid one: man is that unique being who belongs at once to the world of nature and to the world of spirit; but, unlike all other beings of nature, what man is to become is not inscribed in nature, neither in nature in general nor in his own particular nature. Man is to become what he is to become as a result of his own activity (*WG*, 58); man's true humanity is to be the product of his own activity (p. 62), such that man ever remains what he is as human and at the same time constantly becomes more authentically what he is (p. 35). It may, of course, be difficult to conceive, especially in the light of recent history (to which we shall return later), that humanity is constantly rising to higher levels of culture; has it ever in its history risen to a higher level than it did in the Golden Age of Athenian culture? But that is precisely where the important distinction between *Bildung* and *Kultur* comes in: the Greek *Kultur* of the Golden Age reached such an extraordinarily high level because, better perhaps than any other culture in history, it expressed externally the fullness of its own interior *Bildung,* but the *Bildung* it expressed, because merely particular, still had a long way to go in coming to the realization of the spiritual goal of being most fully human, self-determining, self-contained, self-integrated. The disintegration of Greek culture and the reintegration at what has to be called the lower level of Roman culture need be no argument against this. From the bosom of a culture more ancient than that of the Greeks had already emerged a religious principle, the transcendent, unique, spiritual God of the Jews, who was to eclipse the cultures of both the Greeks and the Romans. Admittedly Hegel has a hard time (as has everyone else) coming to grips with the emergence of this principle of human self-consciousness, but he sees in it the preparation for a more adequate *Bildung* of human self-consciousness in the awareness of an Absolute who is not abstractly one, but concretely three-in-one (see *WG*, 722), and thus the more adequate paradigm of human unity in multiplicity, of a universality that conquers the limitations of particularity (see *WG*, 111, 510, 527, 721).

Here, however, we are face-to-face with a Hegelian concept we have not yet called upon, but with which those who know the seventh chapter of Hegel's *Phenomenology* will already be familiar. Not only is the dialectic of spirit's culture one of self-activity, whereby man rises to an ever-higher awareness of what it is to be human (*WG*, 35); not only is the goal to which man is oriented not one that is antecedently inscribed in a blueprint of nature, because the human spirit is to bring into being *freely* that to which it is oriented; but the process toward the goal is at once the activity of the human *and* of the divine spirit. "It is essential to this process that there be levels [of development], and world-history is the manifestation of the divine process, the ascension by stages, wherein spirit both knows and actualizes itself and its truth" (*WG*, 74).

Strong medicine this, it is true; but the question is not at the moment whether the medicine is too strong to take; the question is not even whether what Hegel says is true; it is simply a question of whether Hegel means what he says. We can, if we wish, say that, when Hegel speaks of man as "in himself his own goal" (*WG*, 106), goal nevertheless is not predetermined, as it would be if man were simply a being of nature, and that man is thus his own goal, "only through the divine that dwells in him" (*ibid.*), he is not speaking religious language, that he is using the term "divine" merely metaphorically, but it would seem that the evidence for this contention has yet to be uncovered. When Hegel further says that "the goal of the spirit" is "to give itself consciousness of the Absolute," and that "this consciousness of his is alone true," or that this is at once "honor paid to God" and the "glorification of the truth" (*ibid.*), it is indeed difficult to see why we should not take him at his word. Nor does this take away from—rather it enhances—the dignity of man, since "in honoring God the individual spirit too finds its own dignity," in the recognition that man's "activity for the honor of God is the absolute" [for man] (*ibid.*). Precisely here is where philosophy comes in, for it is "philosophy" that *"thinks* and *comprehends* what is contained in religion in the mode of representation, both sensible and spiritual"[3] (*WG*, 134, see also p. 172). The point Hegel is trying to make, however, is that the activity of honoring God concerns man more than it does God, since "the dignity of man is to be found in honoring the divine . . . such that the divine receives honor through the honor given to the human, and the human receives honor through the honor paid to the divine" (*WG*, 572; see pp. 181, 573).

This last statement, it is true, is made in the context of Hegel's discussion of Greek religion, wherein the beauty of Greek art honors both the divine that it portrays and the human that does the portraying, but it has to be read in continuity with a whole series of texts wherein ever higher forms of religious representation give rise to an ever more purified conceptualization of what it is to be human, to be spirit, since "God is the essence of the human" (*WG*, 575). Nor is this to be separated from man's progressive realization of his own rationality; reason, after all, "is the substance of spirit" (*WG*, 733). But, the rationality of spirit is not to be divorced from the rationality of spirit's object; that object is rational, whether it be present in the explicitly rational form of philosophical thinking or in the implicitly rational form of religious consciousness (*ibid.*), and the move to explicit rationality is accomplished in the progressive overcoming of the naturality in which the human spirit, even religious spirit, is immersed (*ibid.*). *Objective* rationality, whether as the goal of religious or philosophical consciousness, is not the *product* of the human rational process seen as merely subjective activity, as would be, for example, rational conceptualization for Kant.

It may seem that Hegel is taking a very large leap when he moves quite rapidly from this vague religious consciousness of the unity of the divine and the human to the Christian dogma of the unity of the divine and the human in the Incarnation (*WG*, 729). In a sense, of course, it is a leap, but Hegel is convinced not only that the move must be made but also that the move is philosophically defensible. That there are dogmas at all, he claims, is true only because there is philosophical explication of religious belief—nor is the philosophical explication alien to the content of religious belief (*WG*, 742). More than that, although the human and the divine are not simply to be identified (*WG*, 734)—a contradiction that "understanding" sees so readily—a union with the divine is essential to the actualization of spirituality in the human, and this "speculative" thinking can comprehend; it can find that the "essence" of the human is in an intelligible sense "divine."

> Man becomes actual as a spiritual being only when he overcomes his naturality. This overcoming becomes possible only under the supposition that the human and the divine natures are substantially and consciously (*an und für sich*) one, and that man, to the extent that he is spirit, possesses the essentiality and substantiality which pertains to the concept of God (WG, 821).

This human consciousness of union with the divine is neither immediately given nor readily comprehensible; man must grow into it. "The consciousness of this union with the divine is given in Christ. What is important, then, is that man come to grips with this consciousness and that it be constantly awakened in him" (*ibid.*) The "de-naturalization" of the human takes both time and effort, and the model of it is to be found in the God-man.

Now, what is important in all this is Hegel's claim that the whole of post-Roman "European" cultural development has been tied in with and conditioned by Christian religious consciousness and by the latter's explicitation in a philosophical awareness of just what it is to be human, to be spiritual, to be spirit in a way that images in a this-worldly context the spiritual reality of God. The crux of Hegel's claims is his contention that man, as the unique combination of the "natural" and the "spiritual" must by his own activity "overcome" the merely natural in himself and thus actualize the truly spiritual, which is his destiny and his dignity, by being reconciled with God as "Spirit," the paradigm of all spirit (*WG*, 878). The process of this overcoming is the *Bildung* that characterizes Western man, a *Bildung* marked by centuries of vicissitudes whose overtones are moral, religious, legal, and political, but whose orientation is ineluctably the realization of man's true being as spirit, since only spirit is self-determining, free—and this is *human* destiny. Most of us, I venture to say, can see at least the plausibility of the way in which Hegel links religious and cultural developments in the civilizations of China, India, Persia, and Egypt—however fanciful may be the historical account he gives of this linkage. Nor need we be too sceptical about his account of the rise and fall *pari passu* of Greek religion and Greek culture, Roman religion and Roman culture. By the same token, no one, I am sure, will be inclined to deny the enormous influence of the Judaeo-Christian religious tradition on the cultural development of the West. Hegel has, however, left us with two problems that I do not pretend that a paper as limited in scope as this one is can solve: (1) how Christian, in fact, is (or was, in Hegel's day) the culture of the West, and (2) how philosophically necessary is it still to link religious consciousness and cultural development?

For brevity's sake I shall approach the answers to these questions through a detailed analysis of a very short section in the *Lectures on the Philosophy of World History* (6 pages), entitled "The Spiritual Cultivation (*Bildung*) of Europe." If we are to follow even this brief account, however, we must recall that Hegel brings to it two presuppositions: (1) that it is not until the end of the Middle Ages, with the Reformation which, in a certain sense, marks the religious breakup of Europe, that we can begin to speak of Europe as a "cultural unity; and (2) scientific "understanding" (*Verstand*), emerging from the Renaissance, stands on the side of both religious and cultural disintegration, whereas "rational" comprehension (*Vernunft*) stands on the side of religious and cultural reintegration.

The period of which Hegel here speaks, the period following the Reformation, is one in which *Verstand* was formally cultivated. Religion had, so to speak, run its course and had been crystallized in the Lutheran faith. Thus its role had ceased to be that of a cultural force, in the sense that religious development determines cultural development. The role of cultural force was now taken over by scientific understanding. This is not to say that there was to be no internal development within both the Lutheran and the Catholic chruches, but that what came into prominance in the overall development was the culture of learned individuals (*Privatbildung*), and this in such a way that the individual subject, recognized as counting precisely as individual, attained to the "form of universality," in the sense that the whole of a culture was expressed in the activity of individuals, and that the culture took on a value of its own independently of religion. The results was a new attitude toward nature: the human spirit could now trust nature; it was no threat to man but rather was that wherein man could seek both the truth of nature itself and his own truth. Nature had ceased to be no more than a manifestation of the divine but contained in itself its own worth. All of this comes under the heading of "secularization," which was to become the characteristic of modern European culture, a sort of secular "righteousness" to be attained in cultivating natural science, without, however, abrogating its religious dimensions, since faith, precisely as separated from science, continued to see in God the ultimate paradigm of all that was good and "righteous" (*WG*, 910).

The important step that had been taken was that man could turn his attention to the particulars of nature, without seeking the Church's permission to justify this move. The matters of war, industry, business, commerce, and family life came under the aegis of rationality and were no longer under the control of the Church. Rational inquiry, then, was self-contained, based only on experience and reflection, without religious overtones. At this point we begin to find echoes of Hegel's treatment of "culture" in the *Phenomenology:* at the head of cultural development stood France, where the cultivation of scientific knowledge became a concern of the whole nation. The cultivation of the sciences, however, was not to be separated from the cultivation of nobility of character. Still, precisely because cultivation was preeminently that of the natural sciences, and nobility of character was more the topic of cultivated rhetoric than it was the outcome of genuinely ethical responsibility, the "virtues" of French *noblesse* lacked a firm moral foundation (*WG*, 911).

In the movement that Hegel is describing, precisely because the human spirit had lost its fear of being able to reconcile itself with nature, the empirical sciences bloomed. In terms of "culture," however, empirical science meant more than the turn of experience; it meant also that man in his capacity as thinking spirit discovered the "laws" that govern nature and found them *in* nature itself. God was not out of the picture yet, but the emphasis had shifted; it was "science" that gave honor to both God and man. It was as though God were revealing Himself all over again, as though God had re-created a universe, the secrets of which the mind found more and more comprehensible through the workings of *Verstand*. Paradoxically enough, however, the rationality of the world, which scientific thinking was progressively unfolding, was accompanied by the emergence of all sorts of superstition, magic, and witchcraft, the price being paid for the downgrading of religion (*WG*, 912).[4]

What Hegel now saw was on the one hand, a complete secularization of culture, the supernatural reduced to the natural, total disbelief in the miraculous, since nature was taken to be a complete rational system that man could *know*. On the other hand, what was emerging was a complete divorce of culture and religion, one result of which was that the Catholic church looked upon the triumph of science as an insult to God (once again the case of Galileo raises its ugly head) and sought to combat this with an irrational appeal to the Bible. Apart from the political motives (and pressures) that could have induced Hegel to interpret the Catholic church's stance in this way, he did see a certain justification in the attitude of the "Christian" church in relation to the proliferation of "scientific" theories in this period. The temptation is, after all, to look upon the "laws" of nature as ultimate (as though "nature" somehow does its own legislating), and this carries with it a tendency toward materialism and atheism. If "laws" of nature are inscribed in nature by nature itself, there is discoverable in these laws no bridge to God. But, says Hegel, this can happen only where there is too much reliance on the disintegrating force of *Verstand* alone (*WG*, 913). What is more, since a whole culture had been infected with the virus of scientific understanding, even on the religious side, the effort to combat this "naturalism" relied far too much on abstract analysis.

There can be no question that the modern spirit of philosophical inquiry, the beginning of which Hegel finds in Descartes, had effected a separation of the human thinking subject from that which had previously been conceived of as ruling that spirit from above. To find itself, the human spirit now looked to itself alone, and this was the prelude to a thinking that was conceived of as self-determining in itself (*WG*, 914). No longer, to the scientific mind, was there question of the grace of God coming from without to enlighten that mind. It was Descartes who had turned the mind's gaze inward, and his *cogito, ergo sum* is to be interpreted not as an inference from thought to being, but as a recognition that being and thought (human thought) are one. That this insight should be elucidated in the conviction that the external world *must* exhibit the same rationality that human thought does, may itself not be a thoroughly rational conviction. That the universe exhibit this kind of rationality is not, properly speaking, a rational demand—the universe is deaf to such demands—it is a kind of "religious" conviction. One is reminded of A.N. Whitehead's contention that precisely the scientist must begin his inquiry with an "act of faith in the decency of the universe." The pattern now is one of observing nature, discovering that it is regulated by "laws" that constitute its rationality, that imperceptibly become *prescriptive* rather than descriptive. Enter the Enlightenment, and the disintegration is complete (*WG*, 915). Kant, Fichte, Jacobi, and Schleiermacher accept the disintegration as complete, even though they continue to insist that the validity of faith is not compromised thereby.

For a reason that is not too obvious, Hegel does not, in the *Lectures on the Philosophy of World History,* complete the dialectical circle by moving from disintegration to reintegration, unless, of course, he is simply saying that the *future* is not a *historical* question at all. He does, however, throw out some helpful hints in this regard in the very last section of the *Lectures*, entitled "The Present Situation." There he suggests that the disintegration had come about because of the spirit's failure to recognize itself for what it is, a recognition that will come about only if it listens to the testimony of Absolute Spirit, which bears witness to the true reality of human spirit, and this, if we are willing to inquire carefully, Spirit does in "World-History," the history that on the very last page, Hegel calls "the true theodicy, " the "justification of God."

> The spirit is only what it makes of itself; and for that it is necessary that it presuppose itself. Only this insight can reconcile the spirit with world-history and with actuality, the realization that what has happened and what happens at all times not only comes from God and is not without God, but is essentially the work of God himself (WG, 938; see also pp. 78, 81).

But, the answer is not contained here. What Hegel does is to send us back to the final chapter of the *Phenomenology of Spirit,* where religious consciousness and rational self-consciousness are reconciled in "Absolute Knowing," the elaboration of which constitutes the whole of the *Science of Logic* and the "System" that flows from it. The answer, then, depends on the ability of the human spirit to go beyond the "analytic" thinking of *Verstand* to the "speculative" thinking of "*Vernunft*; only in the latter can the spiritual destiny of man (cultural and religious) be realized.

ABBREVIATIONS:

EpW: *Enzyklopädie der philosophischen Wissenschaften.* Frankfurt a.M.: Suhrkamp (with Zusätze), 1970.

GPR: *Grundlinien der Philosophie des Rechts.* Edited by Johannes Hoffmeister. Hamburg: Meiner, 1955.

PdG: *Phänomenologie des Geistes.* Edited by Johannes Hoffmeister. Hamburg: Meiner, 1952.

VPR: *Vorlesungen über die Philosophie der Religion.* Frankfurt a.M.: Suhrkamp, 1969.

WG: *Vorlesungen über die Philosophie der Weltgeschichte.* Edited by George Lasson and Johannes Hoffmeister. Hamburg: Meiner, 1968.

NOTES

1.   It is true, of course, that the overall title of section B, in chapter 6, is "The Self-Alienated Spirit: Culture" (75 pages), but *Bildung* as such is treated only in the briefer subsection.

2.   It could, of course, seem arbitrary that the present brief study confines itself almost exclusively to the text of the *Vorlesungen über die Philosophie der Weltgeschichte.* The The reasons for this restriction, however, are fairly obvious: (1) The full text of these *Lectures*, delivered between 1825 and 1830 in Berlin, has only recently become available, and it gives abundant evidence of emphasis in Hegel's mature thought on the significance of self-cultivation for the development of the human; (2) The *Lectures* develop very cogently the overriding theme in Hegel's thought of the link between human self-development and the "Christian principle," as he calls it, of the self-consciousness that has the realization of freedom as its orientation; (3) Nowhere else is the close connection of religion, culture, and philosophy more prominent.

3.   It might be well to point out that the term *Vorstellung,* which I here translate as "representation," is participial in form and thus connotes process—toward thought and comprehension.

4.   A phenomenon, incidentally, that has been recognized in both the Soviet Union and in the Republic of China.

COMMENT ON
RELIGION AND CULTURE IN HEGEL

by
ROBERT BERNASCONI

I will take up three of the problems and enigmas raised by Professor Lauer in the course of his paper: first, that of the abrupt end of the *Lectures on the Philosophy of World History;* second, that of the brevity of Hegel's discussion of the "key-concept" of culture in the *Phenomenology of Spirit,* which Professor Lauer estimates as some twenty-five pages; and third, that of the place of religion in cultural development.

Professor Lauer makes the point that the abrupt close of the *Lectures on the Philosophy of World History* fails to satisfy our expectations, set by our knowledge of the Hegelian philosophy itself, for reintegration, completion, and fulfillment. This could be explained in a variety of different ways. A contingent explanation might have it that he was running out of time towards the end of the series of lectures; had the lecture schedule provided him with the time, he would have provided us with the reintegration. Or, to give an organizational explanation, one might argue that the absence of reintegration arises from the place of these *Lectures* within the program of the Berlin Encyclopaedia, at the close of the section Objective Spirit that leads into Absolute Spirit. It would be considered quite proper from this perspective that we find not a rounded out conclusion but loose threads that form the passage to the next stage. It is to Professor Lauer's credit that he is clearly looking for philosophical explanation. His paper ends with a proposal that sends us down a different path from either of the above; we must return to the final chapter of the *Phenomenology of Spirit* in order to clarify and supplement Hegel's conclusion to the *Lectures on World History.* This is to give priority to the philosophical task of coming into thoughtful proximity with what Hegel thought. It does not rule out the other two approaches, but we must, for example, avoid the bad habits of past generations of scholars who refer to the plan of the System as so many points on a map,

115

which makes of it a merely formal consideration, disregarding content.

This is clearly not the place to attempt a detailed reading of the final chapter of the *Phenomenology*. Fortunately it is enough for my present purpose to bring to mind two aspects of it. First, the final chapter of the *Phenomenology* attempts to show that absolute knowing is only an integration, a reconciliation, of what the reader has already passed through and attained in the chapters entitled "Spirit" and "Religion." The chapter on religion has attained the *content* of absolute Spirit, but only in the form of representation (*Vorstellung*), the form of objectivity.[1] In the chapter on Spirit, the *form* of absolute Spirit was attained. "The word of reconciliation is . . . a reciprocal recognition which is absolute Spirit."[2] The self-certain Spirit that acts becomes in forgiveness "this *individual* Self which is immediately pure knowing or universal"; it is "the divine's intuition of itself."[3] When the content of the chapter on religion is provided with the shape of the self, we have what Hegel calls absolute knowing: "Spirit that knows itself in the shape of Spirit," or comprehensive knowing (*das begreiffende Wissen*).[4]

The integration of what has gone before occupies the first part of the final chapter of the *Phenomenology*. The second aspect of the chapter, which I want to take up, Hegel's understanding of history, is presented in the final paragraph. There he distinguishes two kinds of history: first, history where the subject matter appears in the form of contingency, and second, comprehended history (*die begriffne Geschichte*), which is the first kind organized by the "Science of Phenomenal Knowing."[5] It is not at first sight easy to see how this distinction might be explicated in terms of the *Phenomenology*, but I have a proposal that perhaps goes part of the way. We all recognize that the chapter on Spirit and that on Religion are in some sense historical, because they follow a very readily recognizable history with which we are already familiar. Indeed we are all too ready when reading those chapters to puzzle about omissions or distortions from what we already know. That would be to remain with history in the first sense. To have a grasp of the second kind of history referred to by Hegel at the end of the *Phenomenology*, is to have the whole, and that is why it comes only with the final chapter when we reconcile the 'history' of Spirit with the 'history' of Religion, the form and content of absolute Spirit. The sense of the whole here has nothing to do with being exhaustive. It is, rather, a matter of it not being one-sided or partial. Completion (*Ergänzung*) in Hegel's sense does not take place through supplementation from outside. It is a question of inner development, the elimination of the aspect of contingency that marks the first kind of history. Reason is the fundamental term for describing this completion, which is also a fulfillment (*Vollendung*), precisely because for Hegel reason contains its end within itself.

Bildung is a crucial term in the explanation of the difference between the two histories.[6] We find this term in a parallel discussion to that in the final paragraph of the *Phenomenology*. I have in mind his distinction between the particular individual and the general or universal individual as it is made in the Preface to the *Phenomenology*.[7] The stages of *Bildung* are stages of the universal Spirit that the individual must pass through, but because this passage has been prepared for, its repetition as *Bildung* is much easier: "What in former ages engaged the attention of men of mature mind, has been reduced to the level of facts, exercises, and even games for children."[8] Although what has to be learned appears to be something external, the ease with which we make it our own shows that it already belongs to us. It belongs to us, he will say, as the substance of the individual, as the universal Spirit. Hegel's basic insight here is not an unfamiliar one.[9] And it leads to the further point that because history is not just objective external data, but accounts for what we have become and in that sense already belongs to us, to study history contributes to our self-possession, to the extent that we find ourselves in that history.

For Hegel this means something more than receptivity of the 'otherness' of the past, as we understand it when it is adopted as an ideal for the historical sciences. This is indicated by the fact that for Hegel self-recognition in otherness and not *Bildung* is the element of the Science.[10] What is at issue is the sense in which through this self-recognition we overcome particularity and are raised to the universal, for *Bildung* also implies an elevation to the universal. Indeed this connotation belonged to the term before Hegel's time.[11] *Buldung,* though an inward process, was not thought of as a private matter but as a qualification for belonging to society and to the humanity of mankind. Hegel's insight, which he developed to a point that took him far beyond his predecessors, was that this took place through the actualisation of something already there latent. What provides for the necessity of the Science, which only "we" who have attained absolute knowing can see, is the emergence of the new object from the old.[12] The daunting phrase "the universal individual" must be thought in terms of that insight: the universal individual is the *Weltgeist* which becomes self-conscious Spirit.[13] This takes place insofar as we recognize that the manner in which that belongs to us as children of the age, of the *Zeitgeist*, is determined for us by the manner in which we are heirs of the past. In my view the term *Bildung* was not invested by Hegel with the full power of this insight. It was retained as a one-sided and thus inadequate characterization of it. This is the explanation of, for example, Hegel's remarks in the Preface that

> This past existence is property that has already been acquired by the universal Spirit which constitutes the substance of the individual and, by thus appearing to him externally, his inorganic nature. In this respect, *Bildung*, considered from the point of view of the individual, consists in his acquiring what is thus given to him; he must digest his inorganic nature and take possession of it for himself.[14]

Bildung takes as its starting point an externality that it believes that it must take possession of; it is blind to that externality as universal Spirit itself. The characterization of the *Phenomenology* as a process of *Bildung* can be regarded as only provisional, partial or external.[15]

If we turn back to the final paragraph of the *Phenomenology* we can see how it is that the concept of *Bildung* is not adequate to *begriffene Geschichte*. *Bildung* refers to an 'inwardising' which raises to the universal. The term *Erinnerung*, which in the passage from the preface we have been discussing bears its nominal sense of memory, serves in the conclusion for the process of recollection as recognition of itself in the other, the external, *Er-Innerung*, internalisation.[16] We are entirely misled about this most important process if we understand it as a making-inward of what is external. The notion of the 'universal individual' was formed by Hegel to emphasize that the process of 'inwardisation' refers to a taking possession of what is already its own through the constitution of the substance of the individual. But it is precisely this that a self-understanding formulated in terms of *Bildung* overlooks; *Bildung* misunderstands itself. Otherwise said, Hegel's use of the term still reflects its usage amongst the preceding generation of German writers, and thus bears only an incomplete understanding of Spirit.

Once this has been understood, it no longer can be regarded as puzzling that the discussion of *Bildung* in the main body of the text is confined to the second of the three parts of the chapter entitled "Spirit." What we must do is understand why it is found there. The clue lies in the conjunction of *Bildung* and alienation. Bildung is not the process of alienation, but the attempt to overcome it; "It has the appearance of self-consciousness making itself conform to actuality."[17] The point is that it accepts the world, which it has produced and to which it is correlated as something foreign; in setting about the task of internalisation, it affirms its self-alienation.

Under the title *Der sich entfremdete Geist. Die Bildung,* we find three sections:

1. The World of Self-Alienated Spirit
2. The Enlightenment
3. Absolute Freedom and Terror.

Although most occurrences of the term *Bildung* appear in the first section, it is a mistake to suppose that it is discussed only in that section. Hegel's comment on *Bildung* resides in the development that takes place in the three stages. When we pass beyond the first stage, the world of *Bildung* that treats of state power and wealth, to the discussion of faith and pure insight in the second stage, 'pure' *Bildung's* failure to overcome externality is emphasized by the Beyond of faith. In a brilliant discussion, Hegel shows that faith and pure insight both share the same structure and formally speaking are thus the same consciousness. But at the same time the limitations of *Bildung* are set; its starting point is externality, which it overcomes by a process of drawing inwards. Absolute Freedom is the most elevated and the final sense of *Bildung*[18] because consciousness here attains to the Universal (General) Will and thus satisfies the task of *Bildung* as raising to the universal. Thus *Bildung* in this chapter marks the break with immediacy and raises to the universal.

In the first part of the *Lectures on the Philosophy of World History,* Hegel writes that "man is only what he should be through *Bildung*. . . . He must throw off the natural."[19] We must be clear that *Bildung* does not make a break with the natural; it marks the break. Later he explains that the overcoming of the natural is only possible on the assumption that human and divine nature are in and for themselves one, and that man, in so far as he is Spirit, possesses the essentiality and substantiality that belong to the concept of God.[20] It is enough here to point out that this takes us far beyond anything that could be recognized in terms of *Bildung*. Hegel emphasizes *Bildung's* limitations; it does not possess that free universality that renders the object of consciousness for itself.[21]

It is clear from the first part of the *Lectures on the Philosophy of World History* that there has been no weakening of the rigor of the concept of *Bildung*, but at the same time we discover on turning to the subsequent parts, that the restriction of the term *Bildung* in the *Phenomenology* ot the period from after the end of the Roman Empire to the French Revolution is lifted. The term is now applied extensively to the Greek world.[22] In the *Phenomenology* the particular external relation with the object which the term implies is characteristic of the period to which it is applied. This is not true of its extension of the Greek world according to Hegel's own characterization of that world. Only in the *Phenomenology* is the usage of the term such that the concept is adequate to the object.

It would be a mistake to regard the major portion of the *Lectures on the Philosophy of World History* as no more than *Bildungsgeschichte*. A proper reading would need to follow its treatment of the theme of the relation between religion and the state. In so far as there is a "reintegration" at the close of the *Lectures on the Philosophy of World History,* it lies in the reconciliation of religion and state through the Protestant church.[23] This theme also clearly associates the discussion of world-history with the *Philosophy of Right* and the *Lectures on the Philosophy of Religion*.[24] Furthermore, I believe that with Professor Lauer that we must emphasize that world-history is for Hegel a theodicy.[25] This role is performed in so far as external necessity and contingency are overcome within its presentation. But the true theodicy is philosophy itself;[26] world-history is theodicy in what Hegel calls in another context 'historical externality'.[27] As theodicy, history must attain the content of philosophy, the divine, which is, as we have seen, the content of religion also.[28] Here, as elsewhere, the concept of reason does service for 'the divine': "Man is an end in himself only by virtue of the divine within him which we have all along referred to as reason (*Vernunft*)."[29]

To the extent that we look to world-history for a theodicy, its inadequacy according to the measure of philosophy becomes apparent. This has already emerged in the extended use of *Bildung*, which is a formal term indifferent to content.[30] We can now state the inadequacy more precisely: if reason appears in history, not in a form adequate to what it is as reason, but only as a content, this is an essential and inevitable consequence of historical externality. It is as true of this kind of history as it is of religion. Indeed in terms of the standard of absolute Knowing as set out in the final chapter of the *Phenomenology,* we can say that the *Lectures on the Philosophy of World History* parallel chapter 7 of the *Phenomenology* ("Religion"); the work of chapter 6 ("Spirit"), which in its decisive discussion of Conscience attains the form of absolute Spirit, has no place there. This remains true notwithstanding the discussion of conscience in relation to Protestantism, for it remains only a discussion *about* conscience. To be sure, the hearer or reader must be presumed to be the heir of that history, but the *Lectures* do not recollect us, do not draw us back to the universal individual as such. In other words, this presentation of history does not attain the form of Spirit that knows itself as Spirit, does not satisfy the demands of *begriffne Geschichte.* This provides a precise sense in which one might talk of lack of reintegration in the *Lectures.* Historical externality is overcome in the *begriffne Geschichte* of Philosophy itself, or the absolute knowing of the *Phenomenology,* through *Er-Innerung.* It is recognized that it is not an indifferent externality, but Spirit's own result.[31]

Finally there is Professor Lauer's question: "How philosophically necessary is it still to link religious consciousness and cultural development?" If I understand him, he takes Hegel's answer to be that neither is intelligible without the other. Furthermore, he would appear to be suggesting that anyone who wants still to link them will find support in Hegel. This answer reflects the extent to which in philosophical circles today religion is on the defensive, but not from Philosophy, as Hegel had predicted. In the *Phenomenology,* Hegel twice makes the point that, although he may touch on religious themes in the discussion of *Bildung,* that discussion is not adequate to the discussion of religion as such.[32] In so far as I have succeeded in showing both that Hegel's program cannot adequately be described in terms of *Bildung,* and that the term *Bildung* can only have a limited place within it (as in the *Phenomenology*), then it follows that an analysis from the standpoint of *Bildung* and in terms of it is inadequate to the discussion of religion in Hegel's sense, is blind to it.

Cultural development (*Bildung*) can never serve as the measure of religion:

this is a lasting conclusion to be drawn from Hegel's texts. We ignore it when almost as a matter of course an external standpoint on religion is adopted. The result is the poverty of philosophy, the despoiling of its proper content. Hegel gives us reason to believe the loss cannot be permanent. His account of the Enlightenment in the *Phenomenology* for example, maintains the futility of attempts to escape religion. It also shows the difficulty of appreciating its true nature. That nature is elucidated in the *Lectures on the Philosophy of Religion:* their importance has never been greater.

ABBREVIATIONS

PG: *Phänomenolgie des Geistes.* Gesammelte Werke Band 9. hrsg. W. Bonsiepen und R. Heede, Hamburg: Felix Meiner, 1980.

PH: *The Philosophy of History.* Translated by J. Sibree, New York: Dover, 1956.

PS: *Phenomenology of Spirit.* Translated by A.V. Miller, Oxford: Clarendon, 1977.

RH: *Lectures on the Philosophy of World History.* "Introduction: Reason in History." Translated by H. Nisbet, Cambridge University Press, 1975.

VG: *Vorlesungen über die Philosophie der Weltgeschichte.* Band I. Die Vernunft in der Geschichte. Hrsg. J. Hoffmeister, Hamburg: Felix Meiner, 1955.

WG: *Vorlesungen über die Philosophie der Geschichte.* Werke Band 12. Frankfurt: Suhrkamp, 1970. (References have been given to this edition rather than the remaining volumes of VG edited by Lasson, because English readers are more familiar with this version. But Lasson's text should also be consulted.)

References are given first to the German texts followed by the corresponding page of the standard translation. The translations have occasionally been altered.

NOTES

1.   PG,422; PS,479. Compare *Einleitung in die Geschichte der Philosophie,* hrsg. J. Hoffmeister and F. Nicolin (Hamburg: Felix Meiner, 1959), p. 191; Q. Lauer, trans., *Hegel's Idea of Philosophy,* (New York: Fordham University Press, 1974), p. 115. See also Q. Lauer, "Human Autonomy and Religious Affirmation in Hegel," and "Hegel on the

Identity of Content in Religion and Philosophy," *Essays in Hegelian Dialectic* (New York: Fordham University Press, 1977), pp. 89–106 and pp. 153–168.

2. PG,361; PS,408.

3. PG,425f.; PS,428f.

4. PG,427; PS,485.

5. PG,434; PS,493.

6. I usually leave the word *Bildung* in German throughout my paper in order to draw attention to my attempt to contribute to our understanding of Hegel's use of it. I shall not make issue with the standard translation of *Bildung* as "culture," because of the difficulty of proposing an alternative, or alternatives. Nevertheless, it seems to me that there are occasions when the term "formation" would be most appropriate. Shafterbury's "form" and "formation" play an important part in the development of the concept of *Bildung*, which, when recalled, helps explicate Hegel's usage. See H-G. Gadamer, *Wahrheit and Methode.* (Tübingen: J.C.B. Mohr, 1972), pp. 7–16; *Truth and Method,* (London: Sheed and Ward, 1975), pp. 10–19.

7. PG,24–25; PS,16–17.

8. PG,25; PS,16.

9. If one is looking for an illustration of this insight philosophically developed elsewhere, one can do no better than turn to Husserl's manuscript "The Origin of Geometry." The text prepared by E. Fink can be found in *Die Krisis der europäischen Wissenschaften und die transzendentale Phänomenologie,* ed. W. Biemel, *Husserlania,* vol. 6 (The Hague: Martinus Nijhoff, 1962), pp. 365–386, translated by David Carr in *The Crisis of European Sciences and Transcendental Phenomenology,* (Evanston: Northwestern University Press, 1970), pp. 353–378.

10. PG,22; PS,14. Gadamer presents *Bildung* as the element of the historical sciences in *Wahrheit und Methode,* p. 12; *Truth and Method,* p. 15.

11. W.H. Bruford, *Culture and Society in Classical Weimar 1775-1806,* Cambridge University, 1975. E. Lichtenstein, "Von Meister Eckhart bis Hegel. Zur philosophischen Entwicklung des deutschen Bildungs begriffs" in *Kritik und Metaphysik. Studien. Heinz Heimsoeth zum achtzigsten Geburtstag,* hrsg. F. Kaulbach und J. Ritter (Berlin: Walter de Gruyter, 1966), pp. 260–298.

12. PG,60–61; PS,55–56.

13. The relations between the *Weltgeist* and self-conscious Spirit is well-illustrated by the fact that in revising the Preface to the *Phenomenology* towards the end of his life, Hegel substitutes the latter term for the former at PG,24, line 15 ("der Weltgeist" *becomes* "der selbstbewusste Geist.")

14. PG,25 (following the revision published in 1832); PM,16. I have here quoted, with minor changes for the sake of consistency, Kaufmann's translation from *Hegel: Texts and Commentary* (New York: Doubleday, Anchor, 1966), p. 44.

15. As in the Introduction where the *Phenomenology* is described as the "detailed history of the *Bildung* of consciousness to the level of Science"—PG,56; PS,50.

16. PG,433; PS,492.

17. PG,268; PS,299.

18. PG,322; PS,362.

19. VG,58; RH,50–51.

20. WG,453; PH,377.
21. VG,172; RH,142.
22. Indeed in this context it appears in conjunction with religion: WG,288; PH,234.
23. WG,529; PH,447; and WG,539; PH,456. Also VG,256; RH,208. It might be added here that Professor Lauer does not clearly explicate in what sense a "reintegration" is missing.
24. Since completing this essay Professor Jaeschke of the Hegel Archiv kindly sent me his valuable essay discussing this theme in the two last mentioned texts: "Christianity and Secularity in Hegel's Concept of the State," *The Journal of Religion*, vol. 61, no.2 (April, 1981), pp. 127–145.
25. VG,48; RH,42. WG,540; PH,457.
26. *Vorlesungen über die Geschichte der Philosophie III*, (Frankfurt: Suhrkamp, 1971), p. 455; *Hegel's Lectures on the History of Philosophy*, vol. III, trans. by E. Haldane and F. Simson, (London: Routledge), p. 546.
27. *"Geschichtliche Äusserlichkeit," Enzyklopädie der philosophischen Wissenchaften*, (1830), hrsg. F. Nicolin and O. Pöggeler (Hamburg: Meiner, 1969), sec. 14, p. 47.
28. See note 1.
29. VG,106–107; RH,90.
30. VG,65–66; RH,56–57.
31. VG,58; RH,50f.
32. PG,226, 287; PS,297,322. I am bound to concede that although Professor Lauer's question refers to "religious consciousness," I am not understanding that in the sense of the faith of the believer; I read there "religion," that is, the self-consciousness of absolute Being (*Wesen*) as it is in and for itself.

HEGEL'S CRITICISM OF THE ETHICS
OF KANT AND FICHTE

by

M.J. PETRY

THE CRITICISM

Sorting out the whole development of the criticism Hegel leveled at the ethics of Kant and Fichte while he was teaching at the University of Berlin is a ticklish and complicated business. To attempt to do so here, within the confines of a single lecture, would certainly make it more difficult to reach a satisfactory assessment of his mature standpoint. We know, for example, that even when he was still a student, he was more interested in Kant's practical philosophy than in his epistemology, and that after he had left Tübingen, Schiller's critcism of ethical rigorism had a great influence upon him. We also know that during his stay in Frankfurt he wrote out an extensive commentary on Kant's *Metaphysics of Ethics,* the manuscript of which has since been lost.[1] The ways in which these early interests can be traced through to the arguments put forward during the last decade of his life are undoubtedly worth looking into, but it is the mature criticism with which I am now concerned, not its origins.

It is evident from the Berlin lectures, especially those on the *History of Philosophy,* that while he regarded Fichte's system as a consistent development of Kant's, he took Kant's to be more important on account of its epistemology and ethics, and Fichte's to be more worthy of close attention on account of its social and political doctrines. His broad criticism of both is that they remain at a level of generalization and abstraction, and they they therefore fail to provide any satisfactory means for comprehending certain specific forms of knowledge and activity. He argues, for example, that Kant's epistemology displays far too strong a tendency to reduce the richness, complexity, and

125

pragmatic effectiveness of intellectual activity to an abstract and merely subjective identity: "What is adhered to is wholly abstract thinking, pure self-identity. The understanding is said to be able to bring forth only the order of things, and this order is said to be merely subjective, nothing in and for itself. For reason, therefore, there remains nothing but the form of its identity, unity; and this extends only to the systematizing of the manifold laws and relationships of the understanding. The understanding discovers the classes, kinds, laws, species, and these are then ordered by reasons, which attempts to draw them into the unity.[2] In a similar vein, he argues that although Kant's ethics had stimulated the need for a general rethinking of human activity, they had failed to provide specific guidelines for carrying it out: "In theology, in governments and their legislation, in national policy, in trades and mechanics, it is said that one ought always to act only in accordance with universal determinations, that is to say, rationally. There has even been talk of a rational brewery, a rational brick-kiln etc. What is in demand here is concrete thinking. The Kantian result was that of the phenomenon however, and all it yielded was an empty thought."[3]

Fichte also regarded the abstraction of Kantianism as a fault, and attempted to provide it with a concrete content. Starting from the ego, he tried, for example, to work out a systematic derivation of plants and animals. In his political philosophy he claimed to have provided deductions of the ego's body and the recognition of the same, the right of compulsion, the establishment of government, the right to ensure that no one shirks the work that has to be done, the correct treatment of outlaws, the proper use of the pillory, the establishment of international and cosmopolitan law, etc.[4] It may be a little difficult to say precisely why, but it is certainly not easy to take this sort of thing very seriously. Hegel calls attention to the artificiality of the deductions involved, and to the inexcusable pedantry of constantly attempting to relate everything back to the abstract subjectivity of ego:

> "Fichte has maintained that the ego is the absolute principle, the direct and immediate certainty of itself, and that all the matter in the universe has therefore to be presented as being produced from out of it. In a similarly one-sided manner he has also maintained that this principle is *one* aspect however: it is by its very nature subjective, conditioned by an opposite, and its realization is a continual rushing onward in finitude, a looking back at what has gone before. The form in which it is presented also has the disadvantage, and indeed the real drawback, of bringing the empirical ego constantly before one's eyes, which is absurd, and very distracting to one's point of view."[5]

Despite the radical nature of this criticism, it is by no means dismissive, for Hegel also ascribes a positive role to Kantian ethics at the relatively abstract level of morality. In the *Philosophy of Right,* he takes the emphasis Kant laid upon the basic importance of the subjective moral will to be a valid theoretical foundation for a general sense of duty and for the exercise of conscience. He denies, however, that this will, by itself, is capable of giving any real guide to conduct within the family, civil society, or the state. He contends that in contexts such as these, a person may well will what is right, pursue what he considers to be good, act according to the dictates of his conscience, and yet behave in a way that is completely antisocial, and therefore, very largely unethical. He argues that the precise reason for this is that the behavioral norms of the family, civil society, and the state are more complex than individual morality, and therefore demand a greater degree of circumspection, a fuller social awareness, a more differentiated sense of duty, than is to be derived from simply consulting one's conscience: "Duty itself, in moral self-consciousness, is the essence or universality of this consciousness, the manner in which it is inwardly related only to itself; all that is left to it, therefore, is abstract universality, and for its determinate character it has identity without content, or the abstractly positive, the indeterminate."[6]

The main thrust of Hegel's criticism of Kantian ethics is, therefore, the contention that they simply tell us that right is right, that they fail to provide the means for specifying this general postulate. He allows them a certain positive significance in that they call attention to the volitional element in morality, but maintains that as a guide to ethical activity or to the comprehension of conduct, they do no more than bring into play the vacuous and inappropriate category of identity. His fundamental contention is, therefore, that they involve a stultifying logical fixation: "To maintain that a planet is a planet, magnetism magnetism, spirit a spirit, is quite rightly regarded as ridiculous, although this is of course most certainly a matter of general experience. School is the only place in which laws of this kind have validity, and together with its logic, in which they are propounded in all seriousness, it has long since lost credibility with both sound commonsense and rationality."[7]

REACTIONS

The reactions to this criticism have been fairly predictable. Kant appeared to have given prescriptive ethics a firm foundation in a critical analysis of human knowledge, and by so doing to have brought to light the fundamental importance of the will in motivating rational activity. He had managed to avoid relativism, hedonism, and the postulation of a moral sense, and had provided a clear and consistent account of the relationship between ethical activity and religious belief. It is not surprising, therefore, that his doctrine should have found widespread acceptance during Hegel's lifetime, and that it should still be regarded as a major contribution to the rationalizing of ethics.

To many of those who have been enlightened by it, Hegel's criticism has appeared to be a regression into relativism or descriptive thinking. The precise motivation for this relapse has, moreover, been difficult to locate. Whereas the complementarity of the critiques of pure and practice reason is clear enough, the nature of Hegel's conception of the relationship between epistemology and ethics has remained obscure. By what standards, then, are the relative merits of the two thinkers to be judged? Is the basic difference between them simply that one is advocating an individualist and the other a collectivist theory of ethics? It can hardly be quite as straightforward as this, since Hegel also states unequivocally that it is "essential to give prominence to the pure unconditioned self-determination of the will as the root of duty, and to the way in which, for the first time, and thanks to Kant's philosophical doctrine of its infinite autonomy, knowledge of the will has found its firm foundation and starting-point."[8] Nevertheless, by distinguishing so sharply between the individualism of morality and the social context of ethics, by confining the significance of Kant's insight to the former sphere and emphasizing the overriding importance of the latter, Hegel certainly appears to be saying that the individual can have no real justification for questioning the presuppositions and mores of the family, civil society, and the state. The seemingly inevitable conclusion would seem to be, therefore, that he took the guiding principle, the lodestar, the centre of gravity of ethical activity to be located in the group, and not in the individual.

Those who have attempted to explain and justify this apparent shift of emphasis in post-Kantian ethical theory have, by and large, fallen into two main groups. On the one hand there are those who have emphasized the importance of Hegel's historical context. They have argued, and with a great deal of justification, that since he was entering into manhood in the years immediately following the French Revolution, since in his own lifetime he experienced the final demise of the Holy Roman Empire, the Napoleonic wars, the constitutional reconstruction of Germany at the Treaty of Vienna, the establishment of an efficient administration in post-war Prussia, he was bound, in his philosophy of action, to ascribe a greater importance to large-scale social entities and movements than to individual decision making. This implies, of course, that there is not much point in attempting to provide any very strictly philosophical justification for his attitude. This argument has often tended, therefore, to give rise to the counterclaim that the intrinsic significance of his thought is embodied in such works as the *Jena Phenomenology* or the *Larger Logic,* that it is these publications that can provide us with the key to his assessment of Kant, the reasons why his criticism of the critical philosophy is still worthy of consideration.

Despite the plausibility of both these lines of argument, neither would appear to have placed the problem in an entirely satisfactory light. It is surely essential that if Hegel's thinking in this particular respect is to be seen as a real advance upon Kant's, it should be shown to be not merely a matter of his reaction to the events of his time, but also the outcome of a universal principle or general approach comparable to Kant's in degree of intelligibility and not inferior to it in respect of cogency. One has to ask, therefore, whether such works as the *Jena Phenomenology* and the *Logic* are able to yield such a principle. Now that the Jena manuscripts have appeared in critical editions and more attention is being paid to the development of the *Encyclopedia* and the various series of lectures based upon it, it is becoming progressively more difficult to rest content with the idea that any one of Hegel's works provides the pattern for the whole. It is becoming increasingly apparent that a particular problem such as his criticism of Kant's ethics has to be approached in the light of a critical analysis of the principles at work within the particular context at issue, that we can no longer hope to pass muster in Hegel studies simply by passing the buck and pretending that the basic issues raised by such problems have been solved elsewhere. In the light of what we now know about the development of the Hegelian system, the general principle at work in the various versions of the *Phenomenology* and the *Logic* are as much in need of clarification as those employed in the particular critique now under consideration.

SYSTEM

It is probably worth emphasizing that there are various versions of both the *Phenomenology* and the *Logic*, that they are by no means identical, and that as in the case of the ethics, enough material is now available for their development to be traced over a period of some thirty years. The mature treatment of all three disciplines is to be found in the *Encyclopedia*, but as has already been observed, this work too has its history, and cannot simply be regarded as the final and irrevisible statement of Hegelianism.

It may be of value to illustrate this development in respect of the disciplines in question. Hegel always a regarded phenomenology as the philosophy of consciousness, as the discipline concerned with the systematic treatment of subject-object antitheses, that is, with the various mental states involving "a being-for-self in the face of its other." It is evident from his early writing, however, that he was unable to decide whether such states were to be regarded as a limited sphere of specialized enquiry, closely related to that of empirical psychology, or as a matter of central philosophical significance. In 1803 he took them to be closely related to subconscious conditions such as animal magnetism and mental derangement, and to include such psychological factors as are involved in language and social relationships. A year later we find him entertaining the idea of their constituting the focal point of the systematic treatment of logical categories, a "metaphysics" or doctrine of consciousness, subdivided into its theoretical, practical, and absolute aspects. In the *Jena Phenomenology* of 1807, consciousness is presented not as the focal point but as the introduction to logic. A year later this conception had already been abandoned however, and in the *Encyclopedia* there is a return to the original assessments, consciousness being treated not only as triadically subdivided, but also as closely related to subconscious states such as habit and mental derangement.[9]

As in the case of consciousness, Hegel's basic conception of logic never changed much. He always regarded it as the philosophy of universals, the discipline concerned with the systematic treatment of categories, that is, with the presuppositions of the natural world and of mental activity. What is more, if we compare his earliest full-scale draft of the discipline with the lectures he delivered on it at the very end of his life, we find that even in the detailed working out of this basic conception, many of its most prominent features are very largely unchanged. The material now available also shows, however, that it was under constant revision, and that no single section of it remained entirely unaltered. One example will have to suffice in order to illustrate this.

In the logic of 1804/1805, Hegel deals with the categories of substantiality, causality, and reciprocity, in that order, as subdivisions of the more comprehensive category of relationship. It is apparent from the material with which he illustrates his exposition, that he then associated these categories principally with the substance of inorganic nature, the causality of the forces then being postulated in physics and chemistry, and the reciprocity characteristic of the inner coordination of the organism. By the time he was working on the logic of 1812/1813, the topics with which he associated this sequence of categories had changed, and this is reflected in the systematic exposition. The major category is no longer relationship but actuality, and the subordinate sequence consists of the categories of the absolute, necessity, and the absolute relationship. The exposition of the first is in fact a critique of the philosophies of Spinoza and Leibniz, that of necessity is largely concerned with the way in which it interrelates with contingency, and it is only in the final category that we find a reemergence of the preoccupations which motivated the exposition of 1804/1805. In the *Encyclopedia*, the major category is still actuality, but it is introduced through a lengthy discussion of necessity and contingency, and expounded in detail as the categories of substantiality, causality, and reciprocity. The criticism of the philosophies of Spinoza and Leibniz now arises out of the treatment of substance, causality is discussed very cursorily, evidently on account of the introduction, and reciprocity is associated not only with the organism, but also with ethical freedom.[10]

Enough material is now available in reliable editions for scores of such developments to be traced and analyzed in every aspect of Hegel's work. In this respect, therefore, the phenomenology and the logic simply illustrate his general philosophical development. Once this has become more widely realized, the generally accepted image of his manner of thinking is certain to change. These two examples show how wide of the mark it is to treat phenomenology as the central discipline of Hegelianism, how completely fluid Hegel's conception of it was until 1808. They also show how little justification there is for the claim that the *Logic*, in the form in which Hegel formulated it, is entirely free of the contingency and historical limitations characteristic of the *Philosophies* of *Nature* and *Spirit*.

It should not be assumed, however, that acceptance of the interpretation forced upon us by the material now available excludes the possibility of there being any stability at all in Hegel's development, or that there is now no prospect of our extracting any general principles from his expositions. His conceptions of consciousness and of actuality may have altered, but they did not change beyond recognition. Subject-object disparities and the category of reciprocity may have been assessed very differently and associated with different issues at different times, but Hegel never abandoned the idea of their being susceptible to systematic exposition.

GENERAL PRINCIPLES

A highly controversial issue such as the nature of consciousness or a rarefied generality such as a logical category are not the ideal subject matter for bringing out the significance of these general principles. I therefore propose to illustrate them with reference to Hegel's famous defence of Goethe's theory of colors. The basic issue then at stake are now easily accessible to scientific analysis, and in this particular case, since Hegel was clearly wrong in his assessment of the basic subject matter, it is possible to draw a sharp and clear distinction between his faulty grasp of what was being dealt with and the validity of the general principles he was employing.

As is well-known, Hegel followed Goethe in rejecting the significance of Newton's discovery that white light is composite, that is to say that it consists of the seven colors into which it is resolved by the prism. Like Goethe, he maintained instead that it is homogeneous, and that it only gives rise to colors once it has been darkened by a medium. This is one of the fields in which we know that he performed experiments himself, both during the Jena period and while he was teaching in Berlin. The conclusion he drew from them was that white light involves such a complexity of motions that it can no longer be classified as an essentiality mechanical phenomenon. As a field of enquiry he therefore took it to be the initiation of the sphere of physics, in the sense that these motions form the absolute presupposition of physical phenomena. Color was also conceived of as a physical phenomenon, but since he regarded it as involving not only white light but also the darkening of white light, it could only be dealt with within a rational or systematic physics once the factors in this darkening had also been given their systematic exposition. In Hegel's *Physics* therefore, the treatment of light is followed by the treatment of specific gravity, cohesion, shape, magnetism, crystallography, transparency, refraction, etc. Only once refraction has been given its systematic exposition, does Hegel present his theory of colors, his criticism of Newton and his defense of Goethe. The implication of this procedure is not, of course, that white light and colors do not occur together in the physical world, but simply that a systematic or philosophical exposition of color involves such an analytical survey of its presuppositions, of the factors in its occurence that have been brought to light by empirical physics.

This systematic distinction between white light and color is to be found in the second and third editions of the *Encyclopedia* and in all three attempts Hegel made at working out a philosophy of the natural sciences during the Jena period. In the first edition of the *Encyclopedia* however, white light and colors are treated together. No explanation for this has yet been found, but it almost certainly illustrates, once again, how ready Hegel was to revise his systematic expositions in response to fresh empirical evidence.[11]

In giving this account of Hegel's restructuring of Goethe's erroneous theory, we have spoken of the relative "complexity" of white light in respect of mechanical phenomena, and of its being regarded as the "initiation" of the "sphere" of physics, and the "presupposition" of color. The meaning of such terminology is the direct outcome of Hegel's general principles. Initially, these involve the acceptance and definition of a "sphere" of enquiry—color, consciousness, or the category of causality. The definition of such a sphere involves distinguishing it from what is less and what is more "complex." According to Hegel, for example, color is more complex than light, transparency, refraction, etc., and therefore "Presupposes" these levels of enquiry. Similarly, light presupposes mechanics and is the presupposition or "initiation" of physics in general; causality presupposes substantiality and is the presupposition of reciprocity; consciousness presupposes anthropology and is the presupposition of psychology, etc.

Hegel's basic principle is therefore the analytical procedure of breaking down spheres of enquiry into their presuppositions or constituent levels. The systematic or philosophical exposition of these spheres then consists of the secondary synthetic procedure of reconstructing them by progressing from the less to the more complex of their presuppositions and constituent levels. These analytical and synthetic procedures clearly have a validity of their own in that they are more general than any of the historically contingent or empirical material to which they are applied.[12] It is, however, this material that provides

Hegel's expositions of logical categories, natural and spiritual phenomena, with their specific significance—hence the seemingly incompatible characteristics of systematic consistency and fluidity of content now being brought to light by the historical analysis of the development of his ideas. His general methodology can therefore be characterized as being empirical in respect of content, analytical in respect of wholes or spheres, and synthetic in respect of parts or levels of enquiry. Considered solely as an abstract or universal structure, the though patterns it gives rise to constitute a sequence or hierarchy of asymmetrical relationships within the whole cycle of the sciences worked out in the *Encyclopedia*. Since triadicity plays a decidedly subordinate role in the formulation of these patterns, it has to be regarded as a strictly secondary procedure, essentially irrelevant to the basic work of analysis and synthesis.

THE ETHICS OF KANT AND FICHTE

What can this characterization of Hegel's general methodology tell us about his criticism of the ethics of Kant and Fichte? We have seen that the criticism was convincing in that it drew attention to the abstract nature of Kantian ethics and to the artificiality of Fichte's attempt to remedy this fault. We have also seen that its apparent weakness lay in Hegel's seeming inability to improve upon Kant's interrelating of epistemology and ethics. How are we to regard his charge that Kant did not provide his ethics with any genuine concrete content if he himself failed to show how this was to be done in the light of an improved theory of knowledge? At first glance it certainly looks as though the emphasis he lays upon the group as opposed to the individual is a matter of arbitrary choice, and if this is so his standpoint can hardly be regarded as an improvement upon Kant's.

Hegel's methodology is not a theory of knowledge in Kant's sense, but then it was never intended to be. It is, however, capable of yielding an appreciative and systematic assessment of Kant's epistemology, and of his interrelating of epistemology and ethics.

Hegel accepts the Kantian claim that it is through the exercise of the will that the ego first overcomes the subject-object dichotomy to which it is necessarily confined in respect of its knowledge of what is objective to it. In the *Berlin Phenomenology* he dramatizes this activity of the will as the struggle that gives rise to the relationship of mastery and servitude, the general development of the intersubjectivity of self-consciousness. Within the systematic treatment of self-consciousness, therefore, the basic tension between two mutually exclusive egoistic wills progresses into the multiple intersubjectivity of "universal self-consciousness." This volitional activity resembles Kant's moral agent in that it is above nature, "absolutely inexplicable from any data of the sensible world,"[13] but differs from it in that it is motivated not by the conscious acceptance of a universal moral law, but, in the first or most basic instance, by nothing more than desire. On Hegel's analysis, therefore, intersubjectivity at this level consists of each ego treating the other not as its equal but merely as an object, in Kant's terms, as a means only, and not as an end in itself. Kant's practical will, stripped of its rationality and circumspection, is therefore presented as a naked drive, a brute desire to act, destroy, find satisfaction and dominate, the purest abstraction of personal freedom. In that it is presented as working itself out into multiple intersubjectivity, however, this primitive volitional activity is also shown to be the immediate presupposition of the rationality that rounds off the sphere of phenomenology, the whole hierarchy of subject-object dichotomies. One might have thought that Hegel would have followed Schelling in treating this rationality as a matter of supreme philosophical significance, and as we have seen, during the Jena period he played with the idea of doing so. In every version of his philosophical system formulated after 1808 however, he makes the point that to regard such subject-object dichotomies as a matter of central philosophical significance is to sink below the animals in degree of rationality, to be on the brink of actually confusing what is subjective with what is objective and relapsing into mental derangement.[14]

Since Hegel's systematic reconstruction of Kant's epistemology precedes his treatment of Kantian ethics, it looks as though he simply accepted Kant's conception of the relationship between pure and practical reason. There is, therefore, good reason for assuming that he first entered upon a systematic analysis of Kant's theory of knowledge as a result of his attempting to sort out the presuppositions of volitional ethics. He evidently began by arguing that volitional intersubjectivity must presuppose the existence of an objective organism. The application of the analytical method to this objectivity then brought to light a sequence or hierarchy of presuppositions, which, when expounded synthetically beginning with the fundamental postulate of the abstract consciousness of the ego, yielded a systematic reconstruction of Kant's non-ego or thing-in-itself. Consciousness of an objective organism, Hegel argued, presupposes the coordination of physical laws. Such laws rest upon necessity. Consciousness of necessity arises out of experiences, the connecting of experiences and being aware of objects and their properties. There could be no experience without consciousness of things, and such consciousness presupposes awareness of space and time, sensations and feelings. When the levels of complexity brought to light by this analytical procedure were reviewed in the reverse order, the result was a reconstruction of what Kant had claimed to be a thing-in-itself, inaccessible to rational enquiry. Hegel observes, moreover, that it is also a recapitulation of the presuppositions of consciousness, the original ego's subconscious and physical foundations, of the subject matter which, in the mature encylcopedic system is provided with a full-scale exposition in the *Logic* and the *Philosophies* of *Nature* and *Spirit*.[15]

In order to bring out the consistency with which Hegel employs the analytical and synthetic procedures that give rise to this treatment of the epistemology and ethics of Kant and Fichte in the *Berlin Phenomenology*, it is useful to compare the critical results of this exposition with his assessment of the Newton-Goethe controversy. As we have seen, in the mature *Physics*, the level at which white light is dealt with is widely separated from that at which color is given its systematic treatment. Yet light and color are also dealt with in connection with electricity, chemical activity, plant life, animal perception and activity, human sensation and psychology, etc., each level being presented as involving a special approach, a particular systematic context, on account of the relative complexity of the further factors it involves. Similarly, the struggle for recognition, the volitional activity and analyzed and systematized within the sphere of self-consciousness, is also dealt with in connection with more complex legal and social topics such as slavery, contract, work, social status, legal formalities, corporations, constitutional and international law, etc., all of which are given their systematic placing, by means of the basic analytical and synthetic procedures, within the general sphere of the *Philosophy of Right*, not the *Phenomenology*.[16] Within a rational physics, it is not a matter of dealing *either* with the color which arises on account of refraction *or* with chemical colors, etc., but of indicating the precise systematic relationship between the levels involved. Similarly, in a rational theory of ethics, it is not a matter of dealing either with a theory of conduct having its center of gravity in the individual *or* with one taking its guiding principle from the group, but of indicating the precise systematic relationship between the decision making of the conscious individual and the various groupings of social life. Chemical color presupposes refraction just as group activity presupposes the individual.

Strictly speaking, therefore, Hegel's objection to the theories of Kant and Fichte is not that they fail to progress into the formulation of any concrete content, but that they are unable, on account of their limited terms of reference, to do justice to the full complexity of the family, civil society, and the state. The crux of his criticism is, therefore, that although their ethical theories overuse the category of identity, their prime fault is not a category but a context mistake. By means of his analytical and synthetic procedures, Hegel was able to show not merely that they had managed to grasp only one subordiante factor in the whole functioning of society, but also precisely how far short of the mark they had fallen in their attempt to work out a philosophy of the state. It could, perhaps, be argued that by confining the essential significance of Kantiansim to the level of subject-object dichotomies, the sphere of phenomenology, he had underrated it. It cannot be said that his criticism is merely the result of his reaction to the events of his time, or that it is simply arbitrary, in the sense that it is not the outcome of general principles.

NOTES

1. Schiller, *Ueber Anmuth und Würde* (Leipzig, 1793); K. Rosenkranz, *Hegels Leben* (Berlin, 1844), p. 87.
2. *Hegel's Lectures on The History of Philosophy,* (translated by E.S. Haldane and F.H. Simson (Londong and New York, 1963), III.455; cf. *Vorlesungen über die Geschichte der Philosophie,* (ed. by Moldenhauer and K.M. Michel, (Suhrkamp Werkausgabe, Frankfurt/M., 1978) III.363.
3. Hegel, *History of Philosophy,* III.478 (iii.386).
4. J.G. Fichte, *The Science of Rights,* translated by A.E. Kroeger (London, 1889); cf. *Grundlage des Naturrechts* (Jena and Leipzig, 1796).
5. Hegel, *History of Philosophy,* III.481 (III.388).
6. *Hegel's Philosophy of Right,* translated by T.M. Knox (Oxford, 1962), § 135.
7. *Hegel's Logic,* translated by W. Wallace (Oxford, 1975), § 115.
8. Hegel, *Philosoophy of Right,* § 135.
9. *The Berlin Phenomenology, translated by M.J. Petry (Dordrecht, 1981).*
10. *Jenaer Systementwürfe II,* ed. by R.-P. Horstmann and J.H. Trede (Hamburg, 1971), pp. 36–75; *Hegel's Science of Logic,* translated by A.V. Miller (London, 1969), pp. 529–571; *Hegel's Logic* § 142–159.
11. *Hegel's Philosophy of Nature,* translated by M.J. Petry, 3 vols. (London, 1970), II.116–160.
12. *Hegel's Science of Logic,* pp. 755–844; K. Düsing, *Das Problem der Subjektivität in Hegels Logik* (Bonn, 1976), pp. 295–335.
13. Kant, *Critique of Practical Reason,* pp. 73–74, translated by T.K. Abbott (1973, 1959) pp. 131–132.
14. *Ther Berlin Phenomenology* svi; 9,26; 67, 13.
15. *Berlin Phenomenology* xlix–lviii; 29–53.
16. *Philosophy of Nature,* § 324, 330, 344, 358, 362; *Philosophy of Subjective Spirit,* translated by M.J. Petry, 3 vols. (Dordrecht, 1979), § 401, 448; *Philosophy of Right,* § 57, 71, 132, 192, 207, 217, 253, 260, 331. Cf. L. Siep, *Anerkennung als Prinzip der praktischen Philosophie* (Munich, 1979), pp. 26–39.

THE "AUFHEBUNG" OF MORALITY IN ETHICAL LIFE

by

LUDWIG SIEP

What does it mean to say that morality is superseded by ethical life? Whether or not Hegel's philosophy of the objective spirit is still worthy of consideration depends to a great extent upon the answer to precisely this question. Ernst Tugendhat, for example, essentially based his devastating criticism of Hegel upon the following answer to it: "Hegel does not allow for the possibility of a self-responsible, critical relationship to the community, to the state. Instead, we are told that the existing laws have an absolute authority, that a community determines what each individual must do, that each individual's own conscience must cease to exist, and that trust must replace reflection. This is what Hegel means when he says that morality is superseded by ethical life." (349)[1] If this answer is correct, one can hardly escape Tugendhat's conclusion that the Hegelian theory of freedom is the summit of a perversion that is no longer merely conceptual, but also moral. On the other hand, Charles Taylor, to whom Tugendhat makes positive reference and who shares Tugendhat's intellectual background in linguistic analysis, finds Hegel's view that ethical life supersedes morality almost unproblematic. He has called interpretations similar to Tugendhat's "ludicrous." (377, cf. 375)[2] It therefore seems appropriate to reexamine the text of the Philosophy of Right[3] and the lecture notes[4] in order to determine what Hegel really means when he declares that morality is superseded by ethical life.

Such an investigation must clarify the following questions:

1. What does Hegel mean by morality?
2. How does he criticize morality?
3. How is morality maintained and transformed in ethical life?

An answer to these questions can be provided only by reconstructing—at least

137

in outline—the course of argument in the chapter entitled "Morality" and then proceeding to examine those passages in the chapter "Ethical Life" that take up once again the problem of morality. It should thereby become apparent that the character of the presentation and criticism of morality is altered in the course of the chapter on "Morality" itself. In the first two sections of this chapter, the development of morality itself is the primary theme; here criticism is limited to "overcoming" incomplete forms of morality. At the end of the second section, criticism takes on a new form. In the conflict between morality and (abstract) right, the one-sidedness of morality in general is demonstrated. However, it is only in the third section that criticism becomes the exhibition of contradictions either between the claim and the performance of moral positions, or between mutually exclusive moral positions that nonetheless lead to one another.

It can be said that there is a change in the meaning of morality that corresponds to the change in the meaning of criticism. Hegel begins with a very broad concept of morality; in the introductory paragraphs to the chapter on morality, morality is equated with subjectivity (§ 108, 112). Morality is not "that which is opposed to immorality" (§ 108), but rather the conscious "self-determination of the will" (§ 107). According to § 113, only the "expression" of such a "moral" will can appropriately be termed an "action." Institutional "actions" (Hegel cites the legal "*actio*" of the courts as an example, cf. § 113) are not in a full sense actions. Initially, the chapter on morality is then a continuation of the theory of will and action contained in the sections "Practical Spirit" in the Philosophy of Subjective Spirit.[5]

In the first section of the chapter on morality, moral action is the conscious expression of an individual will—as opposed to unconscious, merely instinctive or habitually "set" actions. In the realm of objective spirit, action is considered in its "social" effect: it affects other acting individuals. Regarded in this external perspective, it is a "deed" (*Tat*), and the question is, to what extent the deed can be attributed to purpose and intention. The various forms of deeds purposely performed, which are the topic in § § 115 ff., correspond by no means to the "concept of morality" that had "emerged" at the end of abstract right (§ 103), for this had been the "particular subjective will" which wills the "universal as such." This concept is only the "truth" of those forms of volition and action in which the particular will wills itself (cf. § 114), and it is especially relevant at the outset of the third section ("The Good and Conscience") in which Hegel presents and criticizes Kantian ethics. At the end of this section— at the climax of criticism, so to speak—morality once more seems to possess the meaning that Hegel had envisaged in the *Phenomenology* of 1807. Morality characterizes a "self-consciousness" or "world-view" in which the "knowing will" sees itself as "substance and purpose and singular content," as "all reality" (GW 9, 324).[6] Nowhere else in the Philosophy of Right does Hegel deal with both a necessary "side of the concept of freedom" (§ 106) and its unten-able radicalization under the same heading ("Morality") and in the same chap-ter. This has doubtless impaired an understanding of what it means for morality to be "superseded." Abstract right can, of course, also be one-sidedly rendered absolute, but that this is the case can become apparent only in the conflict with other "sides" of freedom, morality, and ethical life. Therefore this one-sideness of abstract right must wait for its exposition until the sections "Intention and Welfare" and "Civil Society." The reason why internal development implies radicalization and its criticism only in the case of "Morality" cannot be explained by general reference to the concept itself. A satisfactory explanation requires that we briefly trace the "process within this sphere" (§ 106). As far as its content is concerned, this process includes a wealth of legal issues (accoun-tability, liability, etc.), moral phenomena (self-realization, hypocrisy, cynicism, self-deception, irony, etc.), ethical conceptions and theories (altruism, eudae-monism, decisionism, probabilism, etc.), and at least an outline of the history of morality from Socrates (cf. 4, 301) up to Friedrich Schlegel. The structure of this process consists in an increasing "identification of the subjective will with the concept of the will" (3, 339). Only by viewing the structured process as a whole can one come to understand what morality is and how it is "superseded."

A

The development of morality begins in the section on "Purpose and Respon-sibility" with the expression of the moral will, action—taken in its most exter-nal sense as an "alteration" upon "the given state of affairs" (§ 115). The subjective will must first of all appropriate its own expressions, so to speak, by coming to recognize itself in them as being "its own" (*ibid.*). I am responsible in the most external sense of the word (as "strict liability") if something that is mine, that is, something that is a part of my property, is involved in such an alteration.[7] But if some deed leading to an alteration can be understood as the expression of a will, then this "acting will" has the right to recognize "in its deed only that which is its own action," i.e., exclusively something that can be traced back to conscious purposes (§ 117). This "reflection" of the difference be-tween deed and action marks the historical transition from the tragic to the moral (subjective) concept of responsibility, as § 118 indicates. However, this is, of course, no more than the point of departure for the legal, and, in a stricter sense, moral problems of accountability that arise as the result of actions com-mitted on purpose.

At the level of purpose, the subject only recognizes the mere "specifics" (§ 119) of the deed (particular consequences of particular purposes) as its action. At the level of purpose, by contrast, the fateful entanglement of individual subjective purposes in the "connectedness and "necessity" of external circumstances and events is supplanted by an internal connection between aims and the anticipation of external occurences. The latter is a universality that originates in the subject's own cognition. But this universalization of volition is at the same time a particularization of the agent out of the "universality which is substantiality," as Hegel stated in his handwritten notes to § 119 (VII, 225). The agent who has certain intentions is concerned with himself and his knowledge of himself, and he attempts to realize this knowledge within the context of social activity, its circumstances, rules, and dependencies. Only, "inasfar as I find satisfaction in it, does my action have an interest for me" (3, 379). This holds for the "most amoral" crimes, such as murder merely for its own sake, as well as for moral actions in a strict sense, such as those performed from altruism or a sense of duty. In the latter case, also, the subject is interested in his own activity as a kind of self-realization. Without interest, the activity of the subject would have no "value" (cf. § 122); lacking interest, one would not be "involved" in one's own actions (3, 382). But in the absence of such involvement in one's own actions, there could be not truly active subject, no person—as Locke had already pointed out.[8] According to Hegel, also, it had become "evident especially in recent times" (3, 377) that the subject "positively fulfills itself" in its actions (3, 373). This produces a new tension in the subject's actions: there is now a tension not only between the amount of purpose involved and the consequences, but also between the motivation and the external aims or "further content" (§ 122) of an action. The aim of any action can become in turn a means of attaining that which I am truly motivated to pursue—in the final analysis this is my own self-realization. I wish to realize myself as something that is active as a subject in general but also as a "natural" individual with concrete "needs, inclinations, passions, opinions, fancies, etc." (§ 123). This implies a first criticism of Kant: Hegel, as opposed to Kant, grants to the "satisfaction of bodily as well as spiritual needs" (3, 383) a positive moral status in the concept of "welfare" or "happiness." To make's one's own welfare one's conscious aim is—in contrast to the instinctive passionate satisfaction of needs—already an element of moral freedom. The reference of various needs "to a whole" (VII, 231), the calculation and postponement of needs for the sake of a lasting happiness, is in itself an indication of a "universality in reflection," and this must be understood as a first step towards acting in accordance with the laws of freedom.

This development towards the willing of something rational and universal is presented by Hegel in § § 125 ff.; however, at least as far as the moral phenomena presented here are concerned, it is not especially convincing. According to Hegel, the universality immanent within reflection leads an individual to proceed beyond his merely private welfare. "The cognitive will determines its volition not according to *its own* welfare, but rather extends it to the welfare of others" (3, 394). But the universality that is contained in the idea of the general welfare is *not* the strict universality of thought. In the lecture notes of 1824/1825, we read: The general welfare is an empty phrase; one must, of course, disregard the dead and those who are to come . . . and how can I further the welfare of those in China?" (4, 338). The logic of this extension consists, according to the text, merely in the fact that "I cannot further my own welfare without furthering the welfare of others" (4, 337; cf. VII, 237 f.). But this kind of universalization cannot assure that the others are intended as free subjects, not even in the mere sense of their legal freedom as persons. Therefore, Hegel is not able to progress any further in the development of moral phenomena or ethical conceptions at this point.[9] Instead, an opposition arises between the benevolent will and formal right. This means that the inadequacy of previous forms of morality is not developed out of internal contradictions but rather from the "collision" between morality and right in which their mutual one-sidedness, the "finitude and thus the contingency of both right and welfare" (§ 128) can be recognized.

What is this one-sidedness? After all, Hegel seems to be able to resolve the conflict between right and welfare by means of a very narrow version of a right of distress, which is restricted to the point at which one's life is endangered. In reality, however, this solution is by no means a mediation between abstract right and morality; it is rather a solution which is strictly limited to right. Furthermore, according to Hegel, it belongs to the area of legal right in a strict sense and is not, as it is in Kant, a part of the *jus latum* which is an "*intermundium*" between morality and right.[10] The right of distress implies only that a free will's right to be present in and dispose over objects may not deprive another person of the possibility to express his will at all ("a loss of rights altogether" § 127). Nevertheless, the unconditional will to freely dispose over objects and the unconditional will of the subject to realize itself in willing the general welfare may be mutually exclusive in a number of cases. Within the realm of morality, as far as it has been developed up to this point, there is no conceivable form of the will that would necessarily unite the two and thus overcome their mutual one-sidedness. Can there by any willing guided by subjective reflection and self-determination that would, at the same time, have to adopt an organization of the rights and duties of all as its unconditional aim? This is precisely the claim that is made by the will to good if the concept of the good is not determined as something alien to the will but rather as the essence of the will itself. The good, as dealt with in the last section of the chapter on morality, is both the essence of the will and the "world's final aim" (§ 129), which ought to be recognized, furthered, and realized by the cognitive will of the subject. This cognitive willing of the good contains all the traits of morality as it has been developed up to this point. The subject realizes itself here (a) as actively "present," (b) as wanting its own welfare as well as that of others, and (c) as its own judge of what is good. "The right of giving recognition only to what my insight sees as rational is the subject's highest right" (§ 132 Rem.). But, at the same time, its concern is that which unconditionally ought to be, that which is the final aim for all and is "absolutely essential" for the subjective will itself: "The subjective will has value and dignity only in so far as its insight and intention accord with the good" (§ 131). One might say that the "modern" concept of freedom contains the demand for self-realization by means of the realization of something that unconditionally ought to be, and that I personally can see as something that unconditionally ought to be. Personal insight, however, is supposed to be founded upon rational grounds and standards. And since these cannot be provided from the stand point of morality, as the third section attempts to show, morality must be transferred into ethical life.

III

I will now first of all consider the transition from morality to ethical life from its negative side, as critique, as the demonstration of contradictions within morality. The aspects of *conservare* and *elevare,* the transformational preservation of morality in ethical life, will be thematized in the following section (IV) of this paper. According to my interpretation, the forms and stages of morality dealt with up until now are not contradictory, but rather only insufficient. This ceases to be valid only at the last stage, the ethics of conviction and conscience, which is a radicalization of "morality."

The "refutation" of this morality can also be considered from various aspects, from the contradictory content of the moral theories and phenomena discussed by Hegel or from their structural or "logical" side. For, in the end, the "transition" from morality to ethical life has to be explained in terms of the "Science of Logic" (cf. § 141 App.).

Let us first consider the aspect of content. What kind of moral concepts and theories are discussed and critized by Hegel? One must distinguish on the one hand between individual facets of ethics and moral theories to which Hegel's presentation applies and which are often mentioned, especially in the lectures; and, on the other hand, positions that are compatible with Hegel's characterization of the good and its relationship to the subjective will. For example, in a broad sense the characterization of the good as that which is "essential" for man (§ 131), or the determination of good actions as "right actions," can also be referred back to Aristotelian ethics (cf. § 134). But if the good is supposed to be the essence or the concept of the will and if the particular will demonstrates "its unity with its essence" (3, 418 f.) by fulfilling its duties, then this cannot be applied to ancient ethics, with the sole exception of Stoic ethics, which Hegel himself expressly exempts. According to the lecture notes of Hotho (1822/ 1823), Hegel explicitly concedes that, in Stoic ethics, man no longer merely discovers "what he ought to recognize as right in a source external to himself, neither in the law nor in customs." Rather, here mankind is aware that right is dependent upon "his essence, the concept of his will. . . . This is the standpoint where one says, 'Duty must be done for its own sake' " (3, 418 f.). Only in positions according to which the essence of will is realized in the fulfillment of particular, but unconditionally valid duties can the contradictions be demonstrated that allow such positions to appear in the last instance indistinguishable from radical amorality, whether relativistic or subjectivistic.

The dynamics of content in this last stage of Hegel's criticism of morality is contained in the assertion that any ethics founded upon the concept of an unconditional will in accord with duty must develop into its "purest" form, Kant's formal ethics. For, there is no other way to solve the problem that a particular duty is "limited" and "does not correspond to the good as such, and inasfar as the particular duty is fulfilled, its value does not consist in the particular character of that duty, but rather in the universality that it is a duty, that it is good. That is, the determination of the good in each particular duty is merely formal" (4, 256). It is precisely this, Kant's unconditional and pure concept of morals that must in the end abandon the determination of the good, as well as its concretion in duties and particular good acts, to the voluntary choice of particular subjects. In the end, this leads to the negation of the boundaries between good and evil, moral and amoral.

Hegel had repeatedly criticized Kantian moral philosophy on this point ever since the *Phenomenology* of 1807. An examination of the justification of this criticism cannot be undertaken here.[11] Instead, it shall be briefly summarized only inasfar as it furthers an understanding of the Hegelian consequence that morality is superseded by ethical life. According to Hegel, the categorical imperative by no means demonstrates that a particular concrete duty can be deduced from the essence of a rational will. Whether or not a maxim is capable of serving as a principle for legislation, depends rather upon the maxim's empirical content. There is no doubt that one cannot consistently wish to possess property and consent to embezzlement, wish to live and, at the same time, consent to murder; or wish to communicate and consent to lying. But this still does not imply that property,[12] communication or human life do or should at all exist (cf. § 135 App.). The presuppositions of such maxims as "one should not do x" are therefore natural, social, and legal contents or institutions. However, these cannot be considered moral if morality consists in the correspondence between the will and its concept; and consequently, this correspondence cannot be guaranteed merely by the manner of judgement itself, i.e., by one's feeling of obligation or by one's conscience. Fichte's reformulation of the categorical imperative in his *System of Ethical Science* is then, according to Hegel's view, completely consistent. It was: "Always act according to your strongest conviction concerning your duty; always act in accordance with your own conscience."[13] Hegel did not however discuss the way in which Fichte, in his *System of Ethical Science* (1798), arrived at social institutions and concrete duties via the intersubjective mediation of ethical consciousness. Hegel is more interested in the principle that established the subject's reflection and decision, the "activity of particularization" (4, 360), as the standard for all morality in place of any particular content of moral action.

This principle contains no criterion, though, for distinguishing the ethical fulfillment of obligations from arbitrary decisions or from blatant or concealed (even from oneself) willing of evil. For Hegel, evil is nothing other than the reflecting will's conscious separation from the universality of mind, i.e., of the *logos* that knows itself as the same in nature, the human world, and individuals. This separation can take various forms. One form is the consciousness that all that matters is a decision one way or the other (decisionism: "every affirmation with regard to the will" is positive, good);[14] another is the consciousness that it depends upon my decision whether or not good or evil will be realized; and still another is the consciousness that every act can be referred to some good aim or reason; and yet another is finally the consciousness that my "voluntary choice . . . is the master over good, right, evil, truth" (4, 389). In this "very summit of subjectivity" (*ibid.*) everything obligatory in the morality of self-realization is rendered the victim of an ironic game: "It is not the thing that is excellent, it is I who am so; as the master of law and things, I simply play with them as with my caprice; my consciously ironical attitude lets the highest perish, and I merely hug myself at the thought" (§ 140 App.).

The ironical subject's "vanity" is a clear demonstration of the essence of subjectivity that is able to abstract from all aims and maxims in which it has posited its determinacy. At the same time, it is an essential attribute of freedom that the universal (at this point subjective) will knows itself to be independent of each of its self-posted or self-appropriated determinacies (cf. Introduction § § 5–7). On the other hand, how can there be an objective good that is obligatory for all, if each individual subject is free from all restraints? The Kantian moral philosophy and its romanticist opposite are merely two sides of the same coin: if the unconditional good is supposed to be free from all empirical determinacy, then "only the good will" can be unconditionally good. But the will that is not empirically bound, is conscious of its freedom to appropriate everything and simultaneously be free from everything. It can play with everything—in the end, it makes no difference—it opts for the greatest possible irregularity in its action, whether it merely imagines anything as a universal law, or even exempts itself from all existing laws (as a sort of "free rider"). The "essence" of the will is the fact that it determines itself, and that it remains free from all of its determinacies in this activity.

The fact that the summit of morality is the dissolution of all obligation and the reciprocal transition from one opposite to the other (the good in itself as opposed to subjective freedom of choice; the good will as opposed to cynicism, etc.) is necessarily due to its "relational structure" (cf. 4, 349, 4, 391). Morality is a relationship in which both sides—the universal, the good, the essence of the will, on the one hand; and the particularity of duty, action, and the will, on the other hand—are supposed to be both "self-sufficient" as well as "identical" (4, 391). The universal will is supposed to become actual through particularization, the particular will is supposed to become "ethical" by corresponding to the universal. But this "becoming," this genesis, cannot reach its goal; otherwise, the good would be rendered finite and the will would be deprived of its ethical striving.

Hegel scholars have not yet reached agreement on the question which logical determinations correspond to the transition from morality to ethical life. U. Rameil recently suggested the corresponding transition is from the Relation of Substantiality to the Concept; L. de Vos, by contrast, proposes that it is the transition from Teleology (the last section of "Objectivity") to the Idea of Life.[15] In Hegel's *Handwritten Notes* (VII, 214) and in Hotho's and V. Griesheim's (3, 470 and 4, 364) lecture notes there are references to the Judgement of Concepts and its transition into Inference. The important thing is that on both sides of this relationship "identity is present" (4, 391 f.). This identity consists in the fact that both the subject and the good are, on the one hand, "self-identical," "solid and immutable"; and, on the other hand, that they are "restlessness, dissolution" (*ibid.*). This is due to the fact that subjectivity at the peak of its amorality wishes to be "free of determination": "this indeterminacy is, however, the very opposite of voluntary choice ("Willkür"); it is the "self-sameness, the universality of the will" (VII, 288). The good turns out for its part to be not only the identical essence of the will but also the dissolution of all determinacies: no determinate will can ever correspond to its pure, indeterminate essence. If this unity is viewed positively, then it is the "system of the particularization of the good" (Handwritten Note to § 142; cf. VII, 289, 292), both "in itself" as "the world" or "the existent mind . . . recognized in other human beings" (VII, 292), as well as in the will of the subject that comprehends this system and wills it as rational. "System" means a totality of determinacies that are organized in a "subject-like" manner, so that the system makes distinctions within itself and represents itself as a totality in each of these distinctions.[15] This totality must be independent of various individuals' contingent and arbitrary opinions, that is, it must be "in itself." At the same time, however, it must become manifest in their deeds and knowledge (the "testimony" of the particular subject, cf. § 147) and this manifestation must occur by means of their free, self-realizaing activity. The "system" of ethical life is not a set of interconnected rules, but is rather a self-developing, common self-comprehension (a "spirit") that can be incorporated in institutions and persons. For this reason, the system as a whole can also be represented by individual particularities: "Individuals are particular in and for themselves and over against other individuals. This whole side of particularity, all of this is the one side in which ethical life is realized" (3, 501).

With regard to Kant's ethics, the transition from morality to ethical life has the following significance: the will does not will its "essence" by making its universality, its conformity to laws, its proper aim. Rather, the will must be directed towards aims that are necessarily bound to everyone's (legal, moral, ethical) freedom in a certain community. Its particular aims must simultaneously further the aims of a totality which is constituted by laws, the will of which is unconditioned and independent of the concrete aims and maxims of individuals. At the same time, however, the community's will is directed towards conditions for free actions. Such conditions must include rules for the free disposal over property, possibilities for self-realization in common tasks, the material presuppositions for self-determinate activity ("subsistence"), etc. This occurs unconsciously in ("functioning") civil society, and consciously in the family and the state.

IV

How is morality superseded and transformed in ethical life? Are its claims merely critically restricted, so that it is granted a limited right at the level of ethical life, so that it parallels, for instance, civil society in the ethicl state; or is it transformed into another, higher form of conduct and consciousness? The beginning of the third section of the *Philosophy of Right* seems to indicate that morality has indeed been superseded by a different, even opposite way of thinking and acting. If the "ethical powers . . . rule the individual's life" with "absolute authority" (§ § 145, 146); and if the "only great ethical totalities" namely "marriage" and "the state" (Handwritten Notes to § 142), determine the individual with their obligations and laws, so that "the individual's private conscience, which had been for itself and opposed to the ethical substance, has disappeared" (§ 152)[16]; then the mere "affirmation" of existing rules and powers appears to have replaced conscience and responsibility.

However, the fact is often overlooked that, for Hegel himself, ethical life is subject to a development within which its relationship to morality changes. In his remarks to § 147, Hegel mentions four stages of the ethical relationship to the substance as represented by habits, customs, ethics, institutions, and laws. The first of these stages is constituted by the subject's feeling within the substance that the substance is like an "element which is not distinguishable from oneself"; the second is "faith and trust, which is no longer "identity," but rather "a relationship"; the third is constituted by "reflection" and "insight due to reasons"; the fourth is "adequate knowledge." Ethical life must proceed through these four stages, the third of which corresponds to morality (cf. 4, 406)—and the second, third, and fourth of them must be preserved in the consummation of ethical life. In Hegel's Handwritten Notes to § 151, it is stated: "Conscience, reflection, morality, is not spirit, but neither is dull innocence" (VII, 301). And the lecture notes from 1822/1823 record in § 147: "Faith, trust are the immediate forms of reflecting understanding; and, as far as their content is concerned, they surpass it. Nonetheless, man must appear before this tribunal, must search for reasons" (3, 487). But reasons that are open to subjective insight can be provided only by adequate knowledge, which recognizes ethics, institutions, and laws as forms of freedom.

Hegel also identified these states in the historical development of ethical life, and, except for the first of them, they provide the systematic basis for the divisions of ethical life—family, civil society, and state. In a brief sketch of the history of ethical life provided in the lecture of 1818/1819, Hegel distinguishes an immediate ethical life, a stage of reflection, which he attributes to Socrates in Greece and to Stoic ethics and Roman law in Rome as "moments of morality and right" (1, 290); and, a stage of "ethical unity," which develops into these moments. This schemework of an immediate ethical life, a stage of reflection that comprehends right and morality, and, as opposed to it, a stage that conjoins the "self-suffiency of individuals" and the "unification in laws" into a "unity as a known, conscious, articulate cognitive unity" (VII, 307) is applied by Hegel in his remarks on § 157 to the threefold division between family, civil society, and state. According to this scheme, civil society is the sphere in which morality is maintained. In the lecture of 1824/1825, it is stated: "Here is where right belongs, here the individual is for himself; just as morality also has its place here: the particular individual's being within himself" (4, 416).

In civil society, Hegel indeed represents morality and right—in this converse order—as forms for cognition, action, and organization in a kind of ethical life that is necessary, though "deficient" to the extent that common life may be sundered so that a consciousness of unity is lost. Morality is then located in the system of needs. Abstract right becomes a "social reality" in the administration of justice (*"Rechtspflege"*), and at the end of this second section of the chapter "Civil Society," the renewed conflict between right and welfare leads to a transition into the highest form of ethical life within civil society, the police or internal administration and the corporation. This time, however, the conflict arises from the side of right. The inadequate attempt to resolve it by the means available to civil society, the common precautions taken by "atomistic" individuals who know themselves to be the only reality, leads to the "transition" (§ 256) from civil society to the state.

The form of moral subjectivity that is once more thematized in the first section of "civil society" is intention and welfare. The system of needs is the sphere in which individuals' particular "plans for self-realization" can be pursued. In this process, there arises a mutual dependency of individuals upon each other, upon the social division of labor, upon the market, etc. This interdependence gives content and reality to the vague moral idea of "the general welfare": The furthering of private prosperity increases the possibility of "satisfying the needs of all others" (§ 199). But the "criss-cross movements of reciprocal production and exchange" (§ 201) also develop a rationality of their own that transcends the mere contingencies of the market: divisions of professions and estates are established that transmit and regulate skills and knowledge, that propagate rules of conduct, develop self-respect and "professional honor," and require mutual assistance for members of a profession. In the free, subjective choice of a profession and estate, which is simultaneously accompanied by particular forms of life, customs, and duties, the individual realizes himself in a moral and ethical manner: "An individual actualizes himself only by becoming something definite, i.e., something specifically particularized" that is represented by a particular estate (§ 207). One's "ethical frame of mind" consists in the disposition "to make oneself a member of a moment in civil society by one's own act" (*ibid.*). This moment, the specific estate, is just as necessary to civil society as civil society is to the rational community. "Morality has its proper place in this sphere" (*ibid.*). This means that the free, conscious choice of an estate and the acceptance of the corresponding obligations are the unification of free self-realization and an adherence to objectivity necessary and actual rules. At the same time, in the obligation to "contingent and singular assistance" (*ibid.*), morality contains a field in which the subjectively determinate, yet concrete furthering of the welfare of others is an altruistic activity that improves the world.

In the third section of "Civil Society" (§ 242), Hegel returns again to this aspect of "moral" engagement in regard to the distress of others, an aspect that was not especially emphasized in the chapter on morality. In this section, however, the organizations, rules, and activities dealt with, are supposed to assure that "particular welfare is treated and actualized as a right" (§ 230). For Hegel, this necessitates a whole range of measures undertaken by private persons, estates, and the social state: "This is the place where morality finds plenty to do despite all public organizations" (§ 242), namely, as "subjective," spontaneous assistance in which the individual discovers his value in alleviating the distress of others. A unity of right, welfare (happiness), and moral value, which would not be subject to the contingencies of circumstances and subjective decisions, can nevertheless only be attained by a will that is exclusively "institutionalized" for this purpose and possesses the highest power in a community. This is the worldly God of the state, which in accordance with its concept can will and realize nothing other than the "supreme good" represented precisely by this unity between freedom and happiness, if it is not to cease to be a state at all.

The manner in which morality is superseded in the realm of civil society is incomplete in two respects. First of all, it contains only the stages, purpose, intention, and welfare, but not good and conscience; and second, it occurs in a domain in which the individual is still "conserved" in his particularity and has not yet been elevated to a common activity aimed toward the unification of everyone in an autonomous community that develops and realizes itself in its own "spirit." Only in the third section of "Ethical lie," in "State," can one thus discover the decisive point where morality is superseded.

In order to avoid repeating too much that is common knowledge, I shall limit myself to a few comments on Hegel's treatment of political sentiment (§ 268, 289), which should be seen as an ethical form of conscience, as the "true conscience" (§ 137). The text in § 268 seems to confirm the "laughable" interpretations regarding morality's being superseded by ethical life. Subjective certainty is replaced by that sentiment that conforms to the "institutions existing in the state," patriotism and "trust." However, an adequate interpretation necessitates the following reservations: first of all, the topic here is not every individual's correct sentiment in every situation and in regard to every specific state, but rather the relationship of subjects who can funamentally be called "citizens" (cf. § 261 Rem.)[18] to the institutions of a community that can fundamentally be called "a state." And, this community can only be one whose constitution and institutions are directed towards the aim of furthering the rights and self-realization of individuals. In such communities, the citizens have a variety of conventions and traditions (Hegel includes "national freedoms" among them, cf. § 258 Rem.) and are therefore able to attain a habitual correspondence to a "political culture" without forsaking reflection upon its foundations. For, each individual as a citizen still "contains" the "one extreme, explicit individuality of conscience and will" (§ 264). Second, the trust that Hegel mentions here is not trust in each law or measure established by governmental authority, but rather only a trust in the correspondence of my "substantial and particular interest" to the interests and aims of the state. An individual's particular interest is his self-realization in fulfilling a certain life plan. This must be furthered by a state that respects and stabilizes the "particular spheres" of the family and of civil society and the estates (§ 289). The substantial interest is an interest in comprehending and realizing oneself as a member of an autonomous legal and cultural community that pursues common aims.[19] For Hegel, the individual is never a *tabula rasa* who approaches a particular community with its customs and laws and then begins to analyse them. An individual is rather the particularization of a community being, a "variation" of a British scholar, a German craftsman, or a Polish laborer. An individual does not comprehend what he is by means of introspection: "Consciousness not in me (Moral reflection), but as existent, i.e., external to me— my unity outside of myself—unity of individuals," as Hegel notes to § 151. But the individual does not realize himself in uniformity with his class, social group, or nation, either, but rather by "determining and creating" the rational spirit of these groups "out of himself as his ownmost and truest" (3, 496). For, without its "ethical character," the substance, also, is a "mere abstraction" (*ibid.,* cf. also 501). In contrast to civil society, the citizen of the state furthers and concretizes the universal, not by means of "subjective selfishness" (§ 199), but rather by fulfilling common public tasks that transcend his private existence, even if these require that he risk his life.[20]

The trust that my private and public self-realization is assured for the most part in an autonomous legal, social, and cultural state, is not to be confused with a blind faith in every kind of governmental authority, laws, or orders. Nevertheless, Hegel's determination of the rational relationship between the citizen and his state presents problems. Two of them should be mentioned here.

1. Hegel's conception of ethical life refers to states, the institutions of which can be comprehended by means of the concept of freedom, institutions in which the particular will is directed towards the universal will and the universal will directed towards the particular. Such institutions were not irrealistic ideals for him: some had occurred historically, others were in the process of being developed. However, there had been states and, more important, there could be states that could not be understood as realizations of the rational concept of freedom. Hegel evades the problem of the citizens' relationship to such states by empirically asserting that "a Christian, European state" (4, 632) or the "cultured" state "in our age" (VII, 404) must contain all the essential moments of rational statehood. Even more questionable is the comparison recorded in the lecture notes of 1824/1825, in which the "defigurated" state is compared to a sick man who still deserves dignity and rights. On the other hand, in his lectures on the Philosophy of Right, Hegel repeatedly granted the possibility of an alienation between an individual and the customs and laws of his community. At times, he even expressly draws a parallel between his own age and the ethical "decay" of Athens in Socrates' age (cf. 3, 436; 3, 474). In the writings of the Jena period, Hegel viewed the cleft between a people's transformed self-comprehension—or that of certain groups within a people—and the existent

institutions and laws as the source of a continuing "progress in the development of right"; however, in the Philosophy of Right, such alienation occurs only as a symptom of world-historical catastrophes. At this point, Hegel is far removed from his position in the Philosophy of Spirit 1805/1806 where he regards the changing "public opinion" as the true "spiritual bond" and as the "true legislative corps," which provide an impulse to alterations in "constitutions" by means of alterations in the forms of life (GW, 8, 263). Hegel emphasizes in the Philosophy of Right that the constitution must be held to be something "absolutely in and for itself"; it "must be viewed as that which is divine and lasting, far beyond the sphere of the created" (§ 128). Perhaps that does not exclude an amendment of the constitution "by constitutional means" (*ibid.*), but in the Philosophy of Right it is not evident by which procedure that could be done. The "legislative power" can merely develop the constitution via the "progressive development of laws," but the constitution itself lies "outside of its (sc. the legislative power's) direct influence" and cannot be altered by the legislative branch. Furthermore, the possibility that the "interests of the communities, corporations, and individuals" (§ 302) can find an expression in legislation is very restricted in the usual case already.[21] The reason for this is that Hegel ultimately entrusted the adequate comprehension of the rational principles of constitution and legislation only to philosophers and philosophically educated officials. He thus draws a sharp distinction between the possibility of an insight into these principles and the empirical insights that a citizen might have.

2. In his lectures on the Philosophy of History, Hegel grants that there is something like a culturally invariant morality, which is independent of the specific customs and laws of a community. There are "moral virtues . . . in all zones, constitutions, and political situations" (XII, 89). In states that have not yet been formed by "consciousness of freedom," a "very pure" morality is still possible, that "expresses the universal duties and rights as objective commandments" (XII, 95). These duties and rights concern the "relinquishment of sensuality," and consciousness of persons as beings who are free "from all particularity" and "infinite within themselves" (*ibid.*). This "merely negative" morality is apparently capable of providing a genuine foundation for human dignity and human rights. As long as the claim is not made that such morals could render the particular constitutions, institutions, and conventions of states superfluous, morality has its place in ethical life, also. Hegel could therefore well have recognized universal moral and legal standards in addition to the "national freedoms" in his Philosophy of Right.

V

If my interpretation of the text is correct, we must interpret the assertion that morality is superseded in ethical life in a more differentiated manner than usual. One must distinguish between various aspects of morality that are criticized, "conserved," and transposed to various degrees. Hegel's criticism of morality is that an ethics of conscience or conviction is incapable of deducing determinate duties from an indeterminate universality (lawfulness in general, the community of all rational beings, conscience as pure decision, etc.). This must lead to a relativity of all duties as imperfect realizations of the universal "good," or as something arbitrarily posited by the subject. And without determinate duties, the only conceivable alternatives are absolute distrust within the state of nature or completely arbitrary rule by a tyrant.

Determinate duties for a "morally" self-determining subject are only possible in relation to a specific community of human beings, which secures the freedom of individuals by simultaneously securing its own freedom from their contingent aims. With respect to the existence of such a community, all rules, rights, and duties, as far as they concern individuals' external conduct, are relative, i.e., they can be restricted for the sake of this existence. But with regard to the freedom of individuals, the community is also relative in its own manner; if it fundamentally or "permanently" ceases to assure the legal, moral, and ethical freedom of individuals, it can no longer lay claim to such duties. (Hegel himself is not very clear on this point, however). This paradoxical relationship between individual freedom and the rules and existence of the community as aims that are both aims in themselves as well as means to one another, can only be realized in communities that fulfill at least the following conditions: First, the individuals must cooperate with each other in opposing forms of organization and conduct (family, civil society, state). Second, there must be a specific relationship between actions, purposes, and rules: rules are not simply theoretically deduced and then applied or put into practice, but are rather generated by unconsciously conforming ways of acting. Rules that have become conscious must be philosophically comprehensible as a system (of conditions of freedom), but within the life of the community, they must be applied "flexibly," and colliding rules and purposes must be adequately compensated for according to the particular situation (cf. for instance, occupational freedom and employment security via the corporations, abstract right and the furthering of the general welfare by the state).[23] And finally, it must be possible for functions and roles to be assigned in which individuals can fulfill common aims by developing a particular character.

Individuals can also question the "practical truth" (as Tugendhat calls it) of such a state, its rules, and its conduct.[24] But the criteria for practical truth or freedom are not such vague concepts as democracy or fraternity, but are rather precisely those structures within the community that can fulfill the paradoxical task mentioned above. For Hegel, such structures have cosmic and logical parallels. His attempt to demonstrate them places him above the suspicion of historicism, but it sometimes also seduces him into a new version of Platonistic rule by those who are the wisest.

In spite of this, one cannot accuse Hegel of eliminating conscience and responsibility. What he rejects is simply the veneration for the decisions of conscience as being beyond criticism. Hegel holds that, according to its very "idea," conscience claims to be the "rule for a rational, universal manner of acting which is valid in and for itself" (§ 137). Hence it cannot be placed beyond all intersubjective standards for examination. One can accuse individual decisions for conscience of being mistaken and punish the acts that follow from them. But this may not be connected with an examination of another's conscience, the attempt to dictate someone else's conscience, or to punish convictions as such, etc.; otherwise, one would indeed commit a "sacrilege" against the "sanctity" of conscience (*ibid.*). Furthermore, the individual does not make his "value" and his guilt ultimately dependent upon an external tribunal, but rather upon an internal one, which therefore remains absolute even in regard to the state.[25] The remaining aspects of morality, also, are not abolished, in Hegel's view, but are instead preserved and complemented. The right to self-realization in conscious actions aimed at one's own welfare and the welfare of others is made concrete by one's conscious, responsible, "productive" (even innovative) conduct within the profession that one belongs to or that one chooses, in privately donating assistance, and in one's support for the institutions of the social state. Complete self-realization can be found only in an autonomous legal and cultural state, for the sake of which one performs certain understandable tasks. But in doing so, one does not cease to be a private, moral, religious individual with particular responsibilities. Viewed in this manner, there are still problems involved in Hegel's conception of morality as superseded by ethical life; but one can hardly still describe this conception as a "moral perversion."

Translated by Thomas Nenon. I am grateful to Raymond Geuss for some improvements in the translation.

NOTES

1.   Ernst Tugendhat, *Selbstbewubsein und Selbstbestimmung* (Frankfurt/Main: Suhrkamp, 1979). Regarding Tugenhat's critique of Hegel, cf. my "Kehraus mit Hegel? Zu Ernst Tugendhats Hegel-Kritik," Zeitschrift für philosophische Forschung, vol. 35, no. 3/4.
2.   Charles Taylor, *Hegel* (Cambridge: Cambridge University Press, 1975).

3. The original quotations were taken from the *Grundlinien der Philosophie des Rechts* according to Eva Moldenhauer and Karl Markus Michel's edition in vol. VII of their G.W.F. Hegel *Werkausgabe* (Frankfurt/Main: Suhrkamp, 1970). The standard English translation, which was used as a guide in this lecture, is T.M. Knox's *Hegel's Philosophy of Right* (Oxford: Clarendon Press, 1952; ppb. Oxford: Oxford University Press, 1967). The body of the paragraphs is cited only according to the paragraph number; the "Remarks" (Rem.) and "Handwritten Notes" are quoted according to the German edition (VII, 1 ff.). Quotations cited with a roman numeral refer to the German *Werkausgabe;* the roman numeral indicates the volume, the arabic numeral indicates the page. For quotations cited with GW followed by an arabic numeral, see footnote 6. Quotations employing only an arabic numeral are explained in footnote 4.

4. The lecture notes are cited according to the edition: G.W.F. Hegel, *Verlesungen über Rechtsphilosophie 1818-1831,* ed. and commentated in six volumes by Karl-Heinz Ilting (Stuttgart/Bad Canstatt: Frommann-Holzboog, 1973 ff.). Both the volume and the page numbers are indicated by arabic numerals.

5. CF. § § 388–399 of the Heidelberg *Enzyklopaèdie der philosophischen Wissenschaften im Grundrisse* (1817); as well as R.P. Horstmann, "Subjektiver Geist und Moralität," in D. Henrich, ed., *Hegel's philosophishce Psychologie,* Hegel-Studien, Beiheft 19, (Bonn: Bouvier, 1969), pp. 190–199.

6. I quote the *Phenomenology* and Hegel's Jena writings according to the Gesamtausgabe of the Rheinisch-Westfälische-Akademie der Wissenschafter (= GW); G.W.F. Hegel, *Phänomenologie des Geistes,* ed. by W. Bonsiepen and R. Heede (Hamburg: Meiner, 1980) (= Gessammelte Werke, vol. 9); G.W.F. Hegel, *Jenaer Systementwürfe III,* ed. by R.P. Horstmann in cooperation with J.H. Trede (Hamburg: Meiner, 1976) (= GW 8).

7. Cf. K. Larenz, *Hegels Zurechnungslehre und der Begriff der objektiven Zurechnung* (Leipzig: A. Deichert, 1927).

8. A precise treatment of the connection between self-interest and self-consciousness is given by R. Brandt, "John Locke," in *Klassiker der Philosophie,* vol. 1 O. Höffe, ed., (Munich: Beck, 1981), pp. 374 ff.

9. In the transition from "welfare" to the "good" via the collision between abstract right and welfare, one can at best discern an attempt by Hegel to employ the means available to his Philosophy of Right in order to adopt Kant's accomplishment of overcoming happiness as the highest principle of morals by the concept of the unconditional good.

10. Cf. Kant's discussion of the right of distress in the appendix to the introduction to the "Doctrine of Right" in the *Metaphysics of Morals,* in: Kant, *Werke* (Akademie Ausgabe) VI, 235 f.

11. A brief, clear and critical portrayal of Hegel's criticism of Kant (with regard to ethics) is given by W.H. Walsh, *Hegelian Ethics* (London/Melbourne/Toronto: St. Martin's Press, 1969), pp. 21–34.

12. In his criticism of Kant's example in which the trust of a depositor is betrayed, which can also be found in the *Phenomenology of Spirit* (cf. GW 9, 233), Hegel did not take into account Kant's philosophical foundation for the right to property.

13. J.G. Fichte, *Das System der Sittenlehre nach den Prinzipien der Wissenschaftslehre,* Second Main Section, § 13, in J.G. Fichte, *Sämtliche Werke,* ed. by J.H. Fichte. vol. IV (Berline: Veit, 1845–1846; reprint Berlin: de Gruyter, 1965), p. 156.

14. Inasfar as "good" is a positive, affirmative determination, every voluntary affirmation of a determination of the will (purpose) appears to be "good." Cf. 4, 372: "Evil has the capability within itself to be able to be presented as good because the good has merely the determination of being affirmative with regard to the will—because it only has the form of an identity of understanding."

15. Udo Rameil, "Sittliches Sein und Subjektivität. Zur Genese des Begriffs der Sittlichkeit in Hegels Rechtsphilosophie," *Hegel-Studien* 16 (981), pp. 129 ff; L. de Vos, "Die Logik der Hegelschen Rechtsphilosophie," *Hegel-Studien* 16 (1981), pp. 107 ff. Concerning the logical categories in Hegel's critique upon the concept "ought to," see B. Bitsch. *Sollenskritik und Moralitätskritik bei G.W.F. Hegel* (Bonn; Bouvier, 1977)

16. Cf. on the point my discussion with Tugendhat cited in footnote 1.

17. One must, however, compare this with the continuation of this statement in Hotho's lecture notes: "one's own conscience, which would oppose the ethical substance, has disappeared; subjectivity no longer wishes the arbitrary choice of determining, but has rather united itself with objectivity and has determined and created this as its ownmost truth" (3, 496).

18. In comparison to the classical tradition of the concept of citizen, Hegel paid little attention to the determination of the individual as the citizen of a state. Only in the Remarks to § 169, *"en passant"* as it were, is the following comment made: "The isolated individual, so far as his duties are concerned, is in subjection; but as a member of civil society he finds in fulfilling his duties toward civil society the protection of his person and property, regard for his private welfare, the satisfaction of the depths of his being, the consciousness and feeling of himself as a member of the whole; and, insofar as he completely fulfills his duties by performing tasks and services for the state, he is upheld and preserved" (VII, 409). Cf. regarding this distinction from that of a citizen ("bourgeois") in civil society (as well as from the concepts of person, subject, human being, etc.), Hegel's Remarks on § 19 in the Philosophy of Right.

19. "Cultural community" inasfar as the state fulfills itself in the products and activities of the absolute spirit: art, religion, and philosophy.

20. Regarding ethical freedom as freedom from one's own desire for self-preservation, cf. my "Zum Freiheitsbegriff der praktischen Philosophie Hegels in Jena," in: *Hegel in Jena,* ed. by D. Henrich and K. Düsing, *Hegel-Studien,* Beiheft 20 (1980), pp. 217–228.

21. By means of the participation of royal power and the government in legislation (§ 300); the appointment of delegates by "societies, communities and corporations" (§ 302) instead of their being elected by "atomistically isolated" citizens; and the crown's right of appointment ("delegates called by power of the crown").

22. A. Peperzak, "Hegels Pflichten und Tugendlehre" forthcoming in *Hegel-Studien*, vol. 17 comes to the same estimation of Hegel's criticism of morality.

23. Cf. my "Intersubjektivität, Recht and Staat in Hegel's 'Grundlinien der Philosophie des Rechts," in: D. Henrich and R.P. Horstmann, eds., *Hegels Philosophie des Rechts,* Veröffentlichungen der Internationalen Hegel-Vereinigung, vol. 11 (Stuttgart: Klett, 1982), pp. 255 ff.

24. Cf. Tugendhat (op. cit.), pp. 31, 47, 351.

25. This has been noted especially by H. Heimsoeth, "Politik und Moral in Hegels Geschichtsphilosophie," in: Hemisoeth, *Studien zur Philosophiegeschichte* (Köln: Universitätsverlage, 1961), pp. 40 ff.

26. One of the most important problems is dealt with by K. Hartmann, "Moralitätat und Konkretes Allgemeines," *Archiv für Geschichte der Philosophie* 60 (1978), pp. 314–324.

HEGEL'S THEORY OF POLITICAL ACTION

by

ERROL E. HARRIS

"Men do not understand how what is at variance with itself agrees with itself—a harmony of opposed tensions, like that of the bow and the lyre'.
Heraclitus (Frag. 51)

The harmony of opposed tensions that is the pervading theme of Hegel's philosophy is the concurrent and alternating objectification of the subjective and subjectification of the objective. The real and the truth is the whole, the Absolute.[1] But the absolute is the Idea, its wholeness can be fulfilled only in the subjectivity of absolute self-consciousness; yet that again is self-complete only as totally self-differentiated, specified, and objectified. This is the comprehensive explanation of what occurs at every stage of its dialectical development. For example: soul is always embodied; idea is always externalized, actualized in self-specified prolificity; subjectivity is always objectified. And this self-external, embodied objectivity, having the Idea immanent in it, always tends unrestrainedly to become aware of itself, to realize itself in subjective self-awareness. Only if we understand this harmony of opposite tensions in which what is opposed to itself agrees with itself, can we understand Hegel's theory of action in general and the concept of political action in particular.

I

The key to the whole of Hegel's system is the Logic, and it sets the pattern for every other philosophical science, so we must seek in the Logic for the principle of explanation of the *Geistesphilosophie* and the *Rechtsphilosophie*. There we find set out in detail the principle of the identity of opposites, as the principle

157

of the dialectic, which is "the principle of all movement, all life and all activity in the actual world."[2] In that statement we have in a nutshell Hegel's theory of action.

The dialectic, however, is the eternal activity of self-realization of absolute Spirit—the whole that is the truth—and that activity is one of self-specification, or of objectification, in which the externalized elements are distinguished one from another and, in their endeavor to maintain themselves, first become opposed to one another, and then their opposition is *aufgehoben* in the harmonious unity of their interrelation in the self-conscious whole of which they are necessary moments; so that the Heraclitean principle is ubiquitously exemplified.

The externality of being-in-itself is thus internalized to being-for-itself, and that as a whole is explicated in the opposed yet mutually indispensable correlations of Essence, which, as Actuality, is led back to the subjectivity of the Concept. Concept, however, is not merely subjective but is also objective, in the categories of Mechanism, Chemism, and Teleology, where it is brought back to objectified subjectivity as Idea. Here it is life, cognitive (subjective) and volitional (objective), and so becomes absolute. Subjective concept in its fulfillment is objective knowledge of an actuality that comes to further fruition in the active realization of subjectively conceived ends, and this takes place in the form of life that is both cognitive and active through volition. Volition (reaction) is thus the objectification of subjective concept as cognized, and cognized by a living being that is an object in the actual world of Nature.

Hence the truth of the absolute Idea is Nature, for Nature is its self-objectification "in the form of other-being" or self-externality. Nature is the utterance (*Äusserung*) of the Idea, which is throughout immanent in it, and, through the natural process, from physical and chemical action to organic life, returns to subjectivity and inwardizes itself as the feeling soul, the germ of self-conscious Spirit.

Once more, Spirit, subjectivized Nature, becomes conscious of itself only to express itself through appetite, generating its self-recognition in its other; and develops its subjective self-awareness in theoretical knowledge only by translating its self-consciousness into practice, the reflective, deliberate, desiring activity of rational conduct. Thus subjective spirit is objectified; and, as it can be subjectively self-conscious only through the recognition of itself in the self-consciousness of others, theoretical mind is from the beginning social, it is throughout other-directed, and the practical life in which it objectifies itself is, from its very initiation, in conflict with and opposition to other conscious beings, and then in mutual recognition and cooperation, as social action. Its objectification, therefore, is a social order, and action properly so called is always social action. As this culminates in institutional organization, it becomes political action, or to express the theory in Hegelian terms, it is sublated (*aufgehoben*) in political action.

II

The Hegelian dialectic is necessarily and inevitably set out serially as successive phases in the concretion of Idea. This consecutive structure is one of its necessary aspects (or moments). But the Idea is essentially a whole, eternally one; and though it is also eternally active and perpetually in process of self-realization (what is precisely its self-objectification) it is also essentially and eternally self-realized. This, Hegel states explicitly towards the end of the Logic (*Enz*, § § 212, 237).

Accordingly, the theoretical and practical, the subjective and objective moments are not simply consecutive but are concurrent, always mutually interdependent; and objectification not merely presupposes the subjective but also actualizes it (as speech actualizes thought[3]), while without the subjective aspect the objective lacks its essential nature. Action, therefore, the utterance or objectification of consciousness, is as necessary to its being as the subjective content is to the action.

Hegel never loses sight of this interdependence, even if he does not always make it obvious in treating the subjective aspect. In his account of Soul, in the Anthropology of the *Geistesphilosophie,* he constantly insists upon the necessity of its embodiment and explains the phases of its development in terms of its outward manifestations. Elsewhere he emphasizes similarly the indispensability of *Gestaltung*—the giving of external shape—to the Concept. It is clear also that the emergence of self-consciousness is dependent upon (is in fact identical with) the conflict of persons, and this is the outcome of appetite, which is at once the externalization of the consciousness of lack and of an other or not-self, that is wanting. It is thus an awareness of a contradiction in the self and its satisfaction is the internalization, or consumption (the enjoyment), of the object. All this is at the same time overt behaviour, i.e., the activity of overcoming and appropriating the object. Likewise the structure of society is the objective self-manifestation of a morality that is rooted in practical feeling and impulse, at once subjective and objectively expressed, as well as illuminated implicitly by reflection and reason. There is more to be said of all this below. First let us take note of its logical basis.

III

The dialectical framwork consists of the two contrasting moments of the Absolute, its universality or unity and its particularity or diversity, and the identity of these moments in and through their opposition, its concrete individuality or wholeness. The first aspect is the whole in its simple immediacy, the second is its self-diremption or specific differentiation, and the third is the explicit identification of the two, in which self is at home with itself in its other.

Generally speaking the second or middle stage is that of objectification. In the Logic, the Doctrine of Essence holds this position, though Hegel there prefers the term *Gesetztsein* (positedness) to objectivity. The categories of immediacy, which, in Being, passed over one into another, here are posited in their interrelation and reflected into each other, as he says:

> In Being everything is immediate, in Essence, on the other hand, everything is relative. *(Enz, § 111, Zusatz)*

Of course, Being is also in a sense objective, but in its sheer immediacy both objectivity and subjectivity are only implicit (*an sich*). The first becomes fully explicit only in Nature and the second only in Mind (*Geist*). The first explication of this implicitness is its *Gesetztsein* in Essence where the quasi-Kantian categories of objectivity are set out.

The dialectic, however, moves through wheels within wheels, not only in its consecutive triads, but also in its major cycles, and the wider relationships are recapitulated in the lesser ones and the earlier in the later. Thus when we come to the Doctrine of the Concept (which is essentially what Logic is)—the union of Being and Essence in explicit self-awareness—the subjective concept (in effect, judgement efflorescing into syllogism or inference) is objectified in the categories of the physical and organic world which culminate as teleology. Teleology, etymologically, is the principle of realization of an end, but genuine teleology is recognized by Hegel as holism, the principle of the totality (or order) by which the parts are determined both in their essential nature and in their mutual relationships. It is the principle by which the ideal (whole) becomes real (thus the principle of Idealism). It is the objectification of the subjective aim (*der Zweck*); so it is the category of purpose and the spring of action. Its realization is that identity of subject and object that is the Idea (or ideal) manifesting itself as life and functioning as cognition and volition—once more action, objectifying the subjective self-awareness of the prior moments (*aufgehoben* within it) as concept and idea.

Life here is treated as a logical category, a thought-determination or *Denkbestimmung*. It is, however, also a natural form and Nature is the Idea in the form or phase of other-being—of self-externality—the objectified Idea. Life is actualized as organism through which the whole of nature is, as it were, focused in the organic relationship of the living being with its environment, and is sublimated as feeling. This is the immediate form of spirit or mind.

In the philosophy of spirit, these logical relationships are repeated on a more concrete level. The second stage of the major triad is that of objective spirit, at which the subjective moment is actualized in external self-manifestation. It is uttered or acted out. But the same relationships are traceable also on the subjective side. Here feeling as primitive sentience is immediate, and properly speaking neither subjective nor objective, although it is always and necessarily embodied and so has external form. But in it the distinction is not yet made between subject and object. It is made first on the level of consciousness, which is the phase of self-differentiation—as Hegel says, the stage of appearance, of correlation and reflection.[4] It is at this level that the world *appears* to the subject as an external object, marking, in the sphere of subjective spirit, the moment of objectification. The object presents itself as external other, though its content is wholly derived from the earlier phase of sentience, for in the realm of spirit the prior phase is always object to the posterior. In this way the identity of subject and object is preserved, and the distinction is made *within* experience. It is a self-diremption. In Fichtean terms, the self by its own activity posits a not-self as its other and encounters its object as an *Anstoss*, a check or opposition to itself.

This opposition develops, on the one hand, as sense-perception (in which the external object appears) and understanding, which distinguishes and relates the appearances, and, on the other hand, as appetite, the sense of deficiency and the inner contradiction consequent upon it, which arise from the extrusion of the other from the self. The self, in effect, claims the other as its own, while it feels it to be opposed to itself. At the same time it finds itself in its object or other, and this in more ways than one. First, the object is the prior phase of itself; second, it is objectified by the very projection into it of the principles of organization and unity (the Kantian categories that are the principles of objective knowledge) that reflect the self-identify and activity of the subject (*qua* synthetic unity of apperception); third, the object (primarily sentience, which is nature internalized—*erinnert*) is organic as well as inorganic and so presents itself also in the guise of other living beings. Thus the other, whether nonliving or living, not only opposes the self, as external to and limiting it, but also contradicts itself, for it is at the same time dependent on and constituted by the self. Such contradictions within both self and other, as well as between them, are insufferable and engender the impulse to remove them—they must be *aufgehoben*, and as always the dialectical principle reveals itself as the spring of action: *"das Prinzip aller Bewegung, alles lebens, aller Betätigung in der Wirklichkeit."*

So arises the struggle for recognition, first for the destruction of the other, its assimilation, extinction and annulment. But as this proves self-frustrating, in that the other is in fact identical with the self, the opposition issues first in dominance over, and finally in equal recognition of, the other. This is the famous master-slave sequence of the *Phenomenology*, and its satisfactory outcome can only be mutual recognition of, and respect for, persons as equals, for the other is actually the self in its other-being. They are in truth identical and each can be fulfilled only so far as the other is also fulfilled. It is the slave who develops all the satisfying and self-fulfilling activities claimed by the master, and it is only when both exert themselves equally in their common interest that proper fulfillment is achieved.

Action here, both as conflict and as cooperation, is the expression of a subjective want or inner contradiction prompted by the self-differentiation that is effected in consciousness by the perceptive understanding. It is a further phase of objectification issuing in the recognition of, and interaction with, persons. But the subjective moment is not temporally prior to the objective, or the passive earlier than the active. They are concurrent and mutually instrumental.

With this recognition of self in other, the subjectification of the object and the consequent objectification of self, self-consciousness is actualized and the level of reason is attained. At the same time, the foundation of morality has been laid, which is rooted in the recognition of persons and is the fruit of rational reflection upon their mutual relations and interaction.

Reason is the proper and genuine form of self-conscious spirit and issues, on the theoretical side, as cognition, or knowledge of the truth, through the media of the subjective faculties of mind, intuition, representation (*Vorstellung*), and thinking. On the practical side, it expresses itself as practical feeling (or moral sense), desire (the rational quest for self-satisfaction) and choice (deliberate decision), and, in sum, the pursuit of happiness.

Practical feeling is not mere instinctive impulse, which belongs to the merely conscious (not yet self-conscious) phase. It is the correlate of intuition, which is an immediate apprehension of things in their mutual relations, prior to analysis. It is the intuition of fitness and unfitness to which modern writers on ethics refer when they speak of what we intuitively feel to be right. And though its primary immediate forms are pleasure and displeasure, it always has moral overtones and might more suitably be called approval and disapproval (of which it is at least the basis). Hegel distinguishes the feelings as such, joy, contentment, gaiety, fear, terror, etc., as contentless, from the moral feelings of complacency, shame and remorse, as those distinguished by their content. But clearly no feeling has significance apart from its object, which must be cognized to be distinguishable. Thus theory and practice are interdependent and concurrent.

This is even more apparent in the case of desire and choice, which obviously depend upon the cognition and theoretical assessment of the object, on comparison and judgements both of fact and of preference. And happiness, as the general feeling of contentment satisfying the self as a whole, implies not only a theoretical judgement of what constitutes happiness, but, in practice, the perception of the harmonious nature of what one calls one's lot, in which satisfaction is taken. Theory and practice are therefore inextricably interwoven, the inner and outer aspects of experience being mutually indispensable.

For this reason it is not sufficient merely to feel nor simply to intend. Feeling and actions to be significant must be expressed in action. In the *Logic*, when he is commenting on the category of inner and outer (under "Essence"), Hegel inveighs against claims to virtue on the ground of good intentions alone, against the pretense that only the inner conception matters, the claim that the man with high ideals, the poet or painter with lofty notions, who never carry them out into comparable actions and products, may nevertheless pride themselves on their high-mindedness.[5] The inner must be externalized, objectified (*äussert*) if it is to count as real.

The activity of the subject is the urge to satisfy its desires, the translation of subjective purposes into objective reality.[6] As before, action is objectification of the subjective content. But practical feeling and its developed forms, while incident to action, remain subjective. They pertain to the individual self and are in principle selfish, contingent, and arbitrary. For this reason, Hegel protests against the elevation, in ethical theory, of feeling above duty and law; or, what amounts to the same thing, contempt of intelligence and reason as superfluous and ineffectual in morality and religion. Volition, we have seen, is the objectification of cognition, and it is now revealed as identical with intelligence; but purely personal and selfish volition is abortive and self-defeating, because, as we have also seen, the recognition and self-awareness of the person is concomitant with and dependent upon the recognition of other persons. Accordingly, inclinations and impulses, which in the nature of the case come into mutual conflict even in the private life of the individual, so that he must choose between them and reduce them to order (subject to some universal and overriding end) in order to attain happiness, come into conflict, further, with the desires and interests of other persons, in conjunction with whom private aims have to be pursued.

IV

It follows that the objectification of subjective purposes is only possible in concert with others and must take the form of social action. Only thus can the aim and content of will be truly universal; for because of the interdependence of persons, self-centered desire is bound to be frustrated by conflicts that arise in the absence of social regulation. The particular will can only be satisfactorily effective, therefore, as a factor in the common, general, or universal will. Thus objective spirit is a structured society and Plato's insight was unerring when, in the *Republic*, he referred us to the larger letters of the *polis* for the discovery of justice.

Self-consciousness, the self-determining subject or the self-differentiating universal (all different ways of expressing the same thing) is the formal definition of free agency. But this self-differentiation is in principle self-objectification. It cannot therefore be merely subjective and contingent; it is not merely natural or biological; hence even the Greeks, who held it to depend on birth, or on education, or subjective attitude (Stoicism) merely, failed to grasp it in its genuine form. It is attainable only in and through social and political organization, so that freedom—even moral freedom—is, in the last resort, political action. This is the objectification of subjective spirit; but, as we shall find, it is not, and should never be, merely, one-sidedly, objective. It is in its truth (or concept) both objective and subjective in one.

As the objectification of the subjective concept issues in teleological or purposive activity, and cognition in the realized idea objectifies itself in volition, so, subjective spirit, expressing its theoretical awareness of the world in practical activity, is objectified in society and the institutional order of the state. As Nature is the Idea externalized, and the forms of nature sublated in organism are *aufgehoben* in sentience and subjective spirit, so all of this is once more *aufgehoben* in objective spirit. So Hegel writes:

Objective spirit is the absolute Idea, but only existing implicitly. (Enz. § 483)

It is with this presupposition that he says of the state, in the introduction to the *Philosophy of History*,[7] that it is the divine Idea as it exists on earth, and that he calls social morality "a second nature"[8]—it is the second externalization of the divine Idea. But as it *exists*, the Idea is only implicit in the state, because it "rests on a basis of finitude" and is externally manifest; for the absolute Idea is fully realized only as the subjectivized object, as absolute Spirit, in art and religion and the pure thought of philosophical comprehension and insight. But none of these can exist or be elaborated in "external appearance" except in an organized social setting.[9]

In the major triad of Objective Spirit, the general rule mentioned earlier, which so far has always held good, seems to have been reversed: i.e., that the dialectical antithesis represents the phase of externalization. Whether inadvertently or deliberately, Hegel has put into the second main division the subjective aspect of social regulation and has begun with the objective. It is clear that abstract legal right, taken in its positive guise (what the jurists call "positive law"), and the morality of conscience (*Moralität*) are opposite but mutually complementary and necessary aspects of social order; but even if one were to interpret the former as the immediate form of regulation and the latter as the mediate or reflective (as indeed they are), it would be difficult to argue that conscience is the *objective* embodiment of the moral law, as opposed to a more subjective legal structure of right. The reverse is obviously the case.

When we come to the union of these two aspects in *Sittlichkeit* (social custom), however, objectivity is much more evident, and the second subdivision, bourgeois society, is definitely the phase of external action and dispersion of activity, in contrast to the community and relative internality of the first, the family. And it is in the bourgeois (or civic) society that the first moment in the larger division—the moment of abstract law, of property rights, contract, tort and crime—is most evidently sublated. But I do not wish to concern myself here with the details of the dialectical structure, so much as with certain genral features of Hegel's theory determining the nature of political action.

Freedom is activity wholly self-determined and this has been identified with self-awareness, as the self-specifying universal. It is the true infinity and its appropriate logical category is *Fürsichsein*. For Hegel, political activity, constituting society and the state (for these exist only in social and political practice) is the actualization of freedom. The self-specifying (or concrete) universal, however, is organized system, in which the principle of order, or wholeness, determines every detail, both as to what it is and how it is related to every other, and governs all processes of development and interaction among its parts or moments. It is this internality of relation and permeation of the whole by the universal principle that is signified by the term *Fürsichsein*, and it is what Hegel calls ideality. In so doing, he is entirely correct, for only in the self-knowledge of a conscious subject is it properly realized. In the externality (*Nebeneinandersein*) of spatiotemporal appearances it is only *an sich*, only implicit. They are governed by it in principle, but express and represent it only *in posse*. But it is only to the extent that they do evince forms of order and wholeness that they actualize freedom.

In terms of human action, freedom is not merely dependent upon, but is synonymous with, rational thought. *Wer das Denken verwirft und von Freiheit spricht, weiss nicht was er redet.* [10] We have already seen that it involves order and regulation of impulse and desire in the pursuit of happiness, and that this again implies accommodation between the interests of self and others. In short, freedom and social order coincide; social anarchy and uncontrolled caprice is the destruction of freedom, it is the Hobbesian state of nature, mere impotence, the negation of action.

The notion that freedom is to be found by the individual in isolation and exemption from government interference is obtuse and fallacious, Thoreau notwithstanding. For the isolated individual is helpless and incapable. In infancy he (or she) cannot survive without tendance, and in adulthood can effect little deprived of the goods and services provided by society. That the benefits of these can be enjoyed (or that they can even at all be provided) without regulation is mere self-deception, which the slightest critical reflection will dispel.

Organized civil society is thus the realization of freedom, and that, without government, is impossible. It follows that political action is the objective reality of Liberty (the subjective or personal pursuit of happiness). This is true in principle as well as in fact, but short of the absolute ideal is a matter of degree. Therefore, in practice, liberty is not always, if ever, fully realized. Here, however we are dealing with the essential principles of social organization. We shall attend presently to its practical failures.

The point to be made is that social organization culminates in the constitution of the state, which unifies a nation and give expression to the national spirit. The institutions of government comprise the sphere of political action *par excellence,* but they cannot be treated in isolation from the other aspects and institutions of society, over which they preside, which are represented in them, and the realization of whose purposes they insure. This is just because the essence of civilized life is social organization, and because that culminates in the state, which unifies the whole society, the state "is the Idea as it exists on earth."

The institutions of government, however, while they epitomize the whole, and, in fact for that reason, may not be divorced from civil society and the family, which are the complementary institutions as well as aspects and consecutive developmental phases of civilized life. The family embodies the natural ties and feelings of kinship and close-knit community, but its wants and the means of its livelihood can be supplied only in wider relationships, in a society of persons performing different and interdependent functions in production, industry, distribution, and exchange. This is the economic aspect of society (*die Bürgerliche Geselschaft*), which is more individualistic and contains looser associations. The higgling of the market and the "cash nexus" in large measure determine its relationships. While the family bonds are love and consanquinity, the ties in civil society are rights, contracts, services, and the interplay of trades and professions. It requires its own peculiar forms of order and regulation, incorporations, administration of law, and policing. But these activities that are primarily self-seeking, pursuing individual or specialized corporate interests, can be concerted and unified in the common interest (without which they tend to conflict and to frustrate one another) only by a universal governing authority with legislative and executive powers. Such authority is embodied in the constitution of the state, which must provide for the representation of estates (*Stände*) and the popular interests, so as to express a general or common will aimed at a common interest; and this interest is primarily the universal interest .in orderly and harmonious government, which makes possible the unhampered pursuit of desired ends.

It is only as organized that the popular will can effectively govern; disorganized the people are a mere mob, whose activity, so far from government, constitutes the breakdown of law and order. But its organized expression constitutes the state whose Constitution *is* the objectification of the popular will. As organized action the state is, therefore, the Concept actualized in political form.

The ultimate unity of political authority is personified in the head of State—in Hegel's eyes, the constitutional monarch—for the state is a corporate person and its acts can be finalized only by the personal authorization of the royal (or, if one prefers, presidential) seal. This is the ultimate political act, and while it is a royal or presidential act, it is also an act of parliament, and it is by that same token an act of the whole people as socially and politically organized. Organization is the constitution of one out of many, a unification of differences. The head of the state personates and embodies the aspect of unity; the legislature represents the elements of diversity, and together they constitute the political whole.

All political action is thus action on behalf, and on the authority, of this public organization or whole, *die Verfassung*, the constitution of government, expressing and seeking to realize common ends of a common will and interest. It is the General Will envisaged by Rousseau, not merely the will of the individual as exercised in the bourgeois society, but that will as modified and corrected, regulated and constrained, by the requirements of the welfare and harmony of the whole organized society, without which no individual will can attain its proper end, or shape itself, as Hegel would say, according to its concept, which is rational self-determination. Thus the general will and the particular will must ultimately coincide in the realization of freedom, through its objectification in the institutions of government.

V

The "realistic" and cynical reaction to all this is that it is romantic idealistic nonsense descriptive of some cloud-cuckoo land remote from poltical reality. Everybody must confess, and Hegel would be the first to admit, that actual states do not, in full measure, actualize the conditions of freedom. Were we not told at the outset that objective Spirit is the absolute Idea only *an sich,* so far as it in the realm of the finite? The mark of finitude is defect and incident upon defect is evil. Finitude characterizes every incomplete phase of self-differentiation of the Idea, and deficiency and inadequacy signify immaturity or corruption. Anything short of the absolute whole will be to some extent subject to these. And that there should be phases short of the whole is inevitable, for without them the whole would be a mere empty abstraction. It would not be self-differentiated and the differences are as necessary to it as is its unity, for they are precisely what it unifies. The reality of evil is, therefore, unavoidable. Moreover, we have seen that the aspect of differentiation is that of objectification, and that the state is freedom *objectified.*

The inner aspect of political action is morality—the personal self-regulation of conduct—and while that is admittedly the pursuit of good and the expression of the rational will, nobody pretends that necessarily and of itself it excludes vice or obviates wickedness. Its categorical imperative is directed precisely against temptation and weakness, and it fails to just that extent that the will it animates is finite and merely instinctive. So too its objectification in the institutions of social and political life is subject to corruption and the degree of its finitude is the measure of its failure.

In this objectification therefore we are bound to find flaws. Actual, historical states will realize human freedom only in some degree, according to historical circumstances, the stage of civilized development reached or the exigencies of the historical period. Further, the political process, political activity within the society, never, in the very nature of the case, runs smoothly. If it did there would be no need for the enforcement of law. Nor is it always (if ever) wholly successful in generating a truly general will or in transmitting faithfully or transforming completely selfish aims to common interests. Accordingly, the state will always be only an imperfect actualization of freedom.

Yet all forms and degrees of failure are possible only as defects and incidents of a structure of organized activity, which precisely is, and is designed to be, the realization of the free, rational will. We cannot speak of political freedom except in the context of ordered, civilized living; and it is only to the extent that rationally ordered civilized life breaks down, is corrupted or misguided, that oppression occurs and liberty is lost. If the state were not, in fact, the objective and institutional form of free activity, maladministration could never thwart its expression. But misgovernment is still government, and its correction is good government, not anarchy. For without social order there is no possibility of freedom and Thoreau's ideal is a fallacious, abstract and self-contradictory fantasy. The failure of the state to embody the freedom of its citizens, when it occurs, is but *corruptio optimi,* and that alone is the source and origin of misgovernment and oppression.

Criticism may further be offered on the lines that Hegel's account of the state, while it might be more or less applicable to Western democracies, cannot account for dictatorships either of the Right or of the Left. This would be a strange cavil in any age when Hegel has been accused of fathering both Marxist communism and Nazi authoritariansim. But such strictures are so loosely grounded in the text as to be beneath the need for refutation. One could argue, as above, that regimes like the Soviet or Fascist dictatorships are modifications of political organization conditioned by the contingent circumstances of history, contingencies for which Hegel's theory makes room. Or one might respond with an *argumentum ad hominem* and charge that the Russian Union of Soviet Republics as little conforms to Marxist doctrine (for example, that of the withering away of the state) as it does to Hegelian. But such answers would be superficial. If we penetrate a little below the surface, we shall find a better defense.

In the Soviet Union, as well as in military and fascist dictatorships, the family persists as the natural basis of society. Without it, in fact, apart from some form of family association, the nation (and, indeed, the race of men as such) would not survive. In these regimes, again, as in any civilized society, there is economic order based on wants, services, the division of labor, and the specialization of functions. Even if this order is centrally planned (as in socialistic systems), it still requires some form of incorporation, whether as cooperatives, communal farms, or (as in fascist regimes) corporations and syndicates; and it requires administrative regulation. Further, all of this is directed by a supreme governmental structure constituted formally—a Chamber of Corporations, a Supreme Soviet, an executive council, however appointed or elected—and presided over, whether only ceremonially or in executive efficacy, but a titular head of state.

If these political structures operate so as in greater or lesser degree to restrict and repress legitimate human rights, it is nevertheless true that no dictatorship can be so absolute and oppressive as to nullify human freedom altogether. Political power, however tyrannous, is never that of one person, or even of a few, and is never sheerly physical force. Socrates reminded Thrasymachus that even among thieves there must be some trust and honesty.[11] And Hobbes wrote:

> Nature hath made men so equal in faculties of body and mind; (that) . . . when all is reckoned together, the difference between man, and man, is not so considerable, as that one man can thereupon claim to himself any benefit. . . . For as to the strength of body, the weakest has strength enough to kill the strongest either by secret machination, or by confederacy with others, that are in the same danger as himself. (*Leviathan, Ch. XIII*)

and Rousseas declared that

> the stronger is never strong enough to remain always the master unless he can transform force into right and obedience into duty. (*Social Contract, Ch. III*)

In the last resort, political power is always bestowed upon the agencies of government by the people who are themselves its subjects, for unless the majority of the populace acquiesce, and unless some considerable number of them approve of the way in which power is exercised, the authority of the governing body will not be recognized, it will be deprived of its weapons, which are provided and wielded only by its own subjects; thus its power will melt away "thaw and resolve itself into a dew," like snow in the midsummer sun.

It is always true, then, as Hegel contends, that political action is the objectification of freedom. For it is the organization of concerted social activity to encompass those ends, without which no freedom at all, not even its rudiments, could be actualized. Hegel was not merely describing the form of political organization that he thought most effective in nineteenth century Europe. Nor was he trying to devise a contemporary form of Utopia. He was analyzing out the presuppositions and underlying principles of civilized living, as was Aristotle, to whose influence Hegel's theory owes much. And Aristotle also distinguishes in the *polis* the *aufgehobene* heritage of its earlier phases—the family, the village community and the state, which "comes into existence for the sake of mere life, and remains in existence for the sake of the good life." Hegel translates this formula into modern terms and clothes it in modern dress. But neither he nor Aristotle is writing history or anthropology. Both are striving to develop a philosophical analysis of political action.

VI

This is by no means to say that Aristotle (or, for that matter, Plato) and least of all Hegel neglected or disregarded history—quite to the contrary. Nothing written above should be taken to imply that in Hegel's theory the structure of the state is deducible a priori from logical principles. The whole Hegelian dialectic is the rejection and repudiation of just such a priori deduction, and Hegel's logic is not a logic of formal deduction at all, but of self-specification of system, the self-differentiation of organic wholeness, which is an entirely different matter. In that there is, of course, an element (or moment) of necessity, for the whole is immanent throughout and the principle of organization governs the structure of the constituent parts as well as the succession of developmental phases. But just because the concreteness of the whole requires radical differentiation, it necessarily involves the opposite moment of finitude and contingency. Accordingly, the self-objectification of subjective freedom, while in it all logical and natural categories are *aufgehoben*, taking the form, as it does, of social structure, itself involves a temporal and developmental process, which is the process of history.

Hegel was deeply convinced that only in and as history were the shapes (*Gestaltungen*) and phases of consciousness actualized. Not only social but also philosophical consciousness is (for him) historically conditioned, but neither is thereby released from the dialectic that permeates history itself. For history is nothing else but the objectification of subjective spirit as it expresses itself in social action and in the development through time of political forms, which display *seriatim* its interdependent moments. So we discover in history the succession of tribalism, despotism and constitutionalism, autocracy, aristocracy and democracy, successive periods giving expression to successive political forms objectifying different and dialectically related political ideas. What has already been said of political failure and corruption accounts for the aberrations, reversions, and degeneracies that history also discloses. Spirit in actualizing itself cannot elude the exigencies and divergences of finite specificities. Contingency is an inevitable incident of the finite and the Absolute specifies itself in finite forms, hence contingency is an ineluctable moment of its self-realization. In the words of Spinoza, God, or Substance, does not lack material for the creation of every degree of perfection from the highest to the lowest; and history, for Hegel, is the march of God upon earth—that is, the finite specifications of absolute spirit as they occur in time in historically conditioned sociopolitical forms.

Hegel's theory of the state and of political action is thus just as much a reflection upon history as it is the application of logical and dialectical principles—for what is his own logic but the fruit of reflection upon common experience, scientific theorizing, moral deliberation, religious contemplation, and the whole history not only of these but of philosophy itself?

NOTES

1. Cf. *Phänomenologie des Geistes,* Preface.
2. *Enzyklopädie,* § 81, *Zusatz: "Das Dialektische ... ist ... überhaupt das Prinzip aller Bewegung, alles Lebens und aller Betätigung in der Wirklichkeit."*
3. Cf. *Enzyklopädie,* § 459.
4. Cf. *Enzyklopädie,* § 413.
5. Cf. *Enzyklopädie,* § 140, *Zusatz.*
6. Cf. *Enzyklopädie,* § 475.
7. Cf. H.B. Nisbet's translation (Cambridge University Press, 1975), p. 95.
8. Cf. *Rechtsphilosophie,* § 4, and *Lectures on the Philosophy of World History,* Introduction.
9. Cf. *Lectures on the Philosophy of World History, Ibid.*
10. Vorlesungen *über die Geschichte der Philosophie,* III, 2, Kap. 2,C,c. Translation by E.S. Haldane and F.H. Simson (London, 1968), vol. III p. 402: "...he who casts thought aside and speaks of freedom knows not what he is talking of."
11. Cf. Plato, *Republic,* I, 351c.

aside and speaks of freedom knows not what he is talking of."
11.   Cf. Plato, *Republic,* I, 351c.

FREEDOM AS INTERACTION:
HEGEL'S RESOLUTION
TO THE DILEMMA OF LIBERAL THEORY

by
RICHARD DIEN WINFIELD

The problem of making freedom the principle of right has dominated practical philosophy ever since the legitimacy of prescribed forms of justice was called into question by the demand that individuals be beholden only to what issues from their own consent. The authority of set virtues, given means of conduct, and any fixed essence of goodness has crumbled before this standpoint of the autonomous will. It has set aside those theories conceiving justice as *praxis*, that is, as conduct that is valid in virtue of embodying predetermined universal modes of action. In their place, it has introduced the problem of establishing what justice is, not by contemplating those given forms that action ought to realize, but by considering what relations emerge from the determining of the will itself. Modern practical philosophy has adopted this framework, where the will stands as the privileged determiner out of which all right is to be derived, and has accordingly set itself the task of working out a theory of justice whose principle is freedom.

Paradoxically, this very attempt to make freedom the principle of valid practical affairs has foundered precisely because taking freedom as a principle contradicts the basic structure of freedom itself.

It does so simply because making the free will a principle from which justice is derived turns into something that determines what is other than itself. To be self-determining, however, the free will must determine its own self and not what is its other. When the will gets treated as a principle, it is rendered a determiner whose character is given prior to its act of determination, and whose act determines something else that is therefore not self-determined, but determined by what is prior to and other than it. By contrast, if the will is to be self-determining, then its own character can not be given prior to its act, but must be determined through it. Consequently, what it determines will be self-determined, for it is nothing other than its own act, that is, itself.

The importance of these elusive contrasts between positing and self-determination is brought into focus when one grasps the universal, particular and individual dimensions of autonomous willing, which together comprise the structure of individuality basic to freedom.[1]

To begin with, the will possesses a dimension of universality to the degree that it is never bound to any particular content, but is always free to will something else and then withdraw itself from that concept to give itself another. Instead of being limited to any specific set of aims, the will rather defines itself by always exhibiting but one particualr *instance* of its self-determination in whatever content it wills. If, on the contrary, the will's character were defined by any specific set of ends, then it would no longer be a self-determining, free agency, but a capacity externally determined by a content other than itself.

Although the quality of universality, of being unrestricted to any particular determination, thus underlies each and every example of willing, it forms only a single component of the will's structure. By itself, this universal dimension comprises as purely negative freedom to which the will cannot be reduced without contradicting its self-determining character. For if the will be defined only in terms of its universality, as a mere capacity to be unbeholden to all given content, then it has no particular content of its own whereby it could actually be self-*determining*.

To be a will, agency cannot just remain unbound to any given determination; it must will *something* and thereby bring a dimension of particularity to its universality. Accordingly, the will has the further aspect of particularity in that, in order to determine itself, it must go beyond its negative freedom and actually give itself a specific content. In so doing, the will does not lose its universal character and become something other than itself. Rather, because the will must will to be what it is, and to will it must will something, the willing of a specific content does not cancel the will's autonomy, but realized it instead. It does so by providing the will not just with determination, but with its own *particularity*, in as much as in willing something the will determines itself in one instance of its general free agency.

In virtue of this component of particularity, it is evident that the will cannot be conceived as a mere faculty or capacity that can be defined prior to and independently of its actual willing of something. Simply to be self-determining agency, the will must have particular determination as part of its essence, and thus must be conceived as actuality.

Its actuality is of a special kind, however, for it integrates both universality and particularity. On the one hand, as much as the will is unbeholden to any given content, it must no less will a particular end in order to be self-determining. On the other hand, although the will necessarily restricts itself to a particular content in willing something, it thereby remains *self*-determined rather than determined by something else precisely because what it has determined is an agency that is never bound to the particular content it has given itself, but can always cast it aside and will another. In these respects, the will combines universality and particularity in its self-determination, and thereby exhibits the further dimension of individuality that contains within it the two others.

The will is individual in this sense, that what it is is not reducible to any prior universal form or capacity, but is only to be had in its actual particularization. Only in giving itself a particular content does the will stand at one with itself, for it has its defining identity as a self-determining agency precisely by determining itself in particular fashion. Consequently, the will is concretely universal, having its general character only in the activity of giving itself a particular content that builds its own free development. As such, the free will thus wills nothing other than itself, for in its individual act, at once universal and particular, what it determines is its own self-determination.

These most rudimentary features of the free will say nothing by themselves of how its agency is actually realized.

However, they do indicate that its own self-determination will be undermined if it be made a principle out of which the forms of justice are derived. In that case, the free will is rendered a merely universal determiner, in that its character is given prior to the form of justice it determines. Since its particular act of determination here falls outside its essence, as a derivative function that adds nothing to its character, the will is stripped of the particular and individual dimensions allowing for any real self-determination. The very freedom whose primacy is here asserted thus loses all actuality precisely be being the prior principle of what it determines. Conversely, the derivative forms of justice cannot be actual realizations of freedom themselves, for they are not self-determined structures, whose essence belongs to their particular existence, but relations dependent upon the prior principle of the will for both their form and content. On both sides, the individuality of freedom is unrealized.

Despite these basic problems, the overwhelming majority of modern thinkers of freedom have ignored its individual character and fallen into the trap of treating the free will as a principle of justice.

There is, however, an alternative conception of freedom, first developed by Hegel, which gives due respect to the individual structure of the will. Although it has fallen into general disregard by both practical philosophers at large and interpreters of Hegel, this conception is well worth reconsidering for the basis it affords for developing the theory of justice today.

Not surprisingly, the importance and necessity of Hegel's concept of freedom are brought to light precisely through following what actually happens when one does attempt to make the free will the principle of valid practical relations. This, of course, is the path of traditional liberal theory, which develops its theory of justice from the postulate of the free will. By tracing the immanent logic of its inquiry, one not only sees what is wrong with the liberal tradition's conception of freedom, but what is required to conceive freedom properly. It is this examination that leads to the concept of freedom as interaction first clearly formulated by Hegel.

I

The Logic and Illogic of the Theory of Liberty

However misbegotten be the problem of making freedom the principle of justice, the problem both motivating and defining liberal theory, it is neither fortuitous nor arbitrary. It must be confronted once it is recognized that valid conduct cannot proceed from prescribed virtues, but must be self-determined, that just public authority cannot be based on a division of ruler and ruled, but must realize self-rule, that in all spheres of practical life what is valid must accord with and realize the autonomy of the will.

From this perspective, freedom must face the given reality of ethical affairs as the one unconditional principle in terms of which that reality must be structured and reconstituted in order to be just. This critical opposition, faced historically by the originators of liberal theory, immediately places self-determination in the position of a given form, out of which the valid relations of practical life are to be determined, rather than a freedom already situated in a world of its own. Although self-determination is properly at one with what it determines, here it is cast in the role of a positor, having both its specific character and existence prior to what it posits.

The ethical problem of freedom arises in terms of this conflation of self-determination and positing,[2] and in this form, it provides liberal theory with its starting point: the will conceived as a given structure, whose character stands defined prior to any actual self-determination, and whose right is to be realized as the first principle of justice.

As something given, the will is here a natural will, whose agency does not arise within any enacted practical relations, but rather precedes them all as an irreducible postulate. In other words, its autonomy exists not in virtue of any agreements or institutions, but in a state of nature that is a "natural" condition precisely by existing independently of the will's self-determination. Since the will itself exists in such a state of nature, being given rather than determined and brought into existence through willing's own act, the state of nature is logically prior to any instituted relations that could be in accord with the freedom of the will.

Further, since this natural will has its own form prior to any particular self-determination, simply by being primoridally given, it is merely universal in form. Lacking particular self-determination as part of its essence, it is not an individual structure, which is inherently actual in so far as it cannot be defined apart from its particular existence. In its given universality, the will is rather a natural *capacity* common to all individuals. As here conceived, the will is a universal faculty which all are born with and naturally possess in equal form. So it provides the canonical first proposition of liberal theory: that all men are free and equal in the state of nature.

The freedom of such a will is accordingly natural *liberty*, the mere capacity of unfettered choice that all enjoy by birth. Because the will is a given universal structure, with no element of particularity within itself, it is not only a mere faculty, but one that must choose from independently given alternatives that can alone supply it with a particular content to will. These alternatives may thus be given either by what exists externally in nature, or by separate subjective faculties, such as reason or desire. However it be supplied, the particular content that the will chooses is independently derived, rather than actually determined by the will itself.

Consequently, although the natural will has the liberty to choose whatever alternatives it wants, it is still always bound to choices that are given to it rather than determined through freedom. From the very start, then, the natural will bears the taint that it can never act with the unconditioned universality required for normativity, since its liberty is relative to the independent alternatives before it. This means at the same time that the natural will can never give itself a particular content at one with its universal form, and thereby attain the individuality of actual self-determination.

On this basis, what alone can provide the real existence of such a will is an embodiment that is external and given, yet stands as the express objectification of a will that must seek its particular content entirely outside itself. This generic realization of the natural will is accordingly a naturally appropriable property, which alone comprises the objectification of that merely universal will that can claim for its own existing self-determination nothing more than some externally given thing. Thus, the liberty all men are born with has its corresponding embodiment in a natural right to property.

This reality of liberty is as much a problem as the general predicament of choice, however, in so far as the individual identity of each natural will is something given. Because the will, as the universal natural faculty of liberty, is a capacity common to all, what individuates one agent from another must be particular desiderata extraneous to the structure of the will itself. This means that individual wills stand differentiated from one another by nature, with their universal form given particular embodiment in different subjects who face one another not through willing and in accord with its common liberty, but in a given condition where what makes each particular is unmediated by freedom. In this way, individuals, born free and equal, immediately oppose one another as independent agents, ready to exercise their separate liberty without any agreements, laws, or other acts of will concomitantly determining their interrelation. Rather, precisely because their respective particularity is something given, their immediate plurality excludes all preestablished harmony. Since each will has its particular identity not in function and in realization of the common form of willing, but as part of a given condition, the distinct individualities from which liberty gets naturally exercised are not already integrated into any system of mutual respect and peaceful coexistence.

Furthermore, because what each individual shall choose to will is a particular content supplied independently of liberty, there is nothing to prevent an unrestrained conflict between the separate volitions of the different agents. Be it given by outer circumstance, inner desire, or rational reflection, whatever content one individual wills can just as much contradict the choice of another. Even if the external alternatives, structure of desire, and reason were to offer the same options to all, the very liberty of each individual to will a given content would rule out any guarantee of harmony.

Consequently, the state of nature necessarily suffers from an endemic lack of concurrence between wills, which leaves in question each individual's ability actually to exercise their liberty and embody it in property without restraint and interference from others. As much as each individual is born free and equal with a faculty of choice generically embodied in property, the state of nature of their liberty is no less a state of war where no will or property is secure from the license of others. Therefore, the will all are born with is not only just a *faculty* of choice bound to given alternatives, but one which enjoys merely the *right* to its own liberty and property. Given the endemic war of all against all, this natural right is not a natural reality, but an imperative, lacking the force of mutual agreement that can supply right with the duty ensuring its respect.

Under these conditions, no "natural law" evident to "right reason" can overcome the insecurity of liberty by mandating rules of respect for right. For any law to command and oblige obedience, it cannot just be revealed by reason, but must issue from a will whose authority each individual has chosen to respect. A "natural" law, however, has no such author, precisely because in a state of nature there is no legitimate lawmaker, but only a plurality of individuals born free and equal. Any attempt to bestow validity upon natural law by ascribing it to a transcendent will of God can only fail, for liberty cannot be made to conform to divine commands, without relinquishing its constitutive character of being unbeholden to any content it has not chosen for itself.

Instead, the predicament of the merely universal will, of freedom taken as a principle, entails a very different course to salvage the reality of freedom and make it the basis of existing justice. This course is mandated in a twofold way:

First of all, because the externally determined particularity of each will in no way resolves itself into the common realization of liberty, the inherently individual structure of the will lacks the individual reality that could secure it actual freedom. Since, however, the given form of willing cannot provide by itself the integration of its particular content with its universal form, it requires some further agency to make the particular act of each will accord with the universal realization of willing.

To overcome the state of war natural to liberty, there must be a higher authority empowered to protect each will and its property by legislating and enforcing the unimpeached coexistence of all individual persons.

On the other hand, given the natural existence of wills and their natural right to exercise their libety, the agency mediating their plurality must issue from the consent of all, if it is not to violate the very autonomy it is called upon to protect. Thus, if the new authority is to serve the liberty that cannot actually exist without it, then all individuals in the state of nature must will it upon themselves and agree to recognize and respect its validity. Consequently, the new order, required to secure natural liberty by suppressing the license of the state of nature, can arise only through a "social contract" in which all agree to join as members of a civil society and institute a public authority ruling over it to whom they give their consent so long as it restricts itself to realizing their liberty and property.

On this basis, however, the social contract has a dual character,[3] which ultimately leaves liberal theory unable to secure freedom an institutional reality in general, as well as to distinguish between civil society and state in particular.

Because the right of person and property requiring security is itself something natural, the public authority is contractually instituted is external and ex post facto to the structure of liberty. Its governing activity does not constitute liberty, but merely preserves person and property as already given in the state of nature.

Consequently, the social contract is not just a mutual covenant between equals, securing each the power to exercise their liberty by accepting the duty of respecting that of others. In so far as the freedom herein realized is neither created by the new authority, nor specific to its institutional practice, but a liberty constituted prior to and separate from it, freedom here does not involve any participation in government. Therefore, at the same time that individuals mutually agree to join together in civil society, they each enter into an equal, nonreciprocal relation to the new authority, a relation between ruler and ruled consisting in their consent to abide by its law and government, so long as it lets them enjoy their personal liberty and private property. Here they agree to hand over the monopoly of public action to the government itself, in exchange for "civil" rights involving no more than the right to exercise their natural rights to liberty and property under the protection of public law and authority.

With legitimate public authority accordingly exercising a power distinct from the liberty of individuals, there is no political freedom to participate in self-government, but only the freedom to institute or replace the ruling regime and then retreat to those essentially prepolitical activities that the public authority allows to be pursued.

As a result, not only is freedom deprived of any political realization, but government itself is merely civil in character, and thereby indistinguishable from civil society. Instead of being a *sovereign* body *politic,* existing for the sake of its own ruling activity and thereby exercising true political self-determination, the instituted government has as its aim the liberty of person and property given to it by nature. Consequently, its rule is relative, receiving its fundamental law from elsewhere—namely, the prepolitical sphere of the state of nature. Like liberty itself, the will of public authority thus has only a formal freedom. It can not determine its own ends, like a truly sovereign state, but can only choose the given means for realizing natural right. In other words, the regime arising from social contract is not a state standing over civil society with aims of its own, but a *civil* government, administering the harmony of civil society against which it has no autonomy.

Nevertheless, as the final arbiter among persons, civil government has a will of its own no less than they do. Accordingly, its first and foremost function is legislative, determining what is publically valid, not as an embodiment of the good or of given means of conduct, but in virtue of being willed by legitimate authority as a law to be obeyed voluntarily by the consenting members of civil society. As such, the laws of justice do issue from a structure of the will, and must also be publicly proclamated since they address persons who follow them only in conscious and willful recognition of their authority.

Although this seems finally to make the free will the real principle of justice, the legislation in question is only a formal lawmaking, suffering from the same falling asunder of particular and universal that afflicts liberty in general. Instead of determining the particular statutes of law from out of its own universally valid will, civil government legitimately enacts only what is given by the "law" of nature, namely, the lawful presentation of person and property. Since its legislation is thereby limited to a merely *civil* law, whose content derives from the character of liberty found in the state of nature, the rule of civil government cannot break the will's bondage to particular determinations that are not its own.

Indeed, it is precisely this dependence upon externally given content that undermines the very power of civil government itself. In virtue of the constitutive conditions of the social contract, the standard of just rule here lies outside the positive institutions of government, in the implicit principles of natural right. As a result, there is no seat of authority within civil government that can certify the legitimacy of its measures in the binding way in which, for instance, the judicial branch of a state exercises its own politically mandated role by interpreting the enacted constitution and thereby determining the legality of government policy on grounds that are political in origin and objectively valid for all citizens. Where freedom is a given principle and justice is no more than the realization of liberty, it must simply be left to personal judgment to decide whether government is properly enacting natural law. With no institutional seat of authority available, individuals have the prerogative to withdraw their recognition of the legitimacy of civil government as soon as they judge it to have transgressed its natural mandate. Their original consent agreement gives them the right to do so, in default of any other nonnatural source of authority. What this means is that the members of civil society are completely at liberty to throw off the obligations of the social contract and revert to a state-of-nature relation to civil authority where no laws or agreements have any binding force upon them.

Consequently, the authority of civil government is itself no more secure than person and property in the state of nature, in so far as respect for both is but a matter of personal choice. Although civil government is instituted to guarantee the exercise of liberty, its very character makes it just as inherently unstable as the right it is meant to realize.

Indeed, the ultimate inability of civil government to have a recognized reality any less contingent than that of harmony in the state of nature, reflects a basic dilemma casting in doubt the very possibility of social contract itself. Namely, just as the authority of civil government depends upon unanimous respect by the members of society, so social contract requires a similar unanimity of willing simply to be entered into. By its very definition, the social contract can only come into being when the prospective members of civil society are already resolved to honor each others' natural rights by taking the common measure of contracting with one another to institute civil government. Such unanimous respect for right, however, is precisely what is lacking in the state of nature, and whose absence requires the founding of public authority in the first place. Without it, the social contract not only has no binding force, but can not even be initiated, whereas only without such prior shared committment, under a state of war, where there is no common recognition of rights, does the need for a social contract arise.

Driven by its own internal logic, the attempt to make freedom the principle of justice here comes to an impasse in these final aporias. Freedom, postulated as liberty, the universal capacity of choice whose particular alternatives are given to it, must be sustained through a social contract precisely because the unmediated plurality of state of nature precludes the general recognition of right. However, because social contract issues from the given liberty of persons, it lacks the preexisting agreement that alone allows it to be convened and binding. Since all higher authority derives from this contract, not only can such authority not be relied upon to enforce the original covenant, but its civil government has no more respected reality than the given wills whose harmony it is designed to ensure. With the authority of civil government necessarily problematic, the realization of the individual will is itself thrown into question, in the absence of any secured recognition by others. As a result, instead of freedom determining an existing system of justice, all that is left is an unrealizable right at both levels of natural liberty and civil society. The quest of liberal theory here grinds to a halt before a hopelessly hypothetical civil government, wherein willing remains a formal imperative of only universal character, facing both are indifferent particularity of its alternative contents and the immediate conflicting particularity of the given plurality of wills.

II

The Indicated Requirements
for Conceiving the Reality of Freedom

If this outcome presents a dead end, it no less lays bare the problems that must be overcome to conceive freedom as a reality of justice.

As might be expected, these problems all revolve around the dilemma of securing individuality for the will's action. At every turn, the course of liberty has set in relief this central difficulty in a dual manner. On the one hand, it has demonstrated how freedom is deprived of reality so long as the particular content of the will and its relation to others is not determined through the will's own universal form. Conversely, it has shown that when the will is reduced to a determiner and the content of justice has the corresponding form of determined, rather than self-determined determinacies, the will can neither achieve any objective existence for itself, nor establish a real community in which freedom is actual.

In terms of the unfolded logic of liberal theory, these insights provide the following lessons:

First, the free will cannot be a natural will, whose defining character is given prior to its actual self-determination. In other words, freedom must not be reduced to liberty, for the autonomous will cannot be conceived as a merely universal faculty of choice, whose particular content and relation to other wills is extraneously given.

By the same token, the free will cannot be a monological structure, that is, a structure of the self, determined independently of the plurality of particular persons in whose context individual identities are distinguishable. Monologically defined, the will is a capacity all selves bear *per se*, and thus cannot serve to differentiate one another. So conceived, the will is automatically reduced to a merely universal faculty with no element of particularity within itself that could individuate one will from another in virtue of self-determination rather than through independently given factors. On this basis, the aspect of particularity, giving freedom the determinacy required for actual self-*determination*, cannot be referred back to the will as determinacy *of* its own *self*, but remains irreducibly a determination of something other. Consequently, any monological conception of the will, be it conceived as a faculty of liberty or an agency determined by practical reason, leaves freedom without reality, and therefore fails to grasp what *is* the free will and the system of justice consisting in its exercise.

These two lessons, that the free will is neither a natural will nor a monological structure, entail a third: Namely, the will is free only by actually giving itself a particular content that derives from willing and willing alone. The free will must will itself and nothing else, but not do so in an empty solipsism of noncontradiction, as in the inner application of a categorical imperative. Rather, it must will its own *particularization*, such that its act of will stands in relation to other wills as an individual one, bearing a particular content specific to itself, yet exhibiting a universal form common to them all.

However, as the aporias of liberal theory have indicated, the free will cannot stand in any immediate, given relation to other wills, for then their particular differentiation from one another is not determined by willing. Consequently, the free will, in willing its own particularization, must also will its relation to others. These others must themselves be free wills as well, for otherwise, the first will, willing its relation to them, will not be able to stand individuated against them, as a particular instance of free willing in general. To be free wills, however, they too must not stand in a relation to others imposed independently of their own willing. Consequently, the free will can will its relation to other free wills only if they concomitantly will that same relation to one another as their own self-determination.

This means that free willing is not the action of a single will alone, but rather a self-determination by one will bound up with the self-determination of another. In order to will itself in a particular manner, the free will must engage in a reciprocal relation to other wills, a relation in which each determines itself as an individual by willing its relation to others in virtue of these others simultaneously willing their own particularization and having it voluntarily establish the same interrelationship. Thus the very exercise of freedom is directly accompanied by the objective recognition of right, since each self-determination is bound up with respect by other wills of its particular realization, as well as with respect for the particular self-determination of these other individual themselves. Accordingly, freedom is not a natural or monological potential, but an actual structure of interaction consisting in the interdirected and mutually respected actions of a plurality of wills.

As such, freedom is not a principle from which the relations of justice are to be derived; rather, freedom is itself an existing relation of right, that is, justice as the very reality of self-determination.

III

Hegel's Conception of Freedom As Interaction

This insight, which by itself says nothing of how such interaction concretely proceeds, has been furthest developed by Hegel, who makes it the very foundation of his entire *Philosophy of Right*. Whether or not he has properly conceived freedom in the full range of its constitutive structures of interaction, he has at the very least supplied the terms for understanding how freedom can be thought as interaction, and what interaction consists in the most basic sense.

The key Hegel provides is the notion that freedom is neither a natural given, nor an attribute of self, but rather an intersubjective process of reciprocal recognition, whose interaction constitutes right.

The individuals involved in this interaction indeed have natural endowments and subjective faculties of knowing and choice, which Hegel himself specifically addresses in his theory of Subjective Spirit. In fact, for the interaction of freedom to proceed, the individuals involved must have a natural corporeal existence in order to act in the world of others and make themselves and their actions recognizable, as well as the ability to choose what they will do and the mental capacities required to recognize the actions of others. Although these are prerequisites for the reciprocal self-determination of free wills, and indeed provide all that is necessary for them to proceed, it is nevertheless the non-natural, nonmonological relation between selves that allows their action to take on the additional character of free and rightful action.

How this actually occurs is the problem that Hegel addresses in his development of Objective Spirit, which comprises the subject matter of the *Philosophy of Right* by being at one and the same time the reality of right and freedom in virtue of the interaction determination of the free will.

Logically enough, Hegel's first concern is establishing the minimal determination of the interaction of freedom, which is to say, the most indeterminate, abstract right of all.

The basic individuality of self-determination and the lessons of liberal theory already point to a notion of reciprocal recognition, but how this realizes itself as the element of freedom must be spelled out.

Hegel provides the required account by simply thinking what interaction must entail to grant the free will its individual reality, in face of the demonstrated limits of natural liberty and its monological willing.

The basic features are already at hand. To begin with, each free will must will its own particularization, not what desire urges or reason compels, but simply an objectification of itself that has a particular content distinct from the objectifications of other wills. This external realization not only must derive its constitutive character from the will itself, but be nothing other than the will's own self-determination, individuating it from other free wills by being a particular sheer embodiment of that will excluding all others from the same domain.

For this to be the case, the respective embodiments of each will cannot stand differentiated from one another as immediately given, indifferent monads in want of a preestablished harmony. Rather, there is actual unimpeded self-determination only when each will establishes its own particular domain in recognition and respect of the objectifications of the others, whose correlatively limited embodiments grant it a recognized objective existence on its part. Thus, each will particularizes itself by giving itself an embodiment limited in accord with those of others, who likewise recognize it by determining their own distinct domains in an unconflicting manner. Self-determination *is* thereby a relation to other, comprising an intersubjective process of reciprocal recognition, where the recognition in question consists both in a theoretical awareness of the objectifications of other wills, and in the practical act of embodying one's own will in such a way that it does not conflict with theirs.

The only matters that need be further specified to complete the actual engagement of this process are the respective characters of the wills involved and the factors providing their objectifications. They, of course, are intimately connected, given the nature of freedom's individuality.

On the one hand, since each will here freely determines itself only in a recognized and recognizing objectification, what gives it its sole recognizable character as a particular free will is the external embodiment others respect as its own. This means that each will has no specific character in itself, but only distinguishes itself in the external domain comprising its respected embodiment. Thus, even though the will is free in this most basic interaction, it is an abstractly individual will, whose self-determined particularity lies outside it in a separate entity.

On the other hand, this external entity, which every such will needs to supply it with the recognizable and recognized medium of its self-determination, has no other status than that of a receptacle for the particularization of the will. Whatever independent characteristics it may have are here a matter of indifference, for the free will has willed itself through it, not by choosing its medium's given determinations, but by rendering them subordinate accidents of its own particular embodiment. Consequently, the basic relation between free wills is mediated through factors that are simply some thing or other in which these wills lay themselves for the sake of their own mutually limited embodiment.

Hegel has drawn all these conclusions,[4] and further recognized that on their basis, the minimal structure of freedom consists in the interaction of persons through property. In contrast to liberal theory, which conceives both person and property as monological relations given within the state of nature, Hegel understands them to be the specific terms of the most elementary interaction of freedom. As such, they cannot be thought apart from an intersubjective process of reciprocal recognition, and therefore, comprise a nonnatural right that actually exists in the constitutive property relations between persons.

This right is what Hegel appropriately calls Abstract Right, and in his development of its relations, he makes clear the elemental character of person and property in their roles within the most indeterminate interaction of self-determination.

As Hegel argues, the person is precisely the free agent who simply wills his own particularization in an external embodiment in virtue of other persons recognizing it to be the domain of his will and not their own. They can afford it the objective respect allowing its owner to be an individuated person only, however, by willing their own property ownership in such a way that it does not conflict with the domain of other persons. This recognizable objectification of the person is property, in so far as it is an external entity whose only relevant feature vis à vis personhood is that it does embody the person's will in a particular object from which all other persons have excluded their self-determination. The taking of property by one person is thus bound up with the taking of other property by other persons. Indeed, only with reference to the intersubjective aspect of recognition, can one distinguish between mere possession and property, for rightful ownership is not a matter of physical grasp, but of respected possession.[5]

Unlike liberal theorists, Hegel takes full account of this in his consideration of how a person takes possession of property in the first place. This act of self-determination is, of course, the starting point of any development of Abstract Right, since all further relations between persons, such as contract and the committing of wrong, involve individuals who have already given their wills a recognized particular embodiment in some previously established property.

Hegel realizes that taking possession of property cannot be understood simply as a relation between a person and a rightless world of things waiting to be appropriated from nature. Rather, the person stands opposite the external factors in which he can objectify his will only in reference to other persons who are themselves in the process of recognizing those factors as his property by correlatively laying their wills in other analogously rightless factors. For this to occur, each person must take possession of property in such a way that his appropriation of the external factor involved is immediately recognizable to others. Consequently, as Hegel makes clear,[6] taking ownership of a factor necessarily involes either some perceivable physical contact with it, a working upon it to alter its outward form, or a marking of it, not because any of these single acts themselves establish rightful ownership, but because they can designate to others that the person has embodied his will in the factor in question.

Since, however, the actual establishment of ownership depends upon how other persons choose to recognize these actions through their own self-determinations, what one individual does to a factor does not have any rightful status unless others are engaged in physically grasping, forming, or marking their own factors in corroboration of a mutual respect for each other's domains. Only within the reciprocity of this interaction do individuals leave behind the unmediated givenness of mere possession and instead take rightful ownership of property, facing one another as free persons, whose distinct particularities are not independently given, but established through their own interrelated willing.

On this basis, a right to property comes into existence in conjunction with the exercise of the duty to respect it. The freedom of the person here manifests its inherent individual actuality, for only through the contrastive recognition process securing it its objective embodiment can it even be exercised.

Nevertheless, the interaction of persons through property is subject to conflicts that cannot be resolved on the basis of its abstract right alone. Hegel is well aware of this, and understands that property relations, as actual as they are, cannot comprise the exclusive reality of freedom, but point instead to further structures of interaction constituting more concrete spheres of right.

What shows the limited character of Abstract Right, and thereby points beyond it to other forms of self-determination, is nothing other than the immediate arbitrariness of all the compenents in its interaction. Simply because the recognition process of personhood proceeds through individuals choosing which factor to make their own and which to honor as someone else's, it is always possible for a nonmalicious wrong to occur where persons disagree over which factor has been rightfully recognized as the property of a certain person. Since, however, the interaction of persons contains no higher authority than that of the mutual respect in which they stand, such nonmalicious wrong cannot be adjudicated if the persons involved do not themselves give up their conflicting interpretations.[7] Similarly, as Hegel explicitly argues,[8] the role of choice within property relations allows both for fraud, where one person intentionally misrepresents his property within a contract in order to use its rightful form of mutual recognition to sanction an improper exchange, and for outright crime, where a person chooses to violate the property rights of others, despite his own need of their recognition to possess rightfully what he himself has. In either case, all persons can do to right the wrong is take an action that may itself stand as a vengeful wrong if others happen not to recognize it as a rightful retribution.[9]

Consequently, although the interaction of persons realizes freedom in an existing right of property relations, these relations stand in need of some further form of interaction to right wrong in an objectively recognized and abiding way.

This does not mean that the elementary interaction of personhood leaves freedom with an insecure reality leading back into the quandaries of social contract theory. Indeed, Hegel does go on to conceive a civil administration of justice that adjudicates disputes among persons through a lawful enforcement of their abstract right. This public authority, however, neither issues from a social contract, nor secures natural rights, nor gets identified with the state. Rather, in Hegel's conception, the civil administration of justice exists as a specific institution of civil society, which regulates the nonnatural personhood and property of its members on the basis of laws it receives from a sovereign state standing over society with political ends of its own. Although Hegel does at times collapse the distinction between civil society and state, most notably in his estatelike characterizations of the three social classes[10] and in his introjection of class distinctions into the structures of the state,[11] his theory of interaction allows him to radically demarcate the two spheres.

The framework of interaction makes this possible because it establishes right as something first determined within the specific structures of reciprocal recognition comprising a certain form of self-determination. Accordingly, the particular components of a sphere of interaction, which could distinguish it from others, have their relevant features not in virtue of any predetermined principle, but through the individual character of the interrelated self-determinations comprising it. Just as the minimal right to objectify one's will in a particular embodiment involves the agency of personhood and the medium of property, which themselves stand determined only within the relations of Abstract Right, so the interactions that could comprise social and political realms of freedom would also have distinct agencies and mediums for their respective rights, which could not be reduced to one another or derived from any prior relation.

In the *Philosophy of Right*, Hegel attempts to develop the specific interactions that do comprise separate spheres of society and state, and does so in terms of components that are irreducible. Civil society is described as the realm in which individuals exercise the specific agency of the civilian or bourgeois, by entering into relationships with others where each individual pursues a particular interest of their own that can only be realized in conjunction with the realization of that of others. On this basis, civil society involves, in the first instance, a system of interdependent needs, whose members exercise the social freedom of pursuing the satisfaction of needs of their own choosing, which can only be satisfied by what others have. Accordingly, the agency of the civilian is immediately bound up with the specific reciprocal self-determination comprising the commodity relations of economic interaction.[12]

By contrast, the state entails an entirely different right, for Hegel, involving its own agency and medium. Instead of comprising a civil government in the service of natural right or any other predetermined principle, it consists in the interactions of individuals through institutions allowing them to relate to one another not on the basis of property relations or their interdependent interests, but through self-determinations that have as their end the policy of government. Here, the freedom at issue is one of participating in self-government, and only in its exercise, which requires specific political institutions, is the person not just a civilian, but a citizen as well.

If nothing else, these brief indications at least suggest how the theory of interaction could address civil society and state without conflating them.

Whether or not Hegel has correctly determined society and state, let alone the other spheres of right, is itself an open question in the absence of any systematic critique of the entire *Philosophy of Right*. Nevertheless, his conception of freedom as interaction has established a new terrain for practical philosophy, where justice can be conceived as the existing reality of self-determination, and where distinct social and politcal spheres of right need not be excluded.

In face of the challenge to renew practical philosophy on its basis, it must not be forgotten that if interaction is itself made an abstract principle, a criterion of justice, or a standard of legitimation from which further institutional structures are derived, then the individuality of freedom is once again forsaken for the dilemmas of liberty.[13]

NOTES

1.   Hegel has sketched out these three constitutive aspects of the self-determining will in paragraphs 5 through 7 in the *Philosophy of Right*, trans. by T.M. Knox (New York: Oxford University Press, 1967), providing the basis for what here follows.

2. For the most complete account of the logical distinction between positing and self-determination, see Hegel's *Science of Logic,* trans. by A.V. Miller (New York: Humanities Press, 1969), where he attempts to present in succession the exhaustive development of the relations of positing (as the Logic of Essence) and self-determination per se (as the Logic of the Concept).

3. Hannah Arendt has discussed at length the importance of the two aspects of mutual covenant within the social contract in *On Revolution*, (New York: Viking Press, 1976), pp. 169 ff.

4. See in particular paragraphs 41–45 of the *Philosophy of Right.*

5. See paragraphs 45–51, *Ibid.*

6. See paragraphs 54–58, *Ibid.*

7. See paragraphs 84–86, *Ibid.*

8. See paragraphs 87–90, *Ibid.*

9. See paragraph 102, *Ibid.*

10. For a detailed critique of Hegel's class conceptions see Richard Dien Winfield, *The Social Determination of Production: The Critique of Hegel's System of Needs and Marx' Concept of Capital,* Ph.D. dissertation, Yale University, 1977, pp. 140–158.

11. See paragraphs 303–308 in the *Philosophy of Right.*

12. See Winfield, *Social Determination of Production,* pp. 74–162, for a detailed critique of Hegel's account of the System of Needs.

13. Such appears to be the mistaken course of Hannah Arendt, Jürgen Habermas, and others who have taken the reciprocal recognition of a plurality of individuals in an uninstitutionalized form and made it the ideal of all institutional life, rather than following Hegel in conceiving interaction as a system of distinct individual structures of reciprocal recognition, each comprising a separate *existing* right with its own agency, medium, and institutions.

COGNITION AS AN ACT OF FREEDOM

by

MURRAY GREENE

There is perhaps no more striking image in philosophical literature than the ascent of the prisoner of the cave in Plato's *Republic*, an ascent towards knowledge that is also toward freedom. That knowledge and freedom go together is almost universally an article of faith. But how do they go together? When we say that knowledge makes us free, do we suppose that knowledge is one thing and freedom another, the one somehow a bridge or means to the other? But how can anything other than freedom be a way towards freedom? Must not knowledge then be freedom, or a freedom? Not all philosophers have viewed the necessary connection of knowledge and freedom as a problem and few seem to have addressed it explicitly. Descartes relates cognition and freedom by viewing judgment as an act of free choice. Spinoza regards human freedom as an activity at once of the pure intellect and the active emotions. Kant restricts theoretical cognition in order to make room for freedom in the practical reason.[1] Does this mean that theoretical knowing is not to be viewed as an act of freedom? According to Hegel, "the principle of liberty is not only in thought but the root of thought."[2] Hegel does not separate theoretical and practical reason in the manner of Kant, and his connecting of cognition and freedom claims to be a thoroughly immanent one. Beginning with some issues arising with the aforementioned thinkers prior to Hegel, I would like to examine how Hegel roots thinking in freedom in such a way that cognition as such is an act of freedom.

That my freedom is exercised in my judgment means for Descartes that I have a spontaneous choice of affirming or denying the truth of my ideas, or, where they are not clear and distinct, abstaining from judgment.[3] This freedom I possess innately from God and I know that I possess it the moment I am aware of my ability to doubt. Since cognition, strictly speaking, has the form of

191

affirmation or denial, cognition entails an exercise of my freedom in judging. Here we have a principle—of paramount importance for later transcendental thinking and Hegel's view of cognition as a freedom—that a logical form, namely, judgment, is a free act of the ego. Nevertheless, as Hegel remarks, while in Descartes the impulse of freedom is fundamental, it remains only implicit.[4] Though according to Descartes my freedom is employed in judging about my ideas, it has nothing to do with my having ideas. Freedom belongs to the will, ideas to the understanding. My freedom lies not in my obtaining my ideas, the most important being anyhow innate, but in my judging about them.

That this is an unsatisfactory connecting of understanding and will, of cognition and freedom, is seen by both Spinoza and Hegel. Knowing is the "actuality" of intelligence, says Hegel, and "to speak of intelligence and at the same time of the possibility of choice (*Willkür*) of knowing" is absurd.[5] For Spinoza, volition and understanding are indeed present in all cognition, not, however, in the manner of a conjunction of faculties or acts, but as aspects, affective and cognitive, of one and the same idea, just as desiring and understanding are aspects of one and the same activity of self-affirmation that constitutes our very being. For Spinoza and Hegel alike, albeit in different ways, freedom is a liberation struggle that involves cognition as an activity of our whole nature. According to Spinoza, I do not decide by a separate act of choice that I will add to my idea of a triangle that its interior angles equal two right angles.[6] Rather my idea itself already contains its necessary determinations, provided it is indeed a pure conception without any of the contingency of an image. My adequate ideas are true in and of themselves, my having such an idea is at the same time my knowing it is true, so that I engage in no separate act of choice in affirming it to be true.[7] Whether I have adequate ideas or confused and contingent images depends on my constitution of mind and body. The truth or falsity of any idea of mine is not a matter of its correspondence with an object, but rather—since very idea of mine corresponds with its object, which is a determination of my body[8]—a matter of my activity or passivity of mind and body. In my pure self-activity, meaning where I depend on myself alone and am the adequate cause of my idea, my ideas is adequate and true; where I am the plaything of my passions and fortuitous external excitations, my idea is confused, fragmentary and false. Thus cognition and freedom are connected in the notion of self-activity more immanently than by Descartes. Any concept of freedom that entails an indifference of choice is discarded by the determinist Spinoza.[9] The mind is no separate substance that stands outside natural causality but rather the idea of the actuality existent body, and any particular idea of mine is as ineluctably part of a causal series as any motion of my bodily parts. The mind too is a part of nature and connected with other modes, every mode being animated in some degree.[10] Thus Spinoza rejects at once the mind-body dualism that is the basis of freedom in Descartes, the artificial severance of man's intellectual and emotional nature, and the soul's standing outside nature's universal determinism. My freedom lies not in my exemption from nature's necessity but in my enlightened acknowledgment of it as the divine reality in which I have my being and embrace in my whole way of living.

But even if in Spinoza my cognition is more intrinsically connected with my freedom than in Descartes, and my free self-activity is actualized as a liberation struggle against my passivity and contingency of mind, the notion of this liberation struggle does not account for my having adequate ideas any more than the faculty of free choice in Descartes. As for the necessary truth of these ideas, it can hardly be said to have been established except through a dogmatism of reason, as Kant would say. In Leibniz such adequate ideas as being, substance, one, etc., are derived from the self-conscious monad's own act of apperception. Here again we have a free self-activity that is at the same time a cognizing of all reality. But the apperceiving principle itself is unaccounted for by the notion of the monadic substance, and the preestablished harmony that guarantees the validity of the ideas of apperception is as much a dogmatism as anything in Descartes and Spinoza.

For both Kant and Hegel the principle of experience affords a liberation from dogmatism, though in different ways. In Kant, cognition becomes in a certain formal sense an activity of freedom insofar as the knowing subject remains with itself in the object known, not as determined by the subject's own pure light of reason but as object of experience. The notion of experience not only brings in a new and purportedly undogmatic criterion of verification. In opening up the subjectivity to the not-I, if I may use an expression not characteristically Kantian, the principle of experience sets the problem of cognition as a freedom into a new framework. My objective unity of experience is for Kant grounded in my subjective unity as transcendental ego. The organizing forms of the objective unity, the categories, derive in some unknown fashion from the identical ego, not, however in the abstract manner of Leibniz but as the spontaneous synthesizing activity of consciousness that first makes experience possible. Yet this subjective activity that is simultaneously a determining of the object is not viewed by Kant himself in terms of an act of freedom.[11] In the first place the subject's knowing of its object is only a phenomenal knowing that makes room for freedom in another employment of reason. But further, the cognizing subject is not a self properly speaking and is not meant to be one. The affective life of the knower, which is so important in Spinoza, is expressly excluded in Kant's notion of cognition.[12] Desire for Kant has nothing to do with the logical constitution of the object, which never means for Kant an object of love or hate or fear, as in Spinoza. The object of cognition is solely a spatial entity structured a priori by my consciousness in such a way that my being able to experience it as an object is my being able to know it under the laws of universal mechanism. The so-called self of self-consciousness, i.e., the identical "I think," is not a selfhood that can be said to be free or unfree. The synthesizing activity of consciousness, which means to say, consciousness's objectivizing of its sensuous manifold, is in no sense a liberation struggle against the passions. The subjectivity of the "I think" is a logical, or rather transcendental logical, requirement of a uniting of a manifold that makes possible a mathematical science of nature. Thus Kant's liberating of thinking from dogmatism through a principle of experience comes at a cost: namely, a truncated subjectivity concerning which it makes little sense to talk about cognition as an act of freedom.

The Kantian connecting of knowing subject and object known, which I termed a freedom only in formal sense, becomes in Hegel a negative self-relation and in this way an actual freedom. Cognition and freedom are for Hegel intrinsically connected in the concept of subjectivity as Notion: the identity that distinguishes itself from itself and returns to itself in its distinction. This identical self-distinguishing is termed by Hegel the former essence of mind, the mind' freedom and the root of its cognitive activity.[13] By conceiving subjectivity as notion, which, through its inner unfolding actualizes itself as unity of subject and object, Hegel incorporates experience as a liberating principle in a way that was not possible for Kant's transcendental apperception. At the same time, since the unfolding process of the subjectivity takes the form of its self-negating, as *Fürsichsein,* of its own naturalness as *Ansichsein,* the relation to nature and to itself as physical is different from the subject-object relation in both Descartes and Spinoza. The *Entwicklungsprozess* in Hegel is a *Befreiungskampf* of the self as a totality, a desiring, knowing selfhood struggling towards self-liberation, as in Spinoza. At the same time it is an experiencing subjectivity whose relation to its object is not dogmatically an identity of idea and ideatum, but an identity that must be attained in and through its experience of the object as a not-I standing over against it.

I

Let us begin our examination of cognition and freedom in hegel with two problems connected with one another and with freedom: (a) the mind's relation to nature generally, which is conceived as a realm of causal determinism by the aforementioned predecessors of Hegel; and (b) the individual's relation to that part of nature that is its own body. The mind for Hegel is not separate from nature like Descartes' thinking ego, but neither is it a particular mode of nature, or, as mind as such, an attribute of substance as in Spinoza. Nature rather belongs to mind: nature *is* mind as the Idea in its other-being or self-externality, hence external to itself and a realm of unfreedom and blind necessity.[14] But as this self-externality that is eternally seeking its own center, nature is an *Entwicklungsprozess* of internalizing and negating itself as *Aussersichsein*, a process consummated in the emergence of subjective mind as nature's truth and prius.[15] Thus in a certain sense we can speak of a continuum of nature and mind, as contrasted with Descartes' separation. But his continuum includes also an opposition. It is not to be viewed merely in terms of an increasing degree of soul or self-activity or clarity and distinctness of perception, as in Spinoza and Leibniz, for whom at some point and in some manner there emerges a power of reflexivity or apperception and herewith the possibility of cognition and freedom. No doubt in Hegel we can speak loosely of the animal's greater degree of internality as compared with the plant. But strictly speaking the animal and the plant are stages of the natural subjectivity that are distinguishable not be degrees but as forms of negative self-relation: to wit, the relation of the subjectivity as *Fürsichsein* to its own corporeal manifold and its inorganic nature as its *Ansichsein*. While nature generally is a realm of unfreedom, this is not the unfreedom of a mechanistic determinism but of a subjectivity that is not yet for itself in its implicit being. In organism we can see the first beginnings of freedom: e.g., in the animal's arbitrary self-movement in which it makes itself its center of gravity,[16] and its sensation, whereby for the first time the natural subjectivity in a truly inward manner is the being-for-self identity of its corporal manifold as its *Ansichsein*. But as natural subjectivity the animal cannot be for itself in its universality; it can only be for itself as sensuous singularity in another singularity of its own kind, i.e., in the *Gattungsprozess* or sex relationship.[17] It's negating power is not sufficient to its preserving itself at once as singular subjectivity and universality. Thus Hegel links the sex relationship and death. The passing of singular natural subjectivity in the abiding universal as *Gattung* constitutes notionally the emergence of the subjectivity as Notion, the individual subjectivity that abides freely with itself in its universality.[18]

   To begin with, or in its immediacy, subjective mind is for Hegel the individual soul, which is not yet mind in its freedom but, as in the beginning on every level, must proceed to make itself free. The soul is for Hegel a psychical subjectivity that is for itself neither in another singularity, like the animal, nor yet in the universal of thought, as in the case of consciousness. The soul is for itself in its preconscious feeling-life (*Gefühlsleben*) in which it has the dreaming presentiment of itself in it totality. The psychical subjectivity is not active like the waking consciousness, which structures its world in categories of thought. As in the case of the dreamer or somnambulist, the subjectivity is passive, lacks self-possession, and is borne along as though held in trance by a subjective power not its own.[19] The development process is its taking possession of itself by making itself master in its own house. Hegel terms this a *Befreiungskampf*,[20] which, as always in Hegel, has the form of a positive self-negating. It is in this way that Hegel conceives the relationship of mind and body: not as a correspondence of idea and ideatum but as the subjectivity's making itself the being-for-self identity of its corporeal manifold as its *Ansichsein*.

The soul's attaining to self-possession in the body is not a negating of the organic multiplicity as in the case of the animal subjectivity, but of the sensations, appetites, and passions, which aim at particular satisfactions that often conflict with one another and disrupt the feeling totality. This negating is not an ascetic extirpation of the passions any more than Spinoza's transformation of the passive to the active emotions under the dictate of reason. But although we are dealing with a universalization of the particular, there are for Hegel many levels to be traversed before the subjectivity attains to the universal of reason. On the level of soul, the universal is the feeling subjectivity that renders its particular determinations a totality in which every corporeal particularity is a moment of the fluid universality in which the soul feels itself and makes itself felt.[21] This means that the psyche does not remain caught fast in any compulsive feeling or obsessive passion, a *befangen bleiben* in a particularity of self-feeling that epitomizes the unfreedom of mind and is for Hegel prototypical of a deranged psyche.[22] The soul's attaining to self-possession is not a turning away from the body but a control through habituation whereby the body is rendered the purposive instrument of soul's own inwardness and the outer sign of its spirituality.

Thus the soul-body relation in Hegel is not that of a correspondence or parallelism, whatever these terms may mean, but the subjectivity's actualizing itself in the body by infusing it with its own ideality. Subjectivity is the power of negativity: the psychical subjectivity's relation to the body is its relating itself negatively to itself in its particularity of self-feeling. Negative self-relation establishes the nature of freedom as a dialectic where such opposites as activity and passivity, engagement and disengagement cannot be held apart as fixed antitheses but are mutually inclusive moments that pass into one another in the course of the developmental process. The soul's actualizing itself in habit is its moving in the boyd as its own free element. The golfer's practice efforts make his swing seem effortless. Mastery of a skill, as in Aristotle's *hexis* as a first grade of actuality, is at once an activenss of control and a passiveness of receptivity. My being able to read at a glance a set of musical notes is an engagement of my capacities that leaves me open for something higher, an engagement of disengagement so to speak.[23] It is in this sense that Hegel speaks of freedom on the preconscious physical level. In coming to self-possession in the body through rendering its feeling-life a fluid universality, the psychical subjectivity has attained what the organic subjectivity could not: it has raised itself above the particularity of feeling and, on the initial level of mind, has made itself the universal that is for itself the universal. This freedom on the psychical level is the basis of cognition and all other freedoms.

II

The soul's self-actualization in the body marks the completion of one stage in subjective mind's liberation from its natural being and the beginning of another. Up to now, the soul has been a self-enclosed monadic subjectivity, its *Ansichsein* coming to it as a dream world, an immediate otherness lacking the mediated connectedness of an objective outer world. The feeling content, in which are interwoven the ties of family and folk, home and homeland, the soul in habit has rendered its own element in which it freely moves and has its being-for-self. The psychical subjectivity, however, is only abstractly a universality. Its immediate unity of feeling is the natural basis for all higher freedom, but at the same time incommensurate with the concrete universality of subjectivity in its notion. Out of this immediate unity emerges a new self-distinguishing and a new and higher freedom struggle. Having permeated its corporeal manifold and made its other-being its own, the subjectivity in its freedom lets its other go free. In this opening up of its monadic self-enclosedness the subjectivity at once raises itself to the ego of consciousness and endows its content with the status of objectivity.[24].

In viewing this emergence of the ego of consciousness in the light of previous considerations, let us note some meanings of the self-distinguishing as an act. In the first place, the subjectivity's letting go of itself in its implicit being is an act of freedom and a ground of freedom: which means to say that the subjectivity has made and is in process of making itself its own ground. Such a speculative conception, whose logical aspects are exhibitied by Hegel elsewhere,[25] is possible neither for a libertarianism such as Descartes', which entails a liberty of indifference, nor a determinism such as Spinoza's for which every event is part of a series of causes and effects. In the self-distinguishing of the subjectivity of consciousness, there is indeed an element of indifference, though not as in the Balaam's ass situation of the reflective understanding, but as a notional moment. In the wholly abstract self-distinguishing of the "I am," the ego posits a difference between the "I" and its being, a difference that is no difference.[26] That the self-distinguishing is an act does not mean that it is a particular event in a temporal series and must have a causal antecedent. The antecedent is the subjectivity itself that has actualized itself as soul. The self-distinguishing is an inner self-unfolding where the distinguished are moments of the subjectivity itself as identity, not independent spatiotemporal entities related as cause and effect. The subjectivity's free act is not a choosing to distinguish itself from itself in the way that the will in Descartes chooses to make a judgment. Rather in its self-distinguishing the subjectivity *is* judgment (*Ur-teil*); it does not possess freedom as a kind of property or determination *in* its nature; freedom is its very nature.[27] In no previous thinker, including Fichte, to whom Hegel is most indebted for the notion of the self-positing ego, do we find the emergence together of the ego and its object as a free act of self-distinguishing that consummates a development of the psyche. The ego is freedom; its objectivity, relative to the self-enclosed feeling-life, is a liberation, which, like health, is ordinarily taken for granted until a moment of breakdown. The distorted perceptions of depression, the phobias of paranoia, the fixed ideas that remain impervious to objective considerations are an imprisonment of mind, shoals on which the feeling-life can become entrapped. They testify that objectivity is a strength of mind and an attainment. Like the upright posture,[28] which enables me to see beyond my immediate environs, objectivity is a stance and a perspective. I have let go the content of my natural feeling-life and set it opposite myself so that in my universality as thinking I may apprehend its universality of meaning.

Habit as an actualization of the soul has been *aufgehoben* to objective consciousness. As individual ego of consciousness I unreflectingly hold myself open to an external world confronting me as a not-I, a world of objects that I can come to know only through experience. Experience is a freedom, but it is different from my *Gefühlsleben* where I can roam in my own inner element of feeling. The world that I find before me possesses a substantial being of its own and has for me a certain necessity that I willy-nilly must accept, although I have the certainty that I can come to know it if I keep myself open to experience. The subject-object opposition of consciousness is for Hegel not the ultimate truth of mind but the becoming, as a coming to appearance, of that truth, a phenomenology of mind.

Although the ego finds its outer world already structured by such universals as thingness, cause and effect, etc., these objective categories derive from the ego's own activity and are therefore necessarily immanent in its experience, as are the categories in Kant. But the situation in Hegel's notion of experience is different from the Kantian in a way that is crucial for the notion of cognition as a freedom. Although the objective outlook is an act of freedom and an achievement in Hegel, the ego's letting the other go free is at the same time an imposing on itself the constraint of objectivity. The subjectivity now confronts an otherness which is must proceed to make its own but not merely within a cocoon of it inner feeling-life. The perspective of objectivity turns out to be a new challenge, one that the subjectivity must accept in its totality as a selfhood, and not merely in a compartmentalization of itself as an "I think."

With regard to the Kantian categories themselves, as universals immanent in experience they are indeed grounded in the identical consciousness as the synthesizing activity of its manifold. As forms of this activity, the Kantian categories are not derived by the philosopher from the notion of the ego of consciousness, as Hegel and Fichte point out, but are taken empirically by Kant from the forms of judgment. But what about judgment itself as an act of the ego? In Descartes, we recall, judgment entailed an act of the free will as a faculty separate from understanding, while Spinoza held there was no such separate faculty or act other than the combined intellectual and affective activity of the mind in its having adequate ideas. In Kant, judgment is a spontaneous act of the understanding, which is separate from sensibility, although the two are said to spring from some common, but to us unknown root.[29] The ego is said by Kant to make use of judgment in its experiencing the external world.[30] Hegel agrees with Descartes in viewing judgment as a freedom. Judgment, however, neither entails a separate faculty of the will, as in Descartes, nor is it separate from sensibility in the Kantian sense. The so-called faculties are, for Hegel, developmental stages of the subjectivity as a totality.[31] The ego is not free in a certain part of itself called desire or will, nor does it "make use" of a part of itself called judgment.[32] Rather the self-distinguishing totality is judgment, is notion. The categories are immanent in experience because they *are* the ego as the self-particularizing universal that is for itself as universal. The judgment "I am," which is the *Aufhebung* of the physical feeling-identity, is implicitly also the judgment "the not-I is." The immediate categories of the experiencing consciousness, such as being, something, other, singularity, etc., thus derive not from understanding as a separate faculty from sensibility but from the self-distinguishing totality whose being for itself as an "I" is at the same time its letting go of its natural being as an other. Having taken up into itself its immediate identity as feeling-totality, the singular consciousness in its immediacy is the sensuous consciousness.

In the phenomenological development of consciousness, the *Befreiungskampf* has also the meaning of a methodology of freedom. Experience as a liberation is a pathway of contradiction in which consciousness suffers violence "from its own self."[33] The immediate abstract categories of the sensuous consciousness are sublated in the more concrete but still sensuously conditioned universals, such as thing and properties, cause and effect, etc., while successively emerge in consciousness' experiencing the contradiction between the be-thinged (*bedingte*) universal, in which it is to be for itself in its knowledge, and its own inherent nature as the self-distinguishing universal that is for itself as universal. That this contradiction is for the subjectivity itself, rather than for the philosopher alone, as in the case of the psychical subjectivity, means that the liberation struggle is implicitly a self-criticism. As against the externality of the Lockean and Kantian critique of the mind as an "instrument" of knowledge, consciousness's experience of the object in its successive forms is an immanent self-critique where the forms of thought criticize themselves.[34] While this self-criticism is consciousness's own destroying of its limited satisfaction, it is also consciousness's liberating itself from its sensuously conditioned forms of thought.

Since freedom for Hegel concerns the subjectivity as totality, there is no

Kantian gap between cognition and action, the theoretical "I think" and the practical "I will." In knowing and doing alike, freedom is the dialectical process of self-distinguishing and return to self of the knowing desiring subjectivity. In this dialectic, freedom never comes ready-made as a gift or inheritance or faculty waiting to be employed. It is never an abstract absence of limitation. Freedom can only be concrete in and through limitation. Limitation is the moment of self-distinguishing, hence, like the privilege of pain or feelig of lack, not an abstract negative but implicitly positive. Insofar as limitation proceeds out of abstract immediate identity, it is a determining of the identity, a step in the concretization of freedom. But insofar as the determining is initially external by way of a relation to other and not yet also a return to self, the limitation has the aspect of an unfreedom. *Gewissheit*, the ego's abstract certainty of self that emerges with the singular ego of consciousness, is an essential moment in the subjectivity's being-for-self and a freedom. But until raised to *Wahrheit* this self-certainty can remain a self-will or a self-conceit, as in the master self-consciousness, which is a cul-de-sac of mind rather than a freedom. Hence what arises on one level as a freedom can be just as well its opposite. The give-ness of the object to consciousness, the fact that it is no mere figment of my inner feelings but something I find confronting me on its own account and which I must respect, bespeaks a certain disinterested of consciousness and an attain-ment. It is a freedom of objectivity, of my having let go a content so that, stand-ing face to face with it, I can "take it truly." But at the same time this giveness and foundness of the object is an unfreedom, and in a deeper sense than what Descartes says that I am not at liberty to deny the object present to my senses. The empirical consciousness that prides itself on its *wahr-nehmen* of the object in fact has already constituted it a thingness, *ein vorgefundenes, ihm, gegenü-berstehendes Seiendes.*[35] Ignorant of its own role as a perceiving conscious-ness, this supposedly free disinterestedness directly find itself in a web of contradictions in which it is anything but free. The *Gefundensein* of the ex-perienced object reveals that the ego's letting go is still a clinging to its own which it is yet unaware of in itself. Thus the disinterestedness of the phen-omenal consciousness is an incomplete freedom and a flawed objectivity.

The ego's taking the other as a thing is in Hegel not only a defect of cognition alone, or rather cognition in the restricted Kantian sense. For Kant my treating another as a means merely, which is to say, as a thing, is a contradiction of the universality of the rational will. But it has nothing to do with theoretical cogni-tion, which, in order to make room for practical freedom, requires a notion of experience that excludes my experiencing of an other as a subjectivity. In Spinoza my knowledge of adequate ideas is at the same time my living in accord with the common bond of humanity. In Hegel, this common bond of the univer-sality of reason must be attained in and through the singular ego's experiencing of contradiction. The ego's taking the other merely as a means for its own satisfaction, as in the desiring and the master self-consciousness, is a necessary step in its verifying its certainty of self but at the same time an unfreedom of mind that needs to be overcome no less than the perceiving consciousness's taking its other as a thing of many properties. Thus in both knowing and acting, the subjectivity's being for itself as universality requires a liberating experience of the contradiction within itself in taking its other in the sensuously conditioned form of thingness.

The ego's letting go of its objects is connected essentially with another moment, which remains but implicit on the level of consciousness, where alteration appears to the phenomenal subject to come from the side of the object.[36] In self-consciousness, which has consciousness as its object, the self-distinguishing of the ego is not only a letting go of the object but at the same time a working off of its own singularity as natural desire and self-will. In comparison with consciousness's taking its object as an independent not-I, self-consciousness has the certainty that in all reality it will encounter again its own self. This idealism of self-consciousness is a higher freedom than that of consciousness. But if consciousness's empiricism is a flawed objectivity, self-consciousness's idealism is an unverified self-certainty that must be worked off and worked up to *Wahrheit* if it is not to remain an unfreedom. The object of the desiring self-consciousness is in itself a negative whose sham independence serves but to whet the ego's appetite to exercise its own sovereign power of negativity. But the object of this ego, like the desiring ego itself, is a sensuous singularity, so that in the satisfaction of its consumption arises again the desire. The master self-consciousness, in risking its life, has worked off its senuous singularity insofar as this entails the particular ties of natural existence. The verification of being-for-self is now to come not in the consumption but the letting go of the other, which is no longer a nullity but also a subjectivity having the negating power in itself. But in exchange for its life the other is to have its being-for-self only in the master self-consciousness which it recognizes as independent. Since the nonindependent self-consciousness is not recognized in turn, however, and to that extent has the form of thingness,[37] the master's letting go remains incomplete; and since the natural object is now mediated by the toil of the other and is still for the master only something to be enjoyed, the master's working off of the immediacy of desire remains abstract. Despite the one-sidedness of the recognition, it is an acknowledgment that freedom is impossible without life. In the quaking fear of the master and its belaboring of the natural object for the enjoyment of another, the nonindependent self-consciousness works off the immediacy of desire and singularity of self-will. Thus the struggle for recognition is a letting go and a working off: the ego's letting go of the other and its working off of its sensuous singularity. Since this double-sided universalizing activity takes place in two self-consciousnesses it constitutes an incomplete self-distinguishing and return to self of subjectivity. But in the acknowledgment of life and provision for the common need, and in the institution of political community, the two self-consciousness are mediated to the self-distinguishing universal individuality that is in and for self universal. Thus the liberation struggle of the phenomenal consciousness is its lived experience of its own contradiction, a simultaneous knowing and acting whereby it overcomes its separation of ego and other and returns to itself as unity of subject and object, or the universality of reason.

At this point let us review some main aspects of the development of consciousness as a liberation struggle. Since cognition and freedom are for Hegel immanently connected in the subjectivity as self-distinguishing, they do not belong to separate faculties of understanding and desire. The unity of the knowing, desiring self was already seen by Spinoza and Leibniz. In Hegel, however, it is demonstrated as an *Entwicklungsprozess* of the subjectivity as Notion. From the immediate feeling unity on the physical level emerges the experiencing ego that cognizes and desires its object as an other. The subjectivity does not merely use universals and judgments in its knowing and acting, any more than is uses its desires or its drive for recognition. The experiencing consciousness is its universals, and as self-dividing it is at once *Ur-teil* and the impulse to overcome its dividedness. On the phenomenal level, the subjectivity lets go of itself as object and works off its limitations as subject. We have made greater use of *entlassen* and *abarbeiten* than of other Hegelian expressions because they seem best to convey the nature of the development as a liberation struggle. As moments of the subjective self-distinguishing and return, letting go and working off are dialectical opposites that coalesce with one another. In consciousness, where alteration appears to come from the side of the object, letting go expresses better the seemingly passive role of the subject. In self-consciousness, where the subjectivity has the certainty of itself as the negating power, working off seems more appropriate. But to the philosopher, if not to consciousness itself, consciousness is not merely passive but also active in the *Fortbestimmung* of the object, and the singular ego's letting the object go from its sensuous grip is simultaneously its working off of its own immediacy as a natural consciousness. Conversely, the desiring self-consciousness's working off of its appetite compulsions through experience of their bad infinity is simultaneously its letting go of the singularity that has served only as an object for consumption. The freedom struggle of consciousness is its progressive letting go of the object to inwardize itself as law and finally life, at which point the inner self-distinguishing universality of the object is identical with that of consciousness itself, and consciousness of the object becomes self-consciousness. The unfreedom of consciousness is its *beharren bleiben* in some incomplete letting go, where the object remains for it a given, a found, a *Seiendes* not mediated through itself. The freedom of self-consciousness is its working off of its natural singularity as ego by directing its negating power against itself as well as its other, until it knows itself in the other as the universal of reason. In this way the universal human bond of free reason is neither connected dogmatically with adequate ideas nor put outside the scope of theoretical cognition but emerges experientially in a liberation struggle as a struggle for recognition. The unfreedom of self-consciousness, e.g., that of the master, is a clinging to itself as a natural singularity of desire or self-will, which means to say, a failing to work off these limitations to ideal moments of its fluid universality.

But whether we focus on the letting go or the working off, there is in consciousness and self-consciousness alike an element that renders the liberation struggle a phenomenological pathway. The self-negating of the subjectivity is not exercised directly upon itself as a pure self-liberating, but mediately through the agency of the other. Even on the level of self-consciousness where the subjectivity has the *Gewissheit* of itself as all reality, the ego does not "freely" give up its natural singularity and self-will. Rather its hand is forced so to speak, as in the fear and enforced toil of the dependent self-consciousness. This is the unfreedom generally of the phenomenal subjectivity. In attaining to the universality of reason, the subjectivity enters a new plane of freedom. As rational intelligence the subjectivity knows that what is is its own, and its own is.[38] On this new level, which Hegel calls free mind, the letting go and the working off obtain a wholly internal character more truly commensurate with the nature of freedom.

III

Through experiencing the contradiction within itself in relating itself to its object as a not-I, the subjectivity has freed itself from its phenomenality and won its way back to the wholeness not of feeling merely, as on the psychical level, but of thinking. Henceforward, as free mind and intelligence, it distinguishes and returns to itself as intuiting intelligence, representing intelligence, and thinking intelligence.[39] These forms of intelligence bear directly the mark of self-determinations that are no less objective than subjective. Mediation is now wholly self-mediation. The liberation process is transparently the subjectivity's own doing, its negating activity directly as self-creating. In this pure medium of self the moments of letting go and working off, externalization and internalization, passive receptivity and formative activity are even more subtly interrelated than before. To begin with, however, free mind gives itself the form of immediacy and the developmental provess consists again in the subjectivity's overcoming of the singularity of sensuousnness, the contingency of foundness, and the externality of thingness as limitations that free mind sets for itself in actualizing itself as reason.

Intelligence in its immediacy is for Hegel intuition, but this is neither the sterling intellectual intuition of Fichte and Schelling nor the Kantian faculty of intuition that is receptive of an external senuous material for a phenomenal knowing. Intuition for Hegel is indeed senuous and receptive of a material, but it is a subjectivity and not a faculty. The intuiting subject is a totality, a feeling intelligence that has incorporated within itself both the inner feeling-life of the pysche and the external world of the experiencing consciousness. These are its materials that it finds within itself, and its receptivity is thus a relation to itself. The content from the soul and consciousness having been raised to reason, the intuitive intelligence concentrates within itself all the representations of the outer world, including those of right, morality, and religion. With this content, in the simple immediacy of feeling, it can stand in utmost closeness. Where such a closeness to the content can be combined with a perspective of the whole, as in the case of a great historian or poet, the intuitive intelligence can mean a depth and breadth of mind. But the immediacy of feeling can just as well be a shallow sentimentalism and a contingency of outlook that is anything but a freedom of mind.

But that the intuitive intelligence's finding of the object bespeaks no mere faculty of receptivity is best indicated in the manner of the finding itself. Here again, self-distinguishing is the primal act of subjectivity, the free act that is its own nature and the ground of all its freedoms. The immediate finding by intuition entails in the first place an attending, a focusing of mind in the absence of which there is nothing to be found. Epistemologists usually take attention for granted as part of awareness generally. Only provided I attend, Descartes should have said, am I no longer at liberty to deny the object set before my senses; for there can be many objects standing before me which I do not see unless I pay attention. In Hegel the dialectic of cognition as a free self-activity is exemplified in attention as a moment of intuition. However much we take it for granted, attention is an attainment of mind, a strength and a freedom. In exhaustion and weakness our power of attention flags; *Faselei,*[40] a continuous mental rambling, is noted by Hegel as a disease of the psyche and as much an unfreedom of mind as the fixed idea. The free mind's attending is termed by Hegel "the active inwardizing, the moment of making unto its own.[41] In attending to the object I exercise my negating power first of all upon myself. I cut myself off from a swarm of distractions, I close my ears to all blandishments. But unlike Odysseus, who stuffed the ears of his crewmen and listened with his own, I combine in myself the shutting off and leaving open. I close myself to the predilections within me that would have me prejudge the object, in order to absord myself in it and let it have its say.[42] Here we have the simultaneous letting go and working off the we noted in the dependent self-consciousness, the receptivity toward the other that is at the same time an activity against the self. Nevertheless in attention as intuition, the moments are still to some extent external to one another, for the intelligence in its self-collectedness is immersed in the out-of-selfness. Hence the objectivity of the content is predominant and the free mind's absorption in the externality of intuition can become a fixation.[43] In its immediacy of apprehension, the intuitive intelligence does not grasp the subject matter as an inwardly articulated systematic totality. Hence intuition is not the end but the beginning of cognitive freedom.

With regard to the content as such, since the intelligence's finding is its appropriating of a material already within itself, the content as a *Gefundenes* is neither the independent not-I of consciousness nor the object of desire that is a self-externality for the subject merely. As extended in space and time, the *Gefundenes* is already external to itself, and in the forms of space and time, wherein the intelligence is intuitive, the subject intuits the object not as a mere appearance of a Kantian thing-in-itself, but rather as the very self-externality that the spatiotemporal object is in itself.[44]

To release itself from its immersion in the externality, intelligence incorporates the intuition within the mind's own inwardness in *Vorstellung*. In the three phases of representation: recollection, imagination, and memory,[45] we can see the process of cognition once again as a letting go and working off of singleness, thingness, and contingency that is simultaneously practiced by the mind upon itself as well as its content, so that it can actualize its cognitive freedom as the universal that is for itself the universal. The content still has the aspect of a *Gefundenes* and a *Seiendes*, but in setting the content before itself, the representing intelligence makes the found its own and establishes itself as its being. The development of the representing intelligence is a working off of the synthetic connecting of representation as such, so that the content can assume the pure forms of thought connected immanently as notions.

In recollection (*Erinnerung*), the initial phase of representation, the intelligence places the feeling content of intuition within the space and time of the mind's own inwardness, the content becoming an image *(Bild)*. The *Gefundenes* of intuition is hereby released from its singleness, detached from the spatiotemporal context in which it happens to have been found, and taken into the universality of the ego, which can form an image even of what is remote from it in time and space. Losing the vividness of the intuition, the image recedes into the subconsciousness—the "night-like pit" of the ego, as Hegel terms it[46]— where it is stored as a material for universalization. In this wealth of materials I am not yet free, for I do not have full command of the images that slumber within me and are therefore only in a formal sense mine. In remembrance, or *Erinnerung* proper, I am stimulated by a given intuition to bring the image to an awareness that is both a recognition of the outer in the inner and a confirmation of the inner in the outer. Repetition of this confirming recognition produces a *hexis,* my taking possession of what was only formally mine, so that my store of images becomes my own free element in which I am no longer dependent on external intuition.

The intelligence that has made the power over its images has raised itself to imagination (*Einbildungskraft*). To the extent that the image retains certain elements of the original intuition, the imagination is reproductive. But the storing of the image within the universality of the ego has also tended towards a dissolving of its original ties and a recomposing of its features. From the associating intelligence the content obtains the form of a general representation. This synthesizing of the images by the intelligence is often viewed by empirical psychology in terms of an association of ideas. Hegel's critique of the so-called laws of association throws light on his own developmental approach to cognition as a free activity. Empirical psychology would explain the formation of general ideas by abstraction as a falling together of many similar images through an alleged force of attraction,[47] which, Hegel remarks wryly, should at least be complemented by a rubbing away of dissimilar features by a force of repulsion. By in fact, says Hegel, the combining and separating of its materials is nothing other than the activity of the self-identical ego. In inwardizing the intuition the intelligence simultaneously generalizes the image and subsumes the single intuition under the internalized image: that is to say, as its return to self in infusing its images with its own ideality, the intelligence is itself the associating, abstracting activity of producing general representations. This return to self in its manifold materials is the free mind's own attainment, not the outcome of a mechanical play of forces.

In the associative imagination I am the subjective bond of the images arising within me, and my moving freely in a medium of my own, as Hegel notes, can express itself in witticisms and punning.[48] But having specific aims and concerns, I express my freedom by more than a mental disporting. In symbolizing, allegorizing, and poetizing I make my storehouse of images my internal studio, whose materials I fashion to my subjective purposes. As creative imagination or *Phantasie* the representing intelligence has worked off the contingent connections of object as a *Gefundenes* to the point where the image serves as a mere outer occasion of an inner universal signification. In the symbol, where the relation of inner and outer is in some degree dependent on resemblance, the intelligence is only partially with its own. In the sign, where the natural object no longer determines the meaning, intelligence has made the intuition its own property. But since the intuition was originally given in space, and now as a sign is no longer a *Seiendes* but an *Aufgehobenes,* the most appropriate medium for the sign-creating intelligence is the vocal note, whose being is directly a vanishing.[49]. In language the intelligence creates its own medium of self-utterance, and in the name, the creative imagination completes its connecting of inner and outer. But the name itself is a contingent externality, so that the unity of inner and outer is itself contingent and therefore outer. In working off this last externality, the representing intelligence constitutes itself as memory (*Gedächtnis*).

In memory we are still dealing with the activity of representation, the inwardizing of the external content of intuition. Whereas in recollection and imagination the intelligence synthesized its materials in the general representation, memory works off the synthetic character of the representation as such. This it proceeds to do, first, by making the synthesis its own through retaining the content and holding it together with the name as sign in the name-retaining memory. In this way the content as inner and the name as outer become one representation that no longer vanishes in time like the spoken word but becomes an abiding inwardness of meaning that has its there-being (*Dasein*) in the intelligence.

The name, now the unity of sign and signification, is ready to hand for intelligence to set before itself in its *Vorstellung*. This synthetic unity, which has the formulalike character of a nonpictorial mnemonic, is termed by Hegel the *Sache*.[50] Needing either outer intuition nor image, the reproductive memory has and recognizes the *Sache* in the name. The name is an intuition produced by the intelligence itself, and the content's existing in this fashion: namely, in a formula of the intelligence's own making, is the mind's own act of making itself external to itself. Its linking of names is intelligence's connecting of its determinations of feeling, representing, and thinking. We think in names, the nonpictorial simple signs that the mind has produced out of itself and set before itself. In producing the name as the externality of its own inwardness, the mind has distinguished itself from itself in order, by returning to itself in the distinction, to actualize itself as a freedom of thinking.[51]

A mere connecting of names is no necessary connectedness of thought. In mechanical memory the fluency in names is but a subjective power, a mere inner that is just as well a mere outer. To free itself from its superficial familiarity with names, the representing intelligence must let go these products of its own making and simultaneously negate itself as a mindless mechanism of memorization. Mechanical or rote memory is representation's highest inwardizing and also the intelligence's utmost self-externalizing. In rote, as a meaningless reciting of names, the intelligence makes itself the mere empty being, the universal space of a series whose insignificant order bespeaks a merely abstract power of subjectivity. Intelligence thus makes itself an externality, and its product becomes again a *Gefundenes*. As in the case of attention, the intelligence has let go its subjectively meaningful associations and made itself an open space for the object. But this self-negating is more radical than in intuition, for the intelligence has made itself the being of the object only after it has worked off the object's spatiotemporal self-externality in Recollection and imagination. Now in mechanical memory it works off the one-sided inwardness of representation generally, so that the intelligence itself is at once the presentation and its meaning. Having freed itself from itself as *Vor-stellung*, i.e., setting the object before itself in order to determine it synthetically, the intelligence is no longer representation but thinking, whose object is determinate not by virtue of synthetic connections but through its own inner self-distinguishing.

The activity of the thinking intelligence is once more a finding, but what is found is no longer an outer intuition or an image. It is the name containing the *Sache*: an intuition that both is, and is the intelligence's own. The finding is thus re-cognitive (*Wiedererkennend*),[52] the found a universal that possesses being. Reason now exists in the subjectivity as the identity of subject and object that knows itself as this identity. As an immediacy, this identity is indeterminate, an unverified *Gewissheit*. But as understanding, the intelligence works off the givenness of its content, the materials of memory's representations, initially by showing that the truth of the content lies in categories and judgments as forms of thought. Finally, as reason the intelligence comprehends the content as a syllogistic closing together with itself in its determinations, thus as the inwardly self-distinguishing universal uniting form and content. With this last sublation of the givenness of its content, thought, whose forms are the free notion, is now also free in its content. At this point the thinking intelligence has actualized itself as free mind. The subject's self-liberating endeavors as soul, ego, and intelligence, which have been directed necessarily upon itself as well as its object, have meant that the content of its knowing has been let free to develop itself according to its own necessity. My own thinking in notions remaining thoroughly immanent in the notional development of the object, my knowing is a looking on which alters nothing by intrusion of my subjective fancies.[53]

Aware that it is determinative of its content as what is and is its own, the cognizing intelligence is will.[54] In cognition the subjectivity has proved itself to be free; in will it makes its freedom its content and aim.

Our study of Hegel's immanent connecting of cognition and freedom has shown how freedom is the root of cognition, and cognition is an essential component of freedom. The connecting is grounded in the notion of subjectivity, which is conceived by all the thinkers we have mentioned as self-relation and the universality of reason. Freedom is essentially a self-relation. But self-relation is and has to be in first instance cognitive. Whether theoretical or practical, self-relation is only possible through the self's knowing or sensing or feeling itself in its activity. Without this primary cognitive relationship that constitutes a self—or whereby the self constitutes itself a self—there can be no self-activity, hence no free activity, but only mechanism. This is the insight implicit in Descartes' separating of the thinking ego from physical nature. But in Hegel, subjectivity, and thereby self-activity, is conceived differently from Descartes, Spinoza, and Kant: namely, as the indentity that distinguishes itself from itself and becomes for itself in its distinction. In this way self-relation becomes a dialectic in which the self and that from which it distinguishes itself are implicitly identical in the very distinguishing. The subjectivity is the identity of its manifold determinations, the inner self-distinguishing universality whose particular determinations are moments of its concrete totality.

By conceiving subjectivity in this way, Hegel is able to view the relation of mind and nature, soul and body as an identity in opposition, whereby the being-for-self subjectivity actualizes itself in its own natural or corporeal being as its being-in-self. The natural subjectivity as soul distinguishes itself from its corporeal manifold and returns to itself as the universal that is for itself in the fluid universality of its inner feeling-life. The ego of consciousness and self-consciousness lets go its natural content of feeling and obtains its being-for-self in its experience of the object as an other. In this way objective experience goes beyond the self-enclosed feeling-life. It is an attainment of the subjectivity in concretizing its universality, and signifies at once a form of cognition and a freedom of mind. To obtain its being-for-self in the other, the ego, through its experience of the contradiction within itself in its certainty of identity with the other, must work off its own sensuous singularity and egocentricity. Only in this way does it attain to the universality of reason postulated by the previous thinkers. The intelligence actualizes itself as this universality in the process of suffusing its inner materials with universality by successively internalizing and externalizing both itself and its content.

That the subjectivity actualizes its being-for-self universality on succeeding levels means that freedom is a process of self-unfolding; and since the process proceeds through limitation and its overcoming, freedom and unfreedom are not fixed opposites but in dialectical opposition. For the mind to experience its content as an independent thing rather than what is immediately its own, is an attainment and a freedom; but at the same time it is a limitation, a contradiction for the being-for-self universality, and an unfreedom. The same is true of desire. Attention is a constraint and a *versenktsein* of the mind in an otherness: yet attention is also an attainment, a freedom, and a basis for all higher freedoms. Rote memory is similarly a freedom and an unfreedom of mind, and the same can be said on each level of the mind's self-determination. Thus the mind's concretization of its self-activity means its letting go of itself in its particular determinations, so that the latter can become a limitation, an other to which the mind submits, abandons, and alienates itself, so that, by its power of negativity, it may work off at once its own limitedness and that of the other in which it is immersed. In this way the self-relation of freedom becomes self-determination, and it is for this reason that Hegel terms cognition a liberation struggle and a freedom.

NOTES

1. *Critique of Pure Reason,* trans. by Norman Kemp Smith (London: Macmillan & Co. Ltd., 1956), B xxx.
2. *Lectures on the History of Philosophy,* trans. by E.H. Haldane and F.H. Simson, 3 vols (New York: Humanities Press, 1955), 3:407.
3. *Mediations on First Philosophy,* Mediation IV: *Principles of Philosophy,* Principles XXXII ff.
4. Hegel, *Lectures on the History of Philosophy,* 3:225–226.
5. *Enzyklopädie der philosophischen Wissenschaften im Grundrisse* (1830), ed. by F. Nicolin and O. Pöggeler (Hamburg: Felix Meiner, 1959), p. 360: remark to #445.
6. *Ethics,* pt. II, prop. 49.
7. *Ethics,* pt. II, prop. 43 and note.
8. *Ethics,* pt. II, prop. 12 and 13.
9. *Ethics,* pt. II, prop. 48.
10. *Ethics,* pt. II, prop. 13, note.
11. "The concept of freedom determines nothing in respect of the theoretical cognition of nature . . . . " *Critique of Judgment,* trans. by J.C. Meredith (London: Oxford University Press, repr. 1969), p. 37.
12. Kant, *Critique of Pure Reason,* A 801 = B 829 (fn.).
13. Hegel, *Enzyklopädie,* #382.
14. *Ibid.,* ##247, 248, 575–577.
15. *Ibid.,* #381.
16. *Ibid.,* #351.
17. *Ibid.,* ##369, 370.
18. *Ibid.,* #376.
19. *Ibid.,* #405.
20. *Hegel's Philosophy of Subjective Spirit,* ed. and trans. by M.J. Petry, 3 vols (Boston: D. Reidel, 1978), 3:212, addition to #402.
21. Hegel, *Enzyklopädie,* #411.
22. *Ibid.,* #408.
23. *Ibid.,* #410.
24. *Ibid.,* #413.
25. Particularly in the transition from substance to subject, necessity to freedom: Hegel, *Enzyklopädie,* ##159–161.
26. Petry, *Hegel's Philosophy of Subjective Spirit,* 3:4, addition to #413.
27. *Ibid.*

28. Hegel, *Enzyklopädie*, #411.
29. Kant, *Critique of Pure Reason,* A 15.
30. Hence we cannot know how our sensibility, understanding, and their ground, the apperception, are possible, since we need to employ them in thinking about them. *Prolegomena to Any Future Metaphysics,* trans. by P.G. Lucas (Manchester: Manchester University Press, 1953), p. 80.
31. Hegel, *Enzyklopädie*, #442 and remark.
32. *Wissenschaft der Logik,* ed. by G. Lasson, 2 vols. (Leipzig: Felix Meiner, 1951), 2:432.
33. Hegel, *Phänomenologie des Geistes* (Hamburg: Felix Meiner, 1952), p. 69.
34. *Ibid.*, p. 71; Hegel, *Enzyklopädie*, #10 remark.
35. Hegel, *Enzyklopädie*, #227.
36. *Ibid.*, #415.
37. Hegel, *Phänomenologie des Geistes*, p. 145.
38. Hegel, *Enzyklopädie*, #443.
39. Petry, *Hegel's Philosophy of Subjective Spirit,* 3:114, addition to #445.
40. *Ibid.*, 2:114, addition to #408.
41. Hegel, *Enzyklopädie*, #448.
42. Petry, *Hegel's Philosophy of Subjective Spirit,* 3:138, addition to #449.
43. *Ibid.*, 3:142, addition to #450.
44. Hegel, *Enzyklopädie*, #448.
45. Petry, *Hegel's Philosophy of Subjective Spirit, vol. 3, ±451 an addition.*
46. *Hegel, Enzyklopädie, #453 remark.*
47. *Ibid.*, #455 remark.
48. Petry, *Hegel's Philosophy of Subjective Spirit,* 3:164, addition to #455.
49. Hegel, *Enzyklopädie*, #459, see also Petry, *Hegel's Philosophy of Subjective Spirit,* 2:198, addition to #401.
50. Hegel, *Enzyklopädie*, #462.
51. "We only know of our thoughts, only have determinate, actual thoughts, when we give them the form of objectivity, of a being distinguished from our inwardness, thus the form of externality, and the very kind of externality that at the same time bears the stamp of the highest inwardness." Petry, Hegel's *Philosophy of Subjective Spirit,* 3:204, addition to #462.
52. Hegel, *Enzyklopädie*, #465. Cf. Plato's *anamnesis,* and Descartes' recognitive knowing of our clear and distinct ideas.
53. Petry, *Hegel's Philosophy of Subjective Spirit,* 1:18, addition to #379.
54. Hegel, *Enzyklopädie*, #468.

BETWEEN THE TWILIGHT OF THEORY
AND THE MILLENNIAL DAWN:
AUGUST VON CIESZKOWSKI AND MOSES HESS

by
LAWRENCE S. STEPELEVICH

In concluding his lectures on the history of philosophy, Hegel noted that "we can be Platonists no longer."[1] Of course, this simply means that the *Zeitgeist* which Plato reflected and that nourished his thought was no more. Now, by the same token I believe that we can be Hegelians no longer. A Hegelian must know that Hegel's Hegelianism cannot be repeated, for no philosophy can transcend its own time, and Hegel's time is no more. To be a Hegelian today must mean in some way to go beyond Hegel. To accept this principle of historicity, of a philosophical *Aufhebung* which generates Hegelianism after Hegel is a decision that makes a so-called "Young Hegelian."

The first generation of Young Hegelians—and they were in fact young men[2]—had directly witnessed Hegel's victorious campaigns upon the fields of speculation, and so were prepared to join battle with the irrational forces so evident within themselves and their work. Naturally, in principle—*sub specie aeternitatis*—the real *was* rational, but *actual* conditions surely appeared—*sub specie temporis*—to be fraught with political fantasies and religious illusions, and the actual seemed far from rational. In the usual terms, theory and practice had yet to be reconciled. Their times, or perhaps merely their judgement upon Metternich's Europe, provoked the Young Hegelians into stepping beyond the line of Hegel's theoretical quietism—as his doctrine appeared—and to set about the incarnation of Absolute Knowledge. Now we, of a later generation of Hegelians, were born during the happy rediscovery of Hegel, participants in the "Hegel Renaissance."[3] But now, Hegel *redivivus*—or at least the immanent exhuming of his complete literary remains—excites a question

213

in us not unlike that which faced the first generation of Hegelians: what are we now to *do* with this recovered wisdom? If we can be Hegelians no longer, can we avoid being Young Hegelians? I believe that the best of today's young Hegelians—the younger generation—are not content to be but the Alexandrians of German Idealism, simply satisfied to follow in the vanishing footsteps of that forgotten generation of "Old" Hegelians. This present discontent sets matters at a crucial stage in the history of *manifest* Hegelianism, i.e., that which goes under the name "Hegelianism." Scholarly exigesis, now almost exhausted in its uncovering of the corpus of Hegel's Hegelianism, can presently either collapse into a heap of dry pedantry or it can, hopefully, rise up to serve as the foundation of an authentic Hegelian philosophy of action. But in any case, I think it can be said that today's Young Hegelians, just as the first generation, have little desire to be impaled upon the horns of Karl Rosenkranz's dilemma; to be either Hegel's gravediggers or his monument builders.[4] The first generation were unafraid, or, if you will, imprudent enough to question the matter of the practical and so future meaning of Hegel's doctrines; and although fault can certainly be found in their premises and logic, we might yet admire their daring, for this factor alone might well be the necessary condition for the extension of the provence of reason beyond the closeted sphere of scholarship, and whatever missteps they took in that dark period that first followed upon the flight of Minerva's Owl, should not deter us from essaying a few forward glances. And so, with the small hope of provoking such an essay, I would like to present two of the earliest pioneers of a Hegelian philosophy of action: August von Cieszkowski (1814–1894) and Moses Hess (1812–1875). They can serve to illustrate some of the brashness and confusion that might always be entailed in "doing something" with the teaching of Hegel. Today, their names are all but forgotten, and yet both, in proposing a future in accord with reason stand at the theoretical centers of two of the most significant forces in the modern world—Marxism and Zionism.

The honor, or notoriety, of being the first of the Young Hegelians is usually accorded to David F. Strauss (1808–1874). His masterful *Leben Jesu*, which appeared in 1835, destroyed the precarious bridge that had linked Hegelianism to the orthodox powers of the Prussian state and Lutheranism. By a bold, and perhaps exaggerated application of Hegel's distinction between the philosophical *Begriff* and the religious *Vorstellung*, Strauss reduced the whole of Christ's miraculous history into a purely mythic, i.e., ideological exercise. But most important for the subsequent history of *political* Hegelianism, he identified Mankind and the Christ. By first evoking the image of a collective salvation through collective action, Strauss prepared the way for the full secularization of the messianic mythology. But in all this, Strauss himself had thought merely to *apply* the principles of Hegelianism to the arena of dogmatic history, and had no intention to *revise* Hegelianism. This was left to August von Cieszkowski. Strauss saw himself to be but Hegel in the garb of gospel critic, but Cieszkowski understood himself to be, in an important respect, Hegel's *successor.*

The body of Cieszkowski's critical revision is contained in his first major work, the *Prolegomena zur Historiosophie,* which appeared in 1838. I would certainly agree with Nicholas Lobkowicz's evaluation of this work, for it is, as he says, "as far as the notion of *praxis* is concerned,. . . the most brilliant and the most important single text published between Hegel's death in 1831 and the *Philosophical and Economic Manuscripts of Marx.*"[5] The *Prolegomena to the Wisdom of History* exercised an early and profound effect upon transforming Hegelian theory into a program of world-revolution, an effect that makes it all more surprising that this seminal work has been all but totally ignored by Hegelian scholars.

Cieszkowski's restructuring of Hegelianism had its deepest motivation in his own millenial optimism, an optimism that he took to be in accord with the essential elements of Christianity, an optimism that remained constant and intense throughout his life, and that infused all of his later writings.[6] He was not, as so many of the Young Hegelians who followed after him, angry, and chose to refer to himself somewhat paradoxically as "a conservative in the fullest and most progessive sense of the term."[7] This conservative and confident side of Cieszkowski seems fitting to his station—he was a Polish aristocrat born to wealth and influence.

The central principle underlying Cieszkowski's particular revision of Hegel's doctrine, and a principle operative throughout Young Hegelianism in general, is announced early in the *Prolegomena:*

> Anyone who establishes a principle is obliged by the same token to acknowledge its most extreme consequences regardless of whether these are drawn out by him or someone else. Woe to him if the principle is overturned—but glory, eternal glory, if the result which he himself was perhaps not able to attain later confirms the new discovery! This is precisely Hegel's lot as well as the fate of all those whom we can call in any way great. Admittedly, Hegel himself was not able to draw out all the consequences of his standpoint, but this does not detract from his merit, and whoever remedies an acknowledged deficiency in his system or even simply develops the system normally by progressing beyond Hegel's point of view will doubtlessly render a far greater tribute to Hegel's genius than someone who sets out to preserve an untouchable tradition. After all, could Hegel, who deduced the laws of development so forcefully and demonstrated them in the genesis of ideas repudiate his own discoveries?[8]

In this, all of the ambiguities entailed in the term "creative disciple" are in evidence.

Now, as Cieszkowski was temperamentally unable to rest content with leaving the inheritance of Hegel an "untouchable tradition" — as the "Old" Hegelians were inclined—so he took upon himself the creative task of remedying the "acknowledged deficiency." This deficiency, first discovered by Cieszkowski, and then revealed in the *Prolegomena*, is simply that "the laws of logic which he [Hegel] was the first to reveal are not adequately reflected in his philosophy of history.[9]

As we know, Hegel divides the course of history into four great periods: the Oriental, the Greek, the Roman, and the Christian-German. Together they form the organism of history—the continuing course of Spirit in it progress to self-revelation. Cieszkowski takes the organic view of history as undoubtedly the correct view, but what of the presence of the dialectic in this advance of the Spirit? Where is the familiar and all-embracing triad of spiritual development? To Cieszkowski, Hegel's fourfold division is not at all in keeping with the very nature of history itself. History is the development of Spirit, and as such that development must be dominated by the triadic dialectic, and not be expressed in a fourfold articulation fitted only to natural, physical phenomena. It appears that Hegel had not reflected upon how the Spirit must operate in its historical course. He had, in short, made a mistake. Cieszkowski might have had in mind Hegel's own statement regarding the exact applications of the triadic dialectic of the Spirit and the fourfold elaboration of the natural. In the *Naturphilosophie* it is said that

> In Nature, as Other-being, the square (Quadrat) or the tetrad (Vierheit) also belongs to the complete form of its necessity, for example, the four elements, the four colours, etc., and further, the pentad (Funfheit) may also be found, for example, the five fingers, the five senses, etc; but in Spirit the basic form of necessity is the triad. In Nature the totality of the disjunction of the Begriff exists as four-ness, the first of which is universality as such. The second term is difference, and appears in nature as a duality, for in nature the other must exist for itself in its otherness.[10]

Hegel, who all too often had been accused of a rigid triadic schematicism — despite his own demurs on the subject[11]—is in the matter of his philosophy of history simply not schematic enough. For those moderate Hegelians who would object to this rigid application of the triadic formula, Cieszkowski responds with the dilemma:

> Either the laws of dialectics are universal and inviolable and should thus find their real manifestation in history; or else they are weak, partial, and inadequate, in which case they should not be proclaimed in other spheres of knowledge and their deduction must everywhere be deprived of all necessity.[11]

Furthermore, not only is Hegel in violation of his own principles, but has—by so doing—distorted the very nature of history itself. History is not merely a past and a present, but it is also a future. To fix history into but a retrospective activity of consciousness is to deny the dynamics of Spirit, and so to close it off from the future. To Cieszkowski, and those who were to follow along his course, such a limited view was as emotionally unsatisfying as it was philosophically untenable. History, as the organic process of the Spirit, must continue beyond Hegel, and it is this future—of which Hegel utters "not a syllable"[12]—that completes the "speculative tricotomy" of history. In Cieszkowski's words,

> The totally of universal history is . . . to be grasped integrally and absolutely as a speculative tricotomy, but if we are to avoid prejudicing the freedom of its development it is history in its totality and not simply a part of history such as the past which we must seize speculatively and organically. The totality of history must consist of the past and of the future, of the road already travelled, as well as of the road yet to be travelled, and hence our first task is the cognition of the essence of the future through speculation.[13]

To those weak of spirit who might object that the future, as such, cannot be known, Cieszkowski reminds them that Hegel's absolute knowledge could not be called "absolute" if the future were to be declared a philosophical *terra incognita*. Again, since Hegelianism could comprehend the Kantian Absolutes of God, Freedom, and Immortality, then there remains no reason why it should not comprehend the future as well. Absolute Knowledge reaches into the realm of the yet-to-be, if not in terms of its existential particulars, then at least in terms of its general structure.

Once history is envisioned in terms of the speculative tricotomy, then Hegel's original divisions of history must be radically revised. Hegel's first three main periods, the Oriental, the Greek, and the Roman, are fused into the thesis of history—the past. Hegel's final period, the Christian-German world, becomes Cieszkowski's second period, which reaches into the present. The future is the synthetic period, whose nature is to be scientifically derived by canceling out the negative and one-sided moments of the past and the present; by elevating and preserving the positive moments of both.

In the past, the future was divined in the imagination of "seers and prophets." In the immediate post-Hegelian present, the future was finally comprehended in thought. But in this very perfection of theory the present age stands at the threshold of the future, of "post-theoretical practice." Knowing, either sensuous or speculative, ends in willing. In Cieszkowski's words, "that which imagination has sensed, and that which thought has come to know, will now be actualized by Absolute Will."[14]

Cieszkowski's view, in both its form and presentation, must recall our memory of Joachim Fiore. The compelling imagry of that grand and fantastic vision of the "Three Kingdoms" of history had certainly—consciously or not—enticed many, not the least being such as Lessing, Fichte, Schelling, and even Cieszkowski's mentor, Hegel. The dialectic of the third part of Hegel's *Religionsphilosophie*, in which the "Kingdom of the Father" passes into the "Kingdom of the Son" and thence—in the truth of its development—into the "Kingdom of the Spirit" could well serve as the bridge between Cieszkowski and the mystical Fiore.

In the *Prolegomena*, the first age is said to be that of the Father, it is the Ancient world dominated by subjective spirit, of personality locked into the limits of sensation, of action unenlightened by theory. It is the age of mere practice, of a *"praxis nur in ihrer schmutzig-jüdischen Erscheinungsform,"* to use Marx's ugly description of this pretheoretical activity.[15] It is the time of art, the ontology of being, and to recall the talk of Professor Lauer, a time in which *Bildung* expresses itself in sensibility. Its ethical life is but the first stage of objective spirit: abstract right. But in the fullness of time, this one-sided thesis gave way to a complimentary but antithetical new age. The birth of Christ sundered world-history, for with Him reflectivity enters upon the world-stage. What was substantial being to the ancients, the practical world, and the beautiful world, becomes, with the advent of the Son, an insubstantial, theoretical, distant, and threatening sensuousness. Subjective morality replaces abstract right, and pure theory displaces direct practice. But with Hegel, the age of speculation comes to an end. What Christ began, Hegel concluded, for thought now comprehends itself, and this perfected theory, this Absolute Knowledge, is now ripe for objectification. The thesis of world-history, practice, now stands fully revealed before theory and the age of spirit is announced. The future will unify practice and theory, being and thought, feeling and knowledge, art and philosophy, and this unity is termed *praxis*, the conscious willing of the absolute good. *Praxis* is, in short, the conscious practice of Absolute Knowledge. In Cieszkowski's words, "the future fate of philosophy in general is to be practical philosophy, or, to put it better, the *philosophy of praxis*, whose most concrete effect on life and social relations is the development of truth in concrete activity."[16]

At this point, we can recall that Hegel did speak of the future, but only one time, when he spoke of America as "the land of the future." We can also recall Professor Plant's brief speculations concerning what sort of a radical turn of the *Weltgeist* Hegel could have had in mind. Cieszkowski might well have proposed, although he did not, that America, once having exhausted its frontiers—both geographical and political—could serve as the spiritual soil upon which the new *Bildung*, the philosophy of praxis, could be erected.

But to Cieszkowski it was the person of Hegel who marked a "turning point," or, in Professor Taylor's phrase, a "provisional end of history." With him, theory was prepared to enter the actual world, and what has up until now been accomplished by the blind impulse of Spirit will be accomplished by conscious action. In the future, to Cieszkowski,

> World historical individuals, those heroes who represent nations in such a way that their own biographies can conviently pass for universal history, should no longer be blind instruments of contingency but conscious artisans of their own freedom. Only can God's will be done on earth as it is in heaven, i.e., with love, consciousness, freedom, whereas until now it has been realized through divine omnipotence without the self-consciousness and self-determined co-operation of humanity."[17]

But just as the coming of Christ marked the end of the ancient practical world and the beginning of the modern theoretical age, so Hegel, in consummating theory stands at the end of his world, at the threshold of action. The Hegelianism of Hegel is dying, and should die so that Hegelian *praxis* can be born.

This prognosis and death sentence would naturally shock Cieszkowski's own generation—still dominated by the thought of Hegel—but, as Cieszkowski observes:

> One may object that instead of dying out philosophy seems, on the very contrary, to be now establishing its hegemony and flowering. This would be as incorrect as if one wanted to consider the sun's zenith as its dawn. When Greece rejoiced in the works of Phidias, the hour of art was already near; Hegel is the Phidias of philosophy.[18]

Indeed, the sorry state of post-Hegelian philosophy does seem to bear out Cieszkowski's contention that philosophy, just as art, has lost its hold upon the Absolute Spirit, a contention that now certainly receives, from among most of today's philosophers, ready acceptance. Speculative philosophy after Hegel does appear—even to those who would wish otherwise, to be but a morbid and disjoined recital of its own sufferings, a recital interrupted all to frequently with suicidal threats.

In our age, the arguments of Cieszkowski might seem to be more inflated than inspired, and yet he did come to grips with a problem that Hegelians in name too often ignore: the future of the actual world. He well understood that the premises of the Christian-German world, which is yet in large measure our own, had exhausted their content; that narcissism or soul tending, otherworldliness, and a stoic carelessness about either the immediate world or its future, were not only becoming ever more unsatisfying, but were morally wrong—a violation of the Spirit and God's will.

In his own age, Cieszkowski's revelation of a future to be acted out in conformity to revealed philosophical principle exercised no small effect upon Germany's frustrated intellectuals. He had given them what their own time had denied them: a world-historical mission. The future, which hitherto had been but the dark provence of those driven half or fully mad by biblical prophecies, or but an empty stage upon which countless fantastic utopias could be erected, was now prepared for rational—i.e. "scientific"—cultivation. In short, Marx's "Scientific Socialism" was conceived during this short juncture of enlightenment optimism and romantic longings.

By the early 1840s the proposal that *praxis* must supplant theory was a ritual maxim among Young Hegelian circles, but it fell to one thinker—Moses Hess—to press Cieszkowski's millenial Hegelianism into an even more radical religious formulation, a formulation that—although its triads and language sometimes resembled Hegelianism—had little to do with it either in it origin or intention. Just as Cieszkowski had revised Hegel, so Hess would revise Cieszkowski, and the resulting doctrine would be passed on to inspire Marx.

From his earliest years, Hess was infused with the despairing sentiments that arose from being of an oppressed people. In a telling anecdote of his youth, he recalled the evenings spent with his beloved grandfather, and of hearing the tales of the long sufferings of the Jewish people. While the grandfather read of the expulsion of the Jews from their home in Israel, "the snow-white beard of this strong old man was covered with tears in the telling of this story, and we children ourselves could not hold back from weeping and sobbing."[19] It seems fitting to remark here that in 1840—the year in which Hess revised the work of Cieszkowski—the Jewish community celebrated the year as 5600, a year that many thought would herald a new, and better age for all Jews.[20] Would not Hess have shared in this hope? It is not hard to imagine that the Rhineland Jews, and Hess was one, had felt their new sufferings under Prussian rule all the more acutely after they had enjoyed a brief moment of right under the Napoleonic code. He was of the same generation of Heine, Lasalle, Börne, and Disraeli, and he suffered the same confused pains of a liberal Jew in a cruel and conservative age, but—even when most in doubt about the role of his faith in the modern world—he never turned against it or its people with the repellent bitterness of a Marx. However, at twenty-three, Hess despaired of Judaism, and declared that since the destruction of the Temple there had been

> no religion, but only a longing after a lost and never-to-be recovered good, and yet even with this powerful longing every trace of that early and authentic Judaism would—and should—vanish.[21]

As I earlier noted, the dominant sentiment of Cieszkowski was optimism. He was confident in the rationality of history, of its organic logic and complimentary moments. In Hess, the sentiment was one of longing—but not for "a lost and never-to-be recovered good"—but for a future of reasoned peace and social harmony in which the angry and competing tensions of this contrary present age would be resolved and forgotten.

Most certainly, Hess had little cause for confidence, and this inquietude rests at the source of his *Philosophie der Tat*.[22] But if young Hess lost his first religion, he soon gained another—Spinozism. To Hess, Spinoza was what Hegel had been to Cieszkowski — not merely a personal inspiration, but a crucial Christ-like turning point in history. In 1837, Hess published his first book, *The Sacred History of Mankind (Die heilige Geschichte der Menschheit)*. He signed it only as "a disciple of Spinoza." Badly written and bearing all the flaws of the autodidact, the work was hardly noticed, yet it can claim to be the first original socialist work to appear in German directed to Germans. Both in form and content it indicated the course that both Hess and German Socialism were to follow in the years to come. It was, as the *Prolegomena*, fixed into the familiar triadic form.

Later, looking back upon its composition, Hess remarked that "Spinoza had elevated my consciousness of God to a height where I—with the bible in one hand and the *Ethics* in the other—wrote *The Sacred History of Mankind.*"[23] There was, he asserted, no further influences working upon him other than these two revered sources; there was "no Swedenborg, no Saint-Simon, no Bentham, no Lamennais, no Hegel, no Heine, no so-called 'Young Germany.'"[24] Historical evidence would support the contention that young Hess knew little of Hegel or Hegelianism at the time he wrote *The Sacred History*. In sum, the triad, which he will henceforth employ—at least in its origins—is not either a conscious or unconscious reflection of Hegel's dialectical form, but is rather grounded in the prophetic tradition of biblical literature. As it will be seen, if it does resemble a Hegelian form, it resembles the developmental form of nature, in which "the second term is a difference, and appears . . . as a duality." This ignorance of and Manichean divergence from the Hegelian mode of development merits notice, for it means that Hess's socialistic dialectic does not originate in Hegel, and to attribute explicit Hegelian influences upon Hess's first and fundamental expression of Communist theory—as Isaiah Berlin has done[25]—is to allow socialist doctrine, at least in this instance, to draw sustenance from the authority of Hegel.

The Sacred History—"sacred" because human history is the manifestation of the divine will—is an unstable amalgam of Enlightenment epistemology and biblical enthusiasm—or inspiration—that traces mankind's historical *via delarosa* to what Hess terms the "New Jerusalem."[26] The first age is, not unexpectedly, the age of the Father—one of innocence, unity, and passivity. In this period, knowledge of God is found in the imagination alone, which picture Him set beyond human reach. This childhood of mankind, reaching from Adam to Christ, was one of implicit equality and freedom—as yet untouched by the evils of private property. The second age, that of the Son, now recognizes the holy as an inward disposition of the soul. Christ was the first to know God in this exclusive manner, privately, in his heart. Quite naturally, this inward feeling of a loving presence led to the evils of egoism. God, as known by the Christian, will be so identified with the private sentiments of the individual that social division must result. The sin of the present is grounded in the Christian's myopic concern with the disposition of his soul, and this egoism readily translates into economic selfishness, Capitalism. To Hess, Christian exclusiveness not only generated the opposing poles of clergy and laity, the poles of medieval aristocracy and peasantry, but—in its final perfection—an aristocracy of wealth set over and against the impoverished mass. Monetary egoism is the final expression of Christianity. All this opposition will pass, however, in the third and final age of man. This age was initiated by Spinoza, who first understood God with an intellectual love unknown to his predecessors, a love which transcended all distinctions and oppositions. This love, a new form of knowledge, will reveal God to all men with a yet unimagined intellectual clarity. This enlightenment, which transcends and synthesizes the shared imagination of the past and the deep private feelings of the present, will enable all men to order their lives according to the recognized precepts of universal reason. To use a Marxian expression, it will be the end of ideology, that false consciousness generated by the alien world of private property. As Adam was but the man of Nature, and Christ the man of God, so—to Hess—is Spinoza, the pure man, the prototype of the future, the discoverer of God in reason. Henceforth, in the light of this reason, man will come to know "how to order his views and deeds according to the all-comprehending Law, and, with the clear consciousness of his eternal life in God, proceed with firm, steady, and manly strides upon the path of understanding."[27] And, in this beatific future, "the whole country will be a great garden. In it everybody will be diligent and happy. Everybody will enjoy life as befits man. One will look for misery in order to remedy it. Yet one will find little of it. Distress will have left man."[28]

In time, Hess' vision of a "sacred history" would lose all of its explicit religious *content,* but the religious or mythic *form* of his thought would remain in his later works, and—if anything—take on even stronger apocalyptic tempers. Hess' secularized content, abstracted and set into its familiar Marxian expression is but the standard socialistic triad: primitive communism, the fallen world of private property, and communism regained through the saving sacrifices of messianic socialism. As in Marx's words, Communism is "the complete return of man to himself as a *social* (i.e. human) being — a return become conscious, and accomplished within the entire wealth of previous development."[29] But yet, through this romantic veil of economics and new understandings, the ancient mythic shape is easily glimpsed: Israel founded, Israel suffering—the diasphora—and Israel regained. This is the fundamental mythical dialectic inspiring Marxism. It is far from being derived from Hegel. In this regard, attention must be drawn to Hess's lifelong interest in what has come to be known as "Zionism." His longing for a Jewish homeland, which was first evidenced in a letter written by Hess when he was but nineteen years old,[30] found its fullest expression over thirty years later, in *Rom und Jerusalem*, published in 1862. This impassioned call for the Jews to return to their ancient land, was, as Isaiah Berlin notes, Hess' "real life work."[31] Hess' continuing work in the cause of Zionism led Theodor Herzl to say that "all of what we sought had already been understood by him—but suffering under Hegelian terminology—Judaism since Spinoza has brought forth no greater spirit than the now forgotten and dimmed figure of Moses Hess!"[32] This obscuring Hegelian terminology was, of course, originally derived from Hess's reading of Cieszkowski.

Early in 1841, just as he personally encountered Marx for the first time, Hess' second work appeared. It was *The European Triarchy (Die europäische Triarchie)*—written in response to a now totally forgotten work, *The European Pentarchy (Die europäische Pentarchie)*. The *Triarchy* was initially to have been entitled "Europe's Rebirth"—just as *Rom und Jerusalem* would later be tentatively entitled "Israel Reborn."[33]

Hess' second work continued along much the same lines as his first, although the *Triarchy* stressed the importance of conscious human action in the construction of the New Jerusalem, whereas the *Sacred History* had cast man principally in the role of an unconscious agent of the divine will. The welcome apocalypse grew ever more immanent, and industrial England was now seen as the Armageddon field in which the inequalities of wealth were to be obliterated. Just as "Germany had given birth to a Reformation that had given man spiritual freedom, and France had generated the Enlightenment and Revolution that had given man moral freedom, so England would bring forth true political freedom with a great social revolution. Hess conveyed this vision directly and convincingly to Marx and Engels.

In the *Triarchy*, Hess fully agreed with the "geistvolle Cieszkowski"[34] in seeing Hegel's philosophy of history as the weakest point of the whole speculative system, but unlike Cieszkowski, he did not charge this to an inexplicable misstep on the part of Hegel. To Hess, Hegel simply lacked the "intellectual love" that inspired Spinoza, a love that would have enabled Hegel to elevate his theory into a philosophy of action. Without this love Hegel could only sink into a despairing reflection upon the "slaughter–bench of history." For this reason, Hess declared that he "could not consider himself a participant in the Hegelian school."[35]

In the course of the *Triarchry*, Hess rather immodestly, if not incorrectly, declared that his first work, the *Sacred History* was, along with Cieszkowski's

Prolegomena, a fundamental work in the needed transformation of abstract German theory into a program of effective and concrete action.[36] Here, it is noteworthy that Hess does *not* consider his more popular later work, the *Triarchy,* to be as important as the *Sacred History*, although this latter work is the first to contain the unmistakeable signs of Hegel. But even these signs were drawn mainly—if not exclusively—from Cieszkowski, for shortly after the publication of the *Triarchy,* Hess confided to his friend Auerbach that he was yet intending to make a fundamental (*gründlich*) study of "German philosophy, namely Fichte and Hegel."[37] In short, whatever Marx acquired from Hess it could not have had much to do with the actual doctrines of Hegel.

Hess, always sensitive to present sufferings and humiliations—which he, as an individual, had sadly encountered[38]—could only see in Cieszkowski's optimistic triad a blindness to the divisive forces rending the present world. The modern age, as antithetical to the past, was not a compliment to that past—as Cieszkowski had thought—but was an age of radical self-opposition. The triad of history presented by Cieszkowski had understood the antithetical period as but the negative compliment of the first period, but Hess took the antithetical period as in itself antithetical—as set over and against itself in the form of class oppositions, of "der Gegensatz der Pauperismus und der Geldaristokratie."[39] Cieszkowski's age of theoretical reflection was transformed into one of material oppositions. Cieszkowski's triad afforded the philosopher of action an optimistic frame, but with Hess's revision, in which the modern period is taken as antithetical *per se*, and wherein present suffering is elevated into a necessitated moment of world-history. This dialectic of "increasing misery," once set upon the track of detecting ever-more-cruel signs of the moment, cannot but have appeal to any discouraged or angry intellectual. *Praxis* soon became the code word for revolution, and has since been translated into terrorism.

As earlier noted, Hess, by all evidence and his own admissions, was never a Hegelian. But he was, in the words of Engels, "The first Communist in the Party." He was an inspired reformer, who, through a reading of Cieszkowski, found himself—in Herzl's words—"suffering under Hegel's terminology." His *Philosophie der Tat* was fundamentally but an exhortation to rid the world of "Other-being." As he said,

> The task of the philosophy of spirit now consists in becoming a philosophy of action. The whole of human action, not only thought, has to be elevated to the standpoint at which all contradiction dissappears.[40]

It was not Hegel but Hess—Arnold Ruge's "Communist Rabbi"[41]—who first introduced Engels and then Marx to a political dialectic that finds its fruition in the "One Substance" of Spinoza.

After Lenin, and the subsequent atrocities committed in the name of Hegel's dialectic, it is small wonder that Hegelians tread softly about the issue of putting Hegelianism into practice. Nevertheless, despite the sorry missteps in this first essay into a philosophy of action, I would still hope that it is in fact possible not only to think but to act as a Hegelian.

I propose that Cieszkowski be reexamined at least in the light of his concern, as a Hegelian, with the future course of history and our role in that future, and that the messianic-socialistic turn forced upon our understanding of Hegelianism by Hess and Marx be recognized for what it is: a retrograde movement of thought in which religious *Vorstellungen*—in this instance the millennial myth—conditionally replaced the *Begriffe* of reason proper to the philosophic discipline.

NOTES

1. *Sämtliche Werke* (Jubilaumsausgabe), 19, 3, 691.
2. Arnold Ruge and Ludwig and Feuerbach were the oldest participants in the Young Hegelian movement—both in their thirties when the produced their most important works. David F. Strauss wrote the *Leben Jesu* in 1835, when he was but twenty-seven years old; Bruno Bauer was twenty-eight years old in 1837, when he first met Marx—who was then nineteen years old. Cieszkowski was twenty-four when he wrote the *Prologemena zur Historiosophie,* and Moses Hess was twenty-five when he wrote *Die heilige Geschichte der Menscheit.*
3. John N. Findlay, "The Contemporary Relevance of Hegel," *Hegel: A Collection of Critical Essasy*, ed. by A. MacIntyre (Garden City, 1972), p. 2.
4. *Hegel's Leben,* xix.
5. Nicholas Lobkowicz, *Theory and Practice* (Notre Dame, 1967), p. 194.
6. For a comprehensive history of Cieszkowski, see André Liebich, *Between Ideology and Utopia: The Philosophy and Politics of August Cieszkowski* (Dordrecht, 1979).
7. Cieszkowski, *Gott und die Palingenesie* (Berlin, 1842), p. 11.
8. Cieszkowski, *Prolegomena zur Historiosophie* (Berlin, 1838), pp. 6–7.
9. Cieszkowski, *Ibid.*, p. 3.
10. Hegel, *Enzyklopädie,* para. 248, *Zu.*
11. Hegel, *Wissenschaft der Logik,* II, 3 Kap.
12. Cieszkowski, *Prolegomena,* p. 8.
13. *Ibid.,* pp. 7–8.
14. *Ibid.,* p. 29.
15. Marx, *Die Frühschriften,* hrsg. von S. Landshut (Stuttgart, 1964), p. 339. This is found in Marx's "Thesen über Feuerbach."
16. Cieszkowski, *Prolegomena,* p. 129.
17. *Ibid.,* p. 129.
18. *Ibid.,* p. 130.
19. Moses Hess, *Rom und Jerusalem,* p. 19. (This, and all following translations from Hess are of the author.)

20. A Messiah was expected who would gather into one community the scattered Jewish communities of the world. See Edmund Silberner, Moses Hess: *Geschichte Seines Lebens* (Leiden, 1966), pp. 63ff.
21. Cited from Silberner, *Moses Hess,* p. 24. Found in Hess's unpublished *Tagebuch,* Sept. 30, 1835.
22. The term "Philosophie der Tat" was first used as a title in one of Hess's articles published in Herweg's *Einundzwanzig Bogen aus der Schweiz* (Zurich, 1843).
23. See Silberner for details of the composition of *Die heilige Geschichte der Menschheit,* pp. 49ff.
24. From Silberner, p. 50. Taken from an unpublished forward written by Hess in 1840.
25. Isaiah Berlin, *The Life and Opinions of Moses Hess* (Cambridge, 1959), p. 6.
26. The closing chapter of The *Sacred History* was entitled "Das neue Jerusalem und die letzten Zeiten."
27. Moses Hess, *The Sacred History of Mankind* (Stuttgart, 1837), p. 176.
28. *Ibid.,* p. 316. For a full description of the "New Jerusalem" see Silberner, pp. 42ff.
29. Marx, *Die Frühschriften,* p. 235.
30. Letter to M. Levy, April 1831 in *Moses Hess: Briefwechsel,* hrsg. E. Silberner, p. 45.
31. Berlin, *Life and Opinions,* p. 29.
32. *Tagebücher,* (manuscript found in International Instituut voor Sociale Geschiedenis, Amsterdam), 2:599.
33. Silberner, *Moses Hess,* p. 74, 391.
34. Moses Hess, *Triarchy,* (Leipzig, 1841), p. 5.
35. *Ibid.,* p. 65.
36. *Ibid.,* p. 13.
37. Letter of March 10, 1841 in *Moses Hess.*
38. See Silberner, p. 60ff.
39. Hess, *Triarchy,* p. 38.
40. Herweg, *Einunzwanzig Bogen aus der Schweiz* (Zürich und Winterthur, 1843), p. 321.
41. Arnold Ruge, *Zwei Jahre in Paris,* (Leipzig, 1946), 1, p. 31. Among other titles Hess was said to be "The Father of German Socialism," (see *Lobkowicz,* p. 231) and was recalled as "The Herald of Socialist Zionism" at the First Zionist Congress held at Basel in 1897 (see *Silberner,* p. 444). Friedrich Engels, in 1843, declared Hess to be "The First Communist in the Party." *Werke* (Dietz, 1964), 1, p. 494.

Index of Names

Althusser, L. 80
Anscombe, E., 6
Aristotle, 3,20
Avineri, S., 49
Bhaskar, R., 77
Bloch, E., 52
Burke, E., 58
Cart, J.J., 41,56
Cieszkowski, A., 214ff.
Condillac, E., 13
Connolly, W.E., 77
Danto, C., 97-100
Davidson, D., 2, 97-8
Descartes, R., 111, 191-200, 209
deVos, L., 145
Dilthey, W., 52, 99
Dunayevskya, R., 94
Durkheim, E., 80
Engels, F., 223
Feinberg, J., 97
Fichte, J.G., 6, 68-9, 125-6, 133, 135,
    144, 198, 204, 218
Findlay, J.N., 94
Fiore, J., 218
Freud, S., 9
Fries, J.F., 37
Giddons, A., 77
Godwin, W., 68
Goethe, J.W., 131-2
Haym, R., 32-3, 41
Heidegger, M., 18, 21, 99
Herzl, T., 224
Hess, M., 214ff.
Hobbes, T., 169
Hotho, H., 143
Kant, I., 4-6, 9, 21, 81, 125-6, 128,
    133-4, 191-4, 191-200, 209
Kelly, G.A., 94

Kleist, H., 5
Kojève, A., 22
Lauer, Q., 115ff., 218
Leibniz, G.W., 3, 193
Lessing, G.E., 218
Locke, J., 14
Louis-Philippe, King. 39
Lukács, G., 52
Macgregor, D.E.S., 49
Marcuse, H., 22
Marx, K., 26, 52-3, 58, 69, 78, 222-3
Melden, A.I. 23
Michel, H., 94
Michelet, K.L., 39
Newton, I., 54, 131-2
Pannenberg, W., 99-100
Paton, H.J., 20
Plato, 55, 57, 64, 163, 170, 191
Plant, R., 218
Pöggeler, O., 51
Polin, R., 94-5
Popper, K., 76
Rameil, U., 145
Ricoeur, P., 23
Rosenkranz, K., 32-4, 53
Rosenzweig, F., 41
Rousseau, J.J., 56-7, 167, 169
Ruge, A., 224
Sartre, J.P., 99
Schelling, F.W., 6, 204, 218
Schiller, F., 125
Schlegel, F., 139
Schopenhauer, A., 6, 9
Smith, A., 21, 53-4, 58-9, 62, 65
Socrates, 85, 139, 169
Spinoza, B., 171, 191-4, 209, 222-4
Steuart, J.D., 53-4, 59ff.
Strauss, D.F., 214
Taylor, C., 28, 99, 137, 219
Tugendhat, E., 137, 152
Whitehead, A.N., 112
Williams, D., 3
Wittgenstein, L., 6, 14